dreams of exile

Henry Holt and Company   New York

dreams of exile

Robert Louis Stevenson: *A Biography*

Ian Bell

Henry Holt and Company, Inc.
Publishers since 1866
115 West 18th Street
New York, New York 10011

Henry Holt® is a registered trademark
of Henry Holt and Company, Inc.

Originally published in Scotland in 1992 by
Mainstream Publishing Company Ltd.

Library of Congress Cataloging-in-Publication Data
Bell, Ian.
Dreams of exile: Robert Louis Stevenson,
a biography/Ian Bell. — 1st American ed.
p.   cm.
Includes bibliographical references and index.
1. Stevenson, Robert Louis, 1850–1894—Biography.
2. Authors, Scottish—19th century—Biography.
3. Travelers—Scotland—Biography.   I. Title.
PR5493.B4 1993
828'.809—dc20
[B]   93-3792
CIP
ISBN 0-8050-2807-2
ISBN 0-8050-3938-4 (An Owl Book: pbk.)

First published in the United States in hardcover in 1993
by Henry Holt and Company, Inc.

First Owl Book Edition—1995

Designed by Paula R. Szafranski

Printed in the United States of America
All first editions are printed on acid-free paper.∞

1   3   5   7   9   10   8   6   4   2
1   3   5   7   9   10   8   6   4   2
(pbk.)

For Mandy, Sean, Lamastre and

Le Monastier

Contents

Life that lives is life successful.

JACK LONDON: THE CRUISE OF THE SNARK

All's misalliance.
Yet why not say what happened?

ROBERT LOWELL: EPILOGUE

It is told of me that I came once to my mother with these words:
'Mama, I have drawed a man's body; shall I draw his soul now?'

R.L.S.: MEMOIRS OF HIMSELF

Preface

A wilful convulsion of brute nature . . ." said the last line of fiction he wrote. Later that day, on the broad verandah of the big new house on a consoling Pacific island, he was infected with high spirits while preparing mayonnaise for a salad. Without warning, his hands went to his head, groping after the haemorrhage. "Do I look strange?" he asked his wife, and sank to his knees. They helped him indoors as consciousness fled. At 8:10 P.M. on 3 December 1894, Robert Louis Balfour Stevenson died, lying on a cot in the hall.

He could not have written his funeral better. The headman of the village below the house brought precious mats to cover him; Catholics chanted over his Presbyterian soul. By dawn the Samoans were cutting a path to the distant summit of the mountain and the room was full of bright flowers. They dressed him in a fine shirt and draped the British ensign over his body. Mourners came and went. On a cool, sunny afternoon the native men shouldered the bag of bones, the untrustworthy flesh that had made living a contest with chance, and carried it to the highland grave. There he lies, the ocean beneath him.

The real surprise was that he had lived so long. In the year before he died, he wrote to George Meredith, his fellow novelist, in an effort to explain how his life had been:

For fourteen years I have not had a day's real health; I have awakened sick and gone to bed weary; and I have done my work unflinchingly. I have written in bed, and written out of it, written in haemorrhages, written in sickness, written torn by coughing, written when my head swam for weakness; and for so long, it seems to me I have won my wager and recovered my glove. I am better now, have been, rightly speaking, since first I came to the Pacific; and still, few are the days when I am not in some physical distress. And the battle goes on—ill or well, is a trifle; so as it goes. I was made for a contest . . .

Like a portrait attempted too often, Stevenson has acquired many faces in the century since his death. None are fixed. He returns your gaze, looks sidelong, bold, sick, wise, skittish, devious, or rapt from canvas, sketch, printed page, and photographic emulsion. We impose R.L.S. on him and take what we need. He is an odd sort of mirror.

The central image persists, though the "brown eyes radiant with vivacity" are dim in the paintings and the old glass plates, like echoes fading. So, too, the versions. Some remembered his speech, the talent to enthral, but they could not report it. Others thought him a self-regarding poseur, the sort who could not pass a looking glass, but they failed to prove it. He was quick to anger, by some accounts; quicker to forgive, by others. In his letters, hundreds of them, there is a sense of suppressed energy, as though the mainspring of his imagination was overwound. He felt intensely, wept easily, loved freely. Sometimes he stared into the encroaching darkness.

He was impossibly thin, so thin the life seemed to have been squeezed out of the chamber of his sunken chest and into the narrow extremities of his face and his long, nervous, tapering fingers. The doctor who came to his deathbed was astonished anyone could write with arms so thin. He reminded some of a stork, febrile and agitated; others of a scarecrow, skin stretched tight over the rickety frame. A bag of bones.

His hair was brown and lank, his face famously boyish, high coloured when not tanned. He spoke with an Edinburgh accent. The trademark wisps of facial hair were all he could ever manage in the way of a beard. Some thought him beautiful.

Narrative: *the orderly description of events.* What happens and what happened. The stories we tell ourselves. "Truth," he wrote in 1888 to Adelaide Boodle, a Bournemouth acquaintance, "I think not so much of; for I do not know it."

"His feelings are always his reasons," said his friend Henry James, summing up the plot in a sentence.

Stevenson was, even without trying, like a character out of time; there was a flamboyance in his nature, a certain taste for self-dramatisation, as though a difficult performance was being perfected. He was a romantic in an age of romantics, yet not typically Victorian; a Scot, yet far from typically Scottish. Sailing to the rim, he was forever looking over his shoulder. His art was a moral argument presented in an entertainer's costume.

Time has played games with his name. Down the years his reputation has survived critical neglect as extreme as the infantile veneration of the decade after his death, when saintliness leeched off those "beloved initials" and sweet martyrdom was proclaimed by a blood vessel exploding in the skull. The worship was as bizarre as the consequent neglect was unusual, and both were inspired by immense popularity. Significantly enough, the best of his peers have thought highly of Stevenson, finding qualities in the mechanisms of prose and the textures of his vision that lesser critics have missed. Others can decide if, to name three, Henry James, Jorge Luis Borges, and Graham Greene were right to put the highest value on his fiction: Stevenson's place is secure, although, as ever, there is no unanimity over what that place might be. R.L.S. was no one's conscript.

His legend—great craft, prodigious effort, incessant travel, and a heroic, lifelong duel with death—is still potent. The romance of nemesis befuddles every commentary, even—especially—for those attempting neutrality. Some find the legend exemplary, others are nauseated: if Stevenson does not ring true, he does not ring at all. Yet the legend and the work are elements not easily separated, nor should they be: most of the legend is fact. Louis the man—mercurial, charming, daring, dying—is the troublesome core.

He was a product of his circumstances, of course. Three, each connected, mattered most: illness, Scotland, and travel. Had he not been born in Edinburgh, he might have enjoyed better health; had he been healthier, he might not have travelled so much; had he not travelled, he would not have written as he did; yet had his health been better, he would not have died with his career only half complete, his potential untested. Fate, if it exists, had fun with Louis.

Victorian Scotland, his society, bred an ambivalent exile with, simultaneously, a taste for escape and a profound love of his country. Exile brought forth nostalgia; recollection brought forth fiction. In his last letters home he was writing of his ancestors, and his last great novel, *Weir of Hermiston*, was of and for Scotland. Like the argument of his life, the book was left unfinished.

Exile is a state of mind, as much a condition of the heart as a physical event. The exile is reminded, more often than the rest of us, to question who he is and what he is. "What am I doing here?" Rimbaud asked himself, deep in the blank expanse of Ethiopia, with all the resonance of a pebble dropped in the ocean. Stevenson was more complicated. He left— was forever leaving—a small northern country long accustomed to casting out its young and unwanted. He had deep roots there that he could not sever. Yet Scotland's exiles have always defined their country. The nation has a relationship of mutual ambivalence with its diaspora; less love and hate than love and valediction; a prolonged goodbye. Louis felt it. Sickness led him on a chase across the globe, yet he chose the journey. Even in the 1880s Samoa was not the only safe haven left on earth for a man with an unreliable respiratory tract. "As regards health," he wrote towards the end, "Honolulu suited me equally well—the Alps perhaps better. I chose Samoa instead of Honolulu for the simple and eminently satisfactory reason that it is less civilised." The impulse was his, whatever the haemorrhages demanded. If Stevenson ever asked himself "What am I doing here?" he probably answered "What was I doing *there*?"

Janus: looking both ways. Rushing towards the promise of health and the possibility of experience; running from a society which seemed eager to stifle him.

The narrative moves along several tracks. Art is on one path, travel another, memory (sometimes the memory of a memory, like a loop) a third, health a fourth.

Sickness tells its own story. Louis's infirmity was mundane, not mythical. He felt himself "physically dishonoured" by his own vulnerability. Illness drained and disgusted him, imposing a fearsome discipline on every action, circumscribing each ambition. If the young bohemian was rebellious as a matter of routine, the mature man was engaged in daily battle with the guerilla actions of his body. Illness was a circumstance to be opposed with will and wit. You cannot write about Stevenson without reporting periodically on his health.

That collapsed, once and for all, on 3 December 1894. Yet without the agency of illness there would probably have been no R.L.S., whatever tragedy can be made out of a talent terminated after only forty-four years and three weeks. Sickness shaped Stevenson, formed his emotions, scented his art, and obliged him to acquire the habit, willing though he was, of travel. The pell-mell flight from physical affliction—and Louis's life often resembles that of a refugee—was also a journey towards something. "The great affair is to move," he wrote in a youthful passage which became a famous, if misunderstood, defence of rootlessness.

It was more than that: Stevenson saw best from a distance, and from a variety of perspectives. The habit found its way into his fiction. Settled circumstances, like the structure of an extended narrative, did not hold his attention for long. His was an intelligence alive in motion, not contemplation. Ill health was the lamentable occasion for travel and escape.

Some memories he carried with him always, like keepsakes. That is important. David Daiches has written illuminatingly of Stevenson's tendency to *anticipate* nostalgia, even in childhood, as a mark of his dual character, "compulsive exile and lover of home."* The trait compensated for his volatility as an artist. Memory, running in a loop, linked him to earth.

Yet he had reason to despise his native Edinburgh. No one has caught the character of its weather—and hence, to some extent, the character of the city—better than he. Few, equally, have had better reason to confuse climate with fate, as though meteorological bigotry had selected him for its special victim. Flint-faced and chilly, Edinburgh did its best to kill him, or so he thought.

*Calder, J. (ed): *Stevenson and Victorian Scotland* (Edinburgh, 1981); p. 13.

It is a cliché to say that a writer can be found, if he can be found at all, in a certain place and at a certain time. It is hardly more profound to say that in a different place, at a different time, you will find a different writer. Yet points in time and space are keys to Stevenson's life, more so than with most writers. It is a hard map to plot, but the characters of Edinburgh, the Cévennes, Silverado, and Samoa are actors as important as any of the people in Stevenson's story. It is in those places that you find him, in buildings and skylines, climate and language, sometimes unexpectedly. His response to place—always immediate, invariably honest—was his autobiography.

Geography mattered in other ways. Stevenson's ability truly to inhabit a place, to comprehend its people and its culture, had something to do with his storyteller's gift. The construction as much as the content of a work like *The Beach of Falesá* was shaped by the environment, the emotional weather, in which the story was made. The story has the texture of myth; it speaks of men adrift in a strange universe. The South Seas gave it that.

Stevenson's was an enthusiasm for the *other*. Mundanely, you are unsurprised to learn that he was an able, instinctive linguist.

Critics have worried for decades that the romance of the life distracts attention from the work, just as his contemporaries muttered that Louis's mind was altogether too agile, too easily diverted, too reluctant to submit to the discipline required for hard, intellectual graft. The errors are equivalent: just as his mind was fired more by immediate experience than by meditation, so the events of Stevenson's short, crowded life were contiguous with his art. Extracting text from context is like expecting the pearl without the grit. R.L.S. rarely wrote under ideal conditions—one reason why the conditions, physical or emotional, are crucial. And if at times the life reads like fiction, one can only say that Louis would have been delighted.

It is beyond doubt, in any case, that another kind of mythmaking has submerged the owner of those "beloved" initials. The enduring popularity of a few R.L.S. stories has made him as much a part of the mass cultures of television, cinema, and tourism as of literature. Today he is a brand name, a guarantee of quality, a looted storehouse of phrases, plots, and characters for a society grown avid for elemental narratives.

Versions proliferate. A "Jekyll and Hyde" will disturb his friends even if none has read a word of *The Strange Case* . . . These days an R.L.S. "heritage trail" winds its ritual way around Edinburgh. Long John Silver, his extraordinary features masked, continues to intrigue functionally illiterate Hollywood executives, while the restless young follow in vagabond Lou's footsteps to camp out under luminous skies. Others tramp Scotland in the wake of David Balfour, or climb the tall mountain on Upolu that supports Louis's thin bones.

There, Mormons have bought a twenty-year lease on Stevenson's old home and plan the "Robert Louis Stevenson Museum/Preservation Foundation Inc.," complete with souvenir shop and a cable car to the grave site on the summit of Vaea. Despised "civilisation" reaches out to R.L.S. even in death.

Elsewhere his relics decay under glass, a trail of debris littering museums across the globe, while *Treasure Island* is turned into pantomime, still more films, or (in an "international co-production") a science-fiction thriller for television. Through it all the writer-as-hero is paraphrased, parodied, adapted, acted, filmed, and imitated, while much of his work remains out of print. The man and his art have become obscure behind an electronic veil.

Old complaints, and R.L.S. is not the only writer to have suffered so. But the purpose of biography is more than curative: clichés will always attach themselves to art, and to a life that has the quality of art. For all his grumbling about reporters, Stevenson did not avoid publicity: his ego (the healthiest thing about him) was large enough to welcome it, and he was astute enough to recognize its market value.

The real question is why he connected with public taste at such a deep level, why his popularity endures. What was it he did in his "children's stories," his "adventure tales," his "romances," that others failed—and fail—to do? The point in writing about Stevenson is to give an account of a man who printed a handful of narratives upon the popular imagination.

~~

Mere narrative, obvious yet mysterious. Stories surround us and we take them, a dirty joke or *The Iliad*, so much for granted, we forget to ask what is going on between speaker and listener, writer and reader. *An account of an actual or fictional event or a sequence of such events . . .* The human appetite for it is ancient and little understood. We can admit that there have been better writers than Stevenson, writers more subtle and ambitious, more tenacious, certainly more profound. Then it is necessary to remind ourselves that many of the names offered have long since faded from the public's memory. Whatever Stevenson had they lacked. The durability and ubiquity of his tales suggest a man touching something basic.

Writing of Prosper Mérimée, creator of Carmen, George Steiner argued: "To have brought off the miracle of persistent life is an artist's supreme achievement . . . But though each period produces innumerable characters in art, poetry or fiction, only a few have in them the spark of grace. Only a few can leap the gulf from momentary substance to lasting shadow." Numbering R.L.S. among these miracle workers, Steiner went on: "The nineteenth century marks the end of the classic status of narrative. Kleist, Poe, Stevenson, Leskov and Mérimée himself are among the last of the pure story-tellers."*

There is more to it than that, but whatever his "merit" as a vehicle for grace, R.L.S. commands a place among the few who have created literature of universal appeal, with characters who have achieved an existence outside the pages of the fictions in which they were born. He was a popular artist: the conjunction has become rare.

Just narrative. He once said that, when he suffered, stories were his refuge. He called them a drug. We want incident, he said, interest, action: ". . . to the devil with your philosophy. When we are well again, and have an easy mind, we shall peruse your important work . . ."

A biographer soon discovers that Stevenson was the consummate autobiographer. His own life fascinated him, and he returned to it time and

---

*Steiner, G.: *Language and Silence* (London, 1967); pp. 289–296.

again in essays, poems, stories, and letters like a dog to a beloved bone. It is an odd sensation to realise that the reader over your shoulder is your subject. I have tried whenever possible to allow him to speak for himself; often it was impossible to keep him quiet.

I make no apology for yielding to his charm. It, like the "duty of happiness" of which he wrote, does not seem to me a negligible thing. Those who fret that Louis's ability to exhilarate by force of personality amounts to a kind of deception worry me more than he ever has. Charm and artistic rigour are not yet incompatible, least of all in a storyteller, and Stevenson's rigour was total.

R.L.S. wrote tales of adventure. That is true enough, but not the whole truth. He is a bridge between the likes of H. Rider Haggard and the achievements of Joseph Conrad, and has something in common with both of them. The times almost trapped him: "Small is the word; it is a small age and I am of it." Many felt the same restlessness during the late Victorian hiatus and sought refuge in fantasy, imperial adventure, or romance. But romance was a native land for R.L.S., and into it he poured resources others might have reserved for more dignified—more "profound"— works. He did not condescend to his material. His character guided his choices but his understanding of impermanence controlled both. There was more to the world than domesticated fiction, or "realism," allowed. He understood it as a reader understands it, and exploited the tension between different ways of telling. *Tusitala*, his Samoan honorific, always meant something more than "teller of tales." Today, if the Samoans use the title at all, they use it of any professional writer. He would have appreciated that.

Oddly enough for a man who made himself at home all over the world, who sprang from a class long thought anglicised by other Scots, he was never comfortable in England. It seems to have been the one country he truly disliked. In this he declared his own independence.

The fact remains: in spite of the difference of blood and language, the Lowlander feels himself the sentimental countryman of the Highlander. When they meet abroad, they fall upon each other's necks in spirit; even at home there is a kind of clannish intimacy in their talk. But from his compatriot in the south the Lowlander stands consciously apart. He has had a different training; he obeys different laws; he makes his will in other terms, is otherwise divorced and married; his eyes are not at home in an English landscape or with English houses; his ear continues to remark the English speech; and even though his tongue acquire the Southern knack, he will still have a strong Scots accent of the mind.

"The Foreigner at Home"

He was a Scottish writer, though his relationship with Scotland, the Scots, and Scottish literature is complex. He was half prodigal son and half deportee; half patriot and half deserter. Listen to the elder Kirstie in *Weir of Hermiston* and you recognise an authentic Scottish voice; but try to place R.L.S. in a line of succession from Scott and you will fail.

Scott, Hogg, Galt, Stevenson, Barrie, Brown, Gibbon, Gunn, Gray, McIlvanney—they are a disparate bunch. Different aspects of Scottish culture claimed, or continue to claim, each of them in very different ways. Mostly, however theirs is an argument with history. Stevenson filtered that history through Protestantism, exile, nostalgia, and his own alienation from the class that bred him.

It was once usual to define him in terms of Scott's achievement. That will no longer do: to the many dualities useful in discussing Stevenson could be added the tensions between nationalism and internationalism, home and exile, then and now. The experience was his alone. He could never use history as the Shirra used it, and never tried to. It had nothing to do with ignorance and everything to do with a distinct view of what history, to a novelist, is *for*. In October of 1891 he wrote to his old friend Sidney Colvin from Samoa. Ten thousand miles from Scotland, he was "teaching" his stepdaughter's young son the volume of Scott he himself had grown up with:

> Now Scotch is the only History I know; it is the only history reasonably represented in my library; it is a very good one for my purpose, owing to two civilisations having been face to face throughout—or rather Roman civilisation face to face with our ancient barbaric life and government down to yesterday, to 1750 anyway. But the *Tales of a Grandfather* stand in my way; I am teaching them to Austin now, and they have all Scott's defects and all Scott's hopeless merit. I cannot compete with that; and yet, so

far as regard teaching History, how he has missed his chances! I think I'll try; I really have some historic sense. I feel that in my bones.

He went deeper into the question of identity, of how it evolves and how it shapes our moral choices, than is usually allowed or realised. Just as important, he rarely made those choices for his readers. Hence the lack of an obvious moral in *Treasure Island* or in *Dr. Jekyll*. For Stevenson character and morality were intertwined. One flowed from the other and both sprang, at source, from circumstance. He understood the closed universe of the reader, character responding to character: the most intimate of all relationships. He understood, too, how narrative shapes that universe.

So many genres have been found to accommodate his varied output that the word loses meaning. Stevenson's true legacy can be unearthed in the foundation works of the popular media, in movies and cheap fiction, where the narrative pulse survives. Most of his stories could be called fables. The word will do.

It is not enough to say that, preoccupied by dualities himself, he sought to reconcile opposites in his fiction. R.L.S. was ready for chaos; he sought it out, lived within it. Inherited concepts of order struck him as fraudulent. He was no more prepared to impose such structures on his prose than he was to impose them on his life. Fiction was a voyage in which all the charts were unreliable. Nothing, life or writing, was seamless, nothing exactly as it seemed. The dreams of a sick child showed that. Why not the novel?

Romance, of course, but hard-won romance. He often said he was good at beginnings, bad at endings. Torpor was the enemy; without apology he chose "a roaring toothache" before renunciation. The task was to take the story forward, to give it sense, to follow it to the finish. So must we.

I: *dreams*

1 Stevensons and Balfours

The name of my native land is not North Britain whatever may be the name of yours.

LETTER TO S. R. CROCKETT

T o look at, the house is much as it was. Its tall windows watch the narrow valley of a private park thick with trees and shrubs, in a street accounted, now as then, one of the finest in a city of fine streets. In sunlight its plain, three-storeyed facade is sand coloured; in the squalls that pass for climate through much of Edinburgh's year, when the rain slants and the wind climbs uphill from the Firth of Forth, it takes on the hue of lead.

It was built as the Napoleonic Wars were ending, to accommodate the desire of the better sort to put distance between themselves and the teeming Old Town. Read as a statement in stone, 17 Heriot Row, with its ornamental balconies, its astragals, high ceilings, fine staircase, and protective gardens, was part of the argument—a matter of class, culture, and anglicisation—that was rupturing the life of Scotland's capital. Where once on the spinal ridge above the old Nor' loch quality had been piled upon commonality in the tottering lands along the Royal Mile, or mixed with them in its pestilential wynds, pends, and closes, there were now two Edinburghs, each aware but wary of the other. "Spatial segregation of the social classes" was civic policy.* Indeed, when in the seventeenth century the city council was first offered land beyond its boundaries by James

*Smout, T.C.: *A Century of the Scottish People, 1830–1950* (London, 1986); p. 55.

VII, the grand scheme had been to build a complete new capital and abandon the Old Town entirely. The proposal failed but its spirit survived.

The city was one of the first of the dualities to preoccupy the writer. Though in later years Stevenson came to believe that Edinburgh's New Town was the perfect antithesis to its Old, as sugar is to salt, the medieval precinct was never his home territory. The youth and young adult would escape to it—lose himself in it—to be fascinated by its malodorous variety; but he was never truly part of it. Its chaos, social and architectural, was an antidote to the clean lines and rectitude of the New Town, but the people there were not his people. He understood them better than most, but not as a native—even if he, like his mother, retained a strong Edinburgh accent throughout his life. To the restless, responsive, middle-class boy, the Old Town was the first of the destinations he found irresistible. In such journeys he defined himself.

The city held perhaps 140,000 people. Spared most of the upheavals of the industrial revolution and already dwarfed by Glasgow, it remained the shadow capital of a spectral nation at a time when life was "competitive, unprotected, brutal and, for many, vile."* Elsewhere, two thirds of Scotland's three million population could be accounted country dwellers, and the myth of the "Scotch peasant"—devout, proud, poor, self-reliant—remained, as one historian has noted, a dominant force in social policy.

The nation was not homogeneous. Town pulled against country, region against region. The question of what it meant to be a Scot could not be answered with nationalistic formulae. In *The Silverado Squatters*, Stevenson indulged his nostalgia with more than usual insight:

> Scotland is indefinable; it has no unity except upon the map. Two languages, many dialects, innumerable forms of piety, and countless local patriotisms and prejudices, part us among ourselves more widely than the extreme east and west of that great continent of America. When I am at home, I feel a man from Glasgow to be something like a rival, a man from Barra to be more than half a foreigner. Yet let us meet in some far country, and, whether we hail from the braes of Manor or the braes of Mar, some ready-made affection joins us on the instant. It is not race. Look at us. One is Norse, one Celtic, and another Saxon. It is not community of tongue.

*Ibid, p. 31.

We have it not among ourselves; and we have it, almost to perfection, with English, or Irish, or American. It is no tie of faith, for we detest each other's errors. And yet somewhere, deep down in the heart of each one of us, something yearns for the old land and the old kindly people.

The decade before Louis's birth was one in which Queen Victoria began her love affair with mist-sodden mountains and cartoon Highlanders, the decade in which a tartan shroud was laid without grace over the old Scotland. In 1846 potato blight destroyed the economy of the West Highlands and launched their population on its long decline. Two years later, in 1848, Scottish Chartists were tried on charges of sedition, and an audience in Edinburgh's Waterloo Rooms was hearing of "a struggle against capital." Sedan chairs could still be seen on the streets.

For much of the urban working class, life was routinely abject. Prostitution, drink, and disease went unchecked. Scots had an *average* life expectancy barely into their forties. In 1842 the *Reports on the Sanitary Condition of the Labouring Population of Scotland* recorded that in Edinburgh the houses ". . . of the lowest grade often consist only of one small apartment, always ill-ventilated, both from the nature of its construction and from the densely peopled and confined locality in which it is ᵗuated. Many of them, besides, are damp and partly underground . . . A te ˙ of the lowest poor have a bedstead, but by far the larger portion have none these make up a kind of bed on the floor with straw, on which a whole family are huddled together . . ."* Such was the Auld Reekie—"there are no stars so lovely as Edinburgh street-lamps"—that enthralled the young Lewis Stevenson.

The New Town, in deliberate contrast, was a comfortable nest for the commercial class, which was bending the economy, architecture, and religious life of the city to its will. This exercise in tyrannical perspective had been constructed as a residential area—effectively as a splendid housing estate—but business soon intruded. With their greater purchasing power, businesses overrode the objections of disgruntled residents. Money talked: by 1850 shops occupied most of the ground floors along Princes Street.

It was, too, a city in which architecture, people, and climate coexisted

*Ibid, p. 30.

in a kind of mutual antagonism. Settled on its hills, with their valleys and buildings making fine funnels for the wind, Edinburgh required all its habitual stoicism. Today, if the weather is kind, the air becomes soft and the stones come alive. When the day is less forgiving, outdoor life can be brutal, akin to living with a northern *mistral*, and indoor life barely more appealing. Edinburgh folk, with their vestigial Victorian faith in fresh air and a no-nonsense attitude to building design, seem reluctant to admit how far north (55° 57′ 23″) they are. The wind, rattling the roofs and chasing red-nosed children to school, reminds them.

The sickly R.L.S. needed no reminder. For him, later, the Edinburgh weather acquired layers of significance to do with home, childhood, character, dreams, and even comedy. In his growing years the northern climate was simply an enemy. If it took a turn for the worse, he knew that his precarious health was about to do the same. The early *Edinburgh: Picturesque Notes* said it best.

> . . . Edinburgh pays cruelly for her high seat in one of the vilest climates under heaven. She is liable to be beaten upon all the winds that blow, to be drenched with rain, to be buried in cold sea fogs out of the east, and powdered with snow as it comes flying southward from the Highland hills. The weather is raw and boisterous in winter, shifty and ungenial in summer, and a downright meteorological purgatory in the spring . . .

Stevenson could not imagine "a more unhomely and harassing place of residence" and recorded, doubtless picturing himself, that

> Many . . . aspire angrily after that Somewhere-else of the imagination, where all troubles are supposed to end. They lean over the great bridge which joins the New Town with the Old—that windiest spot, or high altar, in this northern temple of the winds—and watch the trains smoking out from under them and vanishing into the tunnel on a voyage to brighter skies. Happy the passengers who shake off the dust of Edinburgh, and have heard for the last time the cry of the east wind among her chimney-tops!

In "Ordered South," his first convincing attempt at prose, he admitted that even a slight fall in the Mediterranean temperature would put "a doleful vignette of the grim wintry streets of home" into his head.

The hopeless, huddled attitude of tramps in doorways; the flinching gait of barefoot children on the icy pavement; the sheen of the rainy streets towards afternoon; the meagre anatomy of the poor defined by the clinging of wet garments; the high canorous note of the North-easter on days when the very houses seem to stiffen with cold . . .

For all that, Number 17 was as desirable a residence in the spring of 1857—when Thomas Stevenson moved his household, of which the six-year-old Robert Lewis was the cherished, worrying centre—as it is now. It signified, advertised, and announced; it meant what it seemed to say about the success of its owner. In the middle of the century men like Thomas luxuriated in their certainties and their property, the one an assurance of the other.

The intellectual lustre of the Scottish Enlightenment had faded with the nation's sense of itself. Scotland had retreated to the fringes of European culture. Religion and commerce, moral abacuses and the instruments of an empire in which the Scots bourgeoisie had become enthusiastic shareholders, were dominant. For Thomas Stevenson the study of God's Word, and the millions of words contingent upon the Word which were shaping the Scottish publishing industry, was the highest pursuit. It was an age of tracts, commentaries, and concordances, and Thomas was a fan. His library of religious works was extensive, and he studied it at his ease in Heriot Row with the same quirky originality he brought to the profession of civil engineering.

The family firm, in which his brothers, father, and maternal grandfather had worked, was consultant to the Commissioners of Northern Lights, contracted to design and construct lighthouses and harbours around Scotland's hostile coast. As a thirty-year-old R.L.S. put it: "Whenever I smell salt water, I know I am not far from one of the works of my ancestors. The Bell Rock stands monument for my grandfather; the Skerry Vhor for my Uncle Alan; and when the lights come out at sundown along the shores of Scotland, I am proud to think they burn more brightly for the genius of my father."

There were, ultimately, five generations of "Lighthouse Stevensons." Together they built every lighthouse in Scotland and many more overseas.

Thomas, though younger than his brother David, was the dominant partner in his day.

Previously, the family had bred numerous devout characters. Thomas's
fascination with currents and stresses, lovingly recorded by his son, mir-
rored a distressed obsession with the spiritual tides besetting a soul bent on
redemption. His idiosyncrasies—a low opinion of schools and schoolmasters, an independence of mind that almost matched his son's, unsung
charity work on behalf of "fallen" women, a touch of individualism in his
High Tory politics—render him immune from caricature. But even if he
did refuse lay positions in the Kirk, Thomas took his soul seriously. Scotland being Scotland, he was from time to time at a low ebb when that
black melancholia peculiar to undiluted Calvinism overcame his sunny
disposition. He had, his son wrote later, a "morbid sense of his own un-
worthiness" that tainted his character. He had, too, said Louis, "a gift of
pleasing," but he did not often please himself.

Religion was as potent as whisky in Protestant Scotland then, and im-
bibed as freely. It was sure as gospel that decent folk lived by the Scrip-
tures. The Sabbath was observed with a neurotic devotion. In the cities
of Scotland the (ostensibly) Calvinist middle class dominated, and their
control of local councils meant that much of public life was as orderly as
Sunday school.

There had been an outcry in the 1840s when it was proposed that
trains be allowed to run on Sundays; there was another in the 1860s when
such immorality was at last permitted (though the Sabbath service remained limited for decades).* Many efforts had been made to control
public houses, a campaign which resulted in restrictive legislation in 1853.
Meanwhile, pious councillors strove to turn the tide of sin by reducing
Sunday working. For good measure they closed their own galleries and
museums on the day of rest. Even in the 1880s it could be said of Edinburgh that "One awoke on Sunday morning to a city of silence."†

The "Disruption" of 1843, which saw the Evangelical party march out
of the General Assembly of the Church of Scotland, taking perhaps forty
percent of adherents with them to form the Free Church, had been a na-

---

*Brown, C.: *A Social History of Religion in Scotland since 1730* (London, 1987); p. 133.
†Smout, T.C. and Wood, S.: *Scottish Voices, 1745–1960* (London, 1990); p. 128.

tional cause célèbre, transfixing the upper and middle classes as much for its political subtext as its ecclesiastical text. It was, essentially, a conflict over the rights of patronage in the appointment of ministers which went as far as the civil courts—but the motives of the protagonists made it more than that. For example, Thomas Chalmers, prime mover of the upheaval, believed that the state should give financial support to church extension to allow a truly Christian society to be created beneath the canopy of a free-market system. His funeral in 1847 attracted tens of thousands of mourners: a uniquely Scottish phenomenon.

Charles Guthrie, the student friend of R.L.S. who rose to the bench to become Lord Guthrie long after his "old comrade" conceded that the law was nothing to his taste, caught the temper of the times in a memoir published in 1920. "In early days," Guthrie wrote, "Great Gulfs were fixed between us. Stevenson's father and mother, Tories and State Church people, lived in the New Town of Edinburgh; and Louis went to the Edinburgh Academy. Mine, Liberals and Free Church, lived in the Old Town, and I attended the more democratic High School."

There was no dispute, however, over fundamentals. The Evangelicals venerated the Covenanters, those heroic bigots of the sixteenth and seventeenth centuries, defenders of the Reformation and enemies of episcopacy, who had risen up when Charles I attempted to impose a new liturgy on the Church of Scotland without reference to its General Assembly or to the Scottish Parliament. They were put down after the Restoration during twenty-five years of bloody oppression, but tales of these "Killing Times" were a staple for the young R.L.S. His father, too, was preoccupied with godliness even as he laboured to build lighthouses—though like the state Kirk man he was, he could sometimes indulge in a little theological unorthodoxy, such as the belief that even dogs' possessed souls. Whatever Louis's later reaction to his heritage, his antecedents supplied, from both the paternal and maternal lines, the perfect expression of middle-class Victorian Scotland. "We rose out of obscurity," he said, "in a clap."

The Balfours were churchmen; the Stevensons engineers. Those traditions of solid application and unimpeachable principle could be opposed but never ignored. Likewise the distinctiveness of a Scotland still ambivalent towards its assimilation into English culture (while exploiting the opportunities of the Union at every turn) meant the boy would ensure that the man, wherever he landed up, could never be other than a Scottish writer. The "Dedication of Catriona," written at Vailima on Samoa in 1892, put it best:

> ... I have come so far; and the sights and thoughts of my youth pursue me; and I see like a vision the youth of my father, and of his father, and the whole stream of lives flowing down there far in the north, with the sound of laughter and tears, to cast me out in the end, as by a sudden freshet, on these ultimate islands. And I admire and bow my head before the romance of destiny.

Thomas Stevenson's family had once been farmers in a small way, rising in due course to become millers, doctors, and West Indies traders before grandfather Robert earned grant of coat armour (a heraldic device depicting, naturally, a lighthouse), affirming the tribe's prosperity and sealing its status as pioneers of the mercantile class. Born in 1818, Thomas, like his wife, was one of thirteen children (though in his case only five of the family survived). Raised at 1 Baxter's Place in the shadow of the Calton Hill, with a caged eagle pining for a while in the long back garden, he had most of his fancy notions—including the idea that the writing of fiction could be a suitable pastime—knocked out of him at an early age.

R.L.S. speculated long and often (most notably in the unfinished *A Family of Engineers*) about his Stevenson forebears. "The name has a certain air of being Norse," he thought, and noted that his great-grandfather "wrote the name *Stevenson* but pronounced it *Steenson*." He tried hard to link the brood to the daring Rob Roy Macgregor, yet was obliged to admit:

> On the whole the Stevensons may be described as decent, reputable folk, following honest trades—millers, maltsters, and doctors, playing the character parts in the Waverley Novels with propriety, if without distinction ...

Louis claimed the first of them as, perhaps, one James who may have farmed at Nether Carswell near Glasgow in the mid-seventeenth century. A son, Robert, "possibly a maltster," had a son by his second wife in

1720, another Robert, but "certainly a maltster." This Stevenson married a Margaret Fulton, who bore him ten children.

Two of these, Hugh and Alan, born in 1749 and 1752 respectively, could be traced with more certainty than the patriarchs of R.L.S.'s imagination. "With these two brothers," he wrote towards the end of his life in *A Family of Engineers*, "my story begins," albeit a story derived from "tradition whispered me in childhood," with details filched from the family Bible.

The story went that the brothers owned the isle of St. Kitts. It was at least true that they traded in the West Indies, with Hugh, the elder of the two, on the spot, and Alan managing affairs at home. The latter married Jean Lillie, daughter of a Glasgow builder, and on June 8, 1772, she bore R.L.S.'s grandfather in that city. When the child was barely two, things went amiss with the brothers' business in the Caribbean. Alan, summoned by his brother, left his wife and child in order to deal with the problem and did not return.

Both brothers died, robbed of their business and their fortune; Hugh on Tobago in April 1774, Alan a month later on St. Kitts.

> An agent had proved unfaithful on a serious scale; and it used to be told me in my childhood how the brothers pursued him from one island to another in an open boat, were exposed to the pernicious dew of the tropics, and simultaneously struck down. The dates and places of their deaths would seem to indicate a more scattered and prolonged pursuit.

Meanwhile, Jean Stevenson's father also passed away. Young Robert's childhood thus became a grim round of charity schools and struggle. All of this later agitated the imagination of his grandson, who gloried in tales of lost treasure, infamy, sea-borne pursuits, tropical fevers, and birthrights denied; it could not have been so pleasant for Robert. Fortunately, however, Jean remarried when her son was fifteen. Her second husband was Thomas Smith, son of a skipper at Broughty Ferry on Tayside, who had made his fortune in Edinburgh as a shipowner, underwriter, and owner of a thriving business selling lamps and oils. He also ran a metalworking company.

In 1786, a year before his marriage to the Glasgow widow, Smith had been appointed Engineer to the newly created Board of Northern Light-houses. Thirty-three and twice before married, the devout, High Tory Smith had five children of his own. Nevertheless, he and Robert took to one another. The "Lighthouse Stevensons" were launched.

Robert Stevenson was a Victorian paragon, with all that implies in truth and cliché. Pragmatic, hardworking, conservative, fearless, and de-vout, he spent his summers as a youth travelling Scotland on the firm's business. In winter he studied, first at the Andersonian Institute in Glas-gow, then at Edinburgh University. By the age of nineteen he had super-vised the construction of his first lighthouse, at Little Cumbrae. When he was twenty-four his stepfather took him into partnership; three years later he married the twenty-year-old Jean Smith, his stepsister. On Thomas Smith's death, with the other children provided for, Robert inherited the business, the Baxter's Place property, and the old man's post as Engineer to the Board of Northern Lights.

His skill as an engineer justified R.L.S.'s later pride. An old *Britannica* (to which Robert was a contributor) mentions grandfather and grandson: Thomas earns his place only for siring Louis. His stepfather had replaced primitive coal fires with a system of oil lights but Robert threw a ring of twenty lights around Scotland's treacherous coasts while designing bridges, railways, and roads. In 1807 he commenced work on the Bell Rock light-house near Arbroath, constructing the 115-foot edifice on a reef covered to a depth of 12 feet at every tide. Sir Walter Scott, on tour with the Lighthouse Commissioners in the summer of 1814 and collecting material which would later turn up in *The Pirate*, recorded in his diary that Mr. Stevenson, "the surveyor-viceroy on the Commission," was a modest gen-tleman "well-known by his scientific skill." He called the Bell, first illu-minated in 1811, a "ruddy gleam of changeful light." This marvel of the modern age had cost an enormous forty-two thousand pounds to build. Thomas Stevenson, Robert's seventh and youngest son, was born four years after Scott's visit.

He came into a pious household dominated by the character and achievements of his father. By now Robert was a founder of Edinburgh's Royal Observatory; a member of the Institute of Civil Engineers; and a Fellow of the Royal Society of Edinburgh, of its Antiquarian Society and its Wernerian Society. He was also a Fellow of the Geological Society and the Astronomical Society of London. A man, in other words, of the Establishment.

A "high Tory and patriot," Robert had been ("so I find it in my notes," said R.L.S.) a captain of Edinburgh Spearmen, "and on duty during the Muir and Palmer troubles."

The anecdote places Louis's grandfather on the side of the loathsome Robert MacQueen, Lord Braxfield, the brutal judge who sentenced the advocate Thomas Muir and the Unitarian minister Thomas Fyshe Palmer to deportation in 1793 after what one history calls "a travesty of a trial." The pair had led a reform society, the "Friends of the People"; Muir had circulated a newspaper called *The Patriot* and had made speeches "of a most inflammatory and seditious tendency, falsely and insidiously representing the Irish and Scottish nations as in a state of downright oppression and exciting the people to rise up and oppose the Government."

Braxfield despised the French, from whom all such treason sprang, and Robert Stevenson followed suit: "The people of that land were his abhorrence; he loathed Buonaparte like Antichrist," according to R.L.S.

> Towards the end he fell into a kind of dotage; his family must entertain him with games of tin soldiers, which he took a childish pleasure to array and overset; but those who played with him must be upon their guard, for if his side, which was always that of the English against the French, should chance to be defeated, there would be trouble in Baxter's Place.

Very droll. But it says a good deal about the attitudes of the Stevensons and how they regarded themselves that their founding father sided with a judicial thug like Braxfield. Louis, too, took the Lord Justice-Clerk as a model, utilising him for *Weir of Hermiston*. In the essay "Some Portraits by Raeburn," published in *Virginibus Puerisque* in 1881, he explained something of his own ambivalent feelings towards the judge's "abstract vices."

> It is probably more instructive to entertain a sneaking kindness for any unpopular person, and among the rest, for Lord Braxfield, than to give way to perfect raptures of moral indignation against his abstract vices. He was the last judge on the Scottish bench to employ the pure Scotch idiom. His opinions, thus given in Doric, and conceived in a lively, rugged, conversational style, were full of point and authority . . . He has left behind him

an unrivalled reputation for rough and cruel speech; and to this day his
name smacks of the gallows . . . His summing up on Muir began thus . . .
'Now this is the question for consideration—Is the panel guilty of sedition
or is he not? Now, before this can be answered, two things must be attended to that require no proof: *First*, that the British constitution is the
best that ever was since the creation of the world, and it is not possible to
make it better.'

"It's a pretty fair start, is it not," wrote Louis, "for a political trial?" Yet
while admitting that Braxfield was "an inhumane old gentleman,"
Stevenson still found him "perfectly intrepid." His own politics would
thus be ever a strange mixture of Muir and Robert Stevenson, liberal and
reactionary, part his own sound sense and part the product of tangled
family loyalties. The uproar he was later to cause with his teenage "socialism" can be well imagined.

Robert Stevenson's vigour was utterly Victorian. He it was who
planned and drove the access route from Edinburgh's Princes Street to the
east of the city. Environmental concerns were of no consequence then;
when Robert's carefully calculated scheme for Regent Road encountered
the rocky mass of the Calton Hill, explosives were produced and the
south side of the obstruction blown away. An ancient graveyard was cut
through. The last obstacle, a deep glen, was bridged. It was 1815 and the
bridge was named—doubtless to the satisfaction of the patriotic Mr.
Stevenson—Waterloo Place.

Robert's wife, according to her grandson, was a "pious, tender soul,"
diligent in the reading of her Bible but not bereft of humour. "The marriage of a man of twenty-seven and a girl of twenty who have lived for
twelve years as brother and sister, is difficult to conceive," wrote R.L.S.
But Jean Stevenson—"devout and unambitious, occupied with her Bible,
her children, and her house; easily shocked, and associating with a clique
of godly parasites"—seems to have been a pliant foil to her strong-willed
husband.

He, meanwhile, was "possessed with a demon of activity in travel."
Scotland itself was his drawing board. After 1807, when his stepfather returned to private business, Robert Stevenson became sole ruler of the
lighthouse keepers:

All should go in his way, from the principal lightkeeper's coat to the assistant's fender, from the gravel in the garden-walks to the bad smell in the kitchen, or the oil spots on the store-room floor. It might be thought there was nothing more calculated to awake men's resentment, and yet his rule was not more thorough than it was beneficient . . . When he was at a lighthouse on a Sunday he held prayers and heard the children read. When a keeper was sick, he lent him his horse and sent him mutton and brandy from the ship.

Thomas Stevenson was educated at a private school in Edinburgh's Nelson Street, quite close to Baxter's Place, before being despatched to the Royal High School, first in the Old Town, then at that institution's imposing new quarters on the Calton Hill. No mathematician—and by his own account not much of a scholar—he nevertheless acquired a love of the Latin classics. Louis, something of an expert in such matters, called his father a "mere consistent idler" in his schooldays. Perhaps as a consequence Thomas was bound apprentice to his father's firm when he was seventeen, as were two of his brothers; all three followed their father to become, in turn, Engineer to the lighthouse board. By the age of twenty-eight Thomas was his father's partner.

There were three brothers. Alan, the eldest, was a classical scholar, a linguist who read Dante and Cervantes in the original, a music lover who corresponded with Wordsworth and yet suppressed his cultured nature to become an engineer. He built Skerryvore on the west coast and fathered a son who was to become one of Louis's closest friends. Perhaps as a result (this can only be speculation) of some conflict in his makeup between art and science, or because there were tensions behind the bluff facades of all the Stevensons, he eventually succumbed to a nervous breakdown and died in middle age.

David, the middle son, also entered the family firm but seemed, in years to come, to be overshadowed by his younger brother, Thomas. The father of R.L.S. was the toughest of the trio. An acute, naturally gifted scientist, he invented the first wave dynamometer, devised new portable surveying instruments, and introduced various improvements to light-house lamps.

Like Robert, Thomas seems to have had almost an instinct for engineering. "It cannot be imparted to another," he told Louis, an odd remark considering his later ambition to make his reluctant and unsuitable son part of the family tradition. R.L.S. recorded that his father

> ... would pass hours on the beach, brooding over the waves, counting them, noting their least deflection, noting when they broke. On Tweedside, or by Lyne or Manor, we have spent together whole afternoons; to me, at the time, extremely wearisome; to him, as I am sorry to think, bitterly mortifying. The river was to me a pretty and various spectacle; I could not see—I could not be made to see—it otherwise. To my father it was a chequer-board of lively forces, which he traced from pool to shallow with minute appreciation and enduring interest.

In 1847 Thomas, then twenty-nine, met and fell sincerely in love with Margaret Isabella Balfour, a pretty eighteen-year-old. Their first encounter was on a train to Glasgow; their second at a dance given by his older brother, Alan. In the early summer of 1848 he proposed to the minister's daughter and they were married on August 28 of that year.

Maggie Stevenson was the twelfth child and fourth daughter of the Reverend Lewis Balfour, third son of the laird of Pilrig and minister at Colinton. The village has long since been swallowed by Edinburgh but was then some four miles to the southwest of the city centre at the foot of the Pentland Hills, alongside the Water of Leith. Its manse inspired R.L.S. to some of his most intense bouts of nostalgia.

Lewis Balfour, born at Pilrig in 1777 and married to Henrietta Scott Smith in 1808, had come to Colinton in 1823. As a young man he had thought to become a merchant, but chest troubles—which his daughter and grandson were to inherit—persuaded him into the ministry. He was ordained in 1806 and his first charge was at Sorn, in Ayrshire, where he met his wife. She was herself the child of a local minister who had made the mistake of reproving Robert Burns for his sexual antics, thus earning two mentions in the poet's "Holy Fair." The poet made a pretence of concealment, but his target was clear enough:

> *S**th opens out his cauld harangues*
> *On practice and on morals;*
> *And aff the godly pour in thrangs,*

To gie the jars and barrels
A lift that day.

What signifies his barren shine
Of moral powers and reason?
His English style, and gestures fine,
Are a' clean out o' season.

The Balfour family tree had its roots in Protestant history. Originally from Fife, they were by the late seventeenth century deeply involved in the controversies between Kirk and Crown. One, James, was minister of the East Kirk of St Giles's, Edinburgh, and an associate of Andrew Melville the Reformer, to whom he was related. Such was the zeal of this Balfour that he became one of five ministers summoned to London to answer charges of disobedience to royal authority. Fortunately for the men of God, King James VI did not take the matter too seriously, restricting himself to teasing the Reverend Balfour about the inordinate length of his beard. He did detain the group in godless London for nine months, however.

One son, Andrew, became a minister also, siring another James. That child chose to let the Kirk take its own chances and became the family's first advocate. He also took the precaution of marrying well and, for a time, enjoyed considerable prosperity. Soon he owned lands in Aberdeenshire, soap works, glassworks, and an alum factory in Leith. With partners he acquired a monopoly on the manufacture of gunpowder. In fact, his only slip occurred when he agreed to become a governor of the disastrous Darien Company, the vehicle for Scotland's attempt to become a colonial power. He left his eldest son—yet another James—with a legacy of debt when the crash came.

Fortunately (until the perpetually hard-pressed R.L.S. neither the devout Balfours nor the industrious Stevensons ever seem to have worried for long about money) most of the Balfours' substance was restored in 1707, when a conciliatory England sought to mollify opposition to the Union, in part by repaying those who had suffered in the Darien venture because of London's chicanery. In 1718, with £4,222 of that money, James Balfour purchased Pilrig House, then set among farmland near Edinburgh, while his wife began the task of bearing seventeen children. Thirteen survived, a notable if exhausting achievement for the time.

The eldest of the brood, the second laird and R.L.S.'s great-grandfather, studied philosophy at Leyden before marrying the well-connected Cecilia Elphinstone. One of the lesser intellectual lights of his bright day, he became Sheriff-substitute of Midlothian and took it upon himself to attack David Hume's scandalous *Principles of Morals*. "You have turned your Thoughts too much inward on your Particular Temper; and been less attentive of the great Bulk of Mankind," sniffed this James. Hume dismissed his critic in his usual, icily polite and lethal style, but Balfour was revenged when he was preferred before the infamous sceptic for the chair of moral philosophy at Edinburgh University. Having fathered Lewis, given the world his *Philosophical Dissertations* and composed a quantity of poetry which he chose not to publish, Professor Balfour died, in 1795, aged ninety.

Lewis's oldest brother, another in the long line of Jameses, died aged seventeen, leaving their brother John to succeed as laird. The third son, not so weak in the chest that he would not live, like his daughter, to a ripe old age, took to the Church and, in time, to Colinton. He was, according to Stevenson's *Memoirs of Himself*, "the noblest looking old man I have ever seen . . . one of the last, I suppose, to speak broad Scots and be a gentleman . . ."

In his essay "The Manse," written in 1887, Louis imagined himself walking through eighteenth-century Edinburgh with his grandfather and passing "kinsmen of mine on the other side," though "they were of a lower order, and doubtless we looked down upon them duly." Nevertheless, by the time the young engineer married "the Minister's white-headed lassie," both Balfours and Stevensons were eminent among the middle classes of Edinburgh. To be eminent in that city was, it went without saying, to be eminent everywhere.

The rise of the Scottish professional classes is nowhere better seen than among Maggie Balfour and her siblings. One brother became Physician in Ordinary to the Queen in Scotland; another was in the medical service of the East India Company; a third Engineer to the Crown Colony of New Zealand. Her sisters married men of a similar stripe, as she married

Thomas Stevenson, even if the Balfours were, as R.L.S. liked to joke, better born.

The bride was thought comely, sweet-tempered, and averse to disagreements. Certainly she was free of her husband's black depressions, though she had to struggle with them. He was, or tried to be, as stern with himself as he was with others. David Angus, the great Victorian railway engineer who began his career as a junior assistant with the Stevensons (and filled the uncomfortable chair once reserved for R.L.S.), found that Thomas demanded the utmost from his employees. Angus's biographer records that "there was an established family tradition of relentless hard work" and "a commitment to high standards and high personal integrity." Thomas "kept a tight rein on his assistants no matter what less important task he had set them." He is described, particularly in his relationship with his brother David, as exerting a "dictatorship" over the firm's affairs.

Yet he was not entirely the bleak patriarch such an account implies and several writers on R.L.S. have suggested. The public rectitude of Victorian middle-class men was often matched by a private sentimentality or eccentricity. Friends described "Tom" as cheerful and somewhat droll; Fanny Vandegrift thought her father-in-law adorable from their first meeting onwards; he left money in his will for a "Magdalen" establishment to assist "fallen women." For all their later battles, Thomas was capable of spending hours amusing his sick child in the early years. His sense of fun was open and honest, as the process of *Treasure Island*'s composition was to show.

A man of immense self-possession with a strong, square face utterly unlike his offspring's feline profile, Thomas had a sure sense of honour. Like his brothers he refused, for example, to take out patents on any of his many inventions, preferring to share them with the world. Again, for all their conflicts, he never wavered in the pride he took in his son or in his support for him, even in the years when affection was tested and the financial cost was high. But there was a distress at the heart of Thomas, a species of doubt that belied his faith. His occasional depressions seem like the responses of a man manacled to his beliefs and duties. It was not that he opposed the articles of faith around which his life was built; rather that he knew his own character to be deeper, more generous, and more natural, than his Calvinism allowed. He had been shaped by his relationship with his father, as Louis was to be by their own relationship. Robert Stevenson, that ramrod of a man, had demanded much of his three sons, and they had accepted their obligations, curbing whatever other inclinations they had in the process. Thomas had helped to make his own fetters, but they chafed. Perhaps that was why he indulged his own child. In times to come his behaviour was such that he seemed almost to harbour a sneaking regard for his son's rebellions, a tolerance born of understanding. Not always, however.

Maggie had been known in Colinton as "daft about weans," but her own weak health meant that she could bear, or would choose to bear, only one child, and a miserable specimen at that. She often seemed weak and foolish, but there was an essential strength to her that the pose could not conceal. She became one of the three women who formed the tripod that supported her son throughout his life. Few others of her age and class would have upped sticks for the South Seas as she eventually did at the age of fifty-nine. Like the other women, she outlived her son.

Lineage mattered. Throughout his life Louis took his forefathers as guiding spirits; as guarantors. He objected and rejected but he gloried in the bloodlines. The past, the confluence of forces and events, helped to give him a Scottish sense of himself. Lewis, son of Thomas, son of Robert; Stevenson and Balfour. Character was a consequence of history.

As strictly raised as her husband, Maggie ensured that their child was dosed with approved religion but spared the dead weight of Thomas's bleak meditations. Louis discovered the meaning of those for himself, in his own time, in his nursery bedroom on the third floor of 17 Heriot Row.

2 1850–1865

. . . another air that I remember, not regret, was the solo of the gasburner in the little front room; a knockering, flighty, fleering, and yet spectral cackle. I mind it above all on winter afternoons, late, when the window was blue and spotted with rare raindrops, and looking out, the cold evening was seen blue all over, with the lamps of Queen's and Frederick's Street dotting it with yellow, and flaring eastward in the squalls. Heavens, how unhappy I have been in such circumstances . . .

*R*obert Lewis Balfour Stevenson was born on November 13, 1850. He was allowed two years of relative good health and suffered nine of intermittent illness in the embattled, isolated country of his childhood. The experience marked him, an only child transformed by loneliness, piety, and fever into "an ardent and uncomfortable dreamer," more deeply than even a Freudian might allow.

He was born north of the New Town proper, at 8 Howard Place, near the same Water of Leith that ran in a younger form past his grandfather's manse, in a ground-floor bedroom at the rear of the house. Among the decorations was an engraving of the Balfours' old opponent, David Hume, a figure greatly admired by the mischievous Thomas Stevenson. Nevertheless, he told one visitor that he would take the picture down "when the boy is old enough to notice it, for I should not like him to think Hume was one of my heroes."

One of his mother's bridesmaids described the child as "a fractious little fellow . . . though decidedly pretty." The names given to him were easy enough to explain: the first and last for his paternal grandfather, dead three months before the child was born; the middle pair for the maternal, aged when R.L.S. knew him. The Reverend Balfour christened the child in the house—an old, unexceptional Scottish practice but a symbolic one: everything was inheritance. Religion was assumed just as the future was assumed; with his lineage Smout, as the family nicknamed him after the young of the salmon, would grow up to become an engineer, a Presbyterian, and a New Town man of substance. Not even David Hume could have doubted it.

Nevertheless, his parents did not regard their wishes as commands, believing rather that what they offered was the best they had. For all the storms of adolescence to come, they loved the child. That he was the only one they had or would have made him the centre of the household. When he, too, began to suffer a series of illnesses, the devotion of his parents was redoubled.

Maggie and Tom Stevenson were robust, energetic individuals who lived long lives. Yet both seemed to indulge in hypochondria as though it were a morbid hobby. It is easy to misjudge the Victorian obsession with health: death came easily in those days, even in the best homes. But the Stevensons seem to have fretted more than most over the threat of illness. Thomas, to judge from some of his letters, his arguments with his son, and his depressions, had a neurotic streak. Maggie was often vapid, absent even when she was present, and coddled. Throughout Louis's childhood it was her habit to remain in bed until noon, whether she was ill or not.

Deeply in love as they were, the pair can at this distance seem self-involved to the point of childishness. It is assumed, for want of evidence, that Maggie Stevenson's health prevented her from having more than one child. Both Balfours and Stevensons were notably fecund, and "weakness" seems the only explanation. But it is hard to believe that she was as frail as she liked to believe, given her longevity and her later adventures. Illness may have been a pretext, used consciously or not, to prevent her husband's attention being diverted to a brood of children. Louis certainly believed that his parents had a relationship on which he intruded merely by being born. In any case, even if he had been the finest of physical specimens, he would still have grown up in a household preoccupied with human frailty. As a young man he wrote in a gloomy letter of a "gloomy family always ready to be frightened about their precious health."

His mother succumbed first, falling to the respiratory weakness which had sent her father to the Isle of Wight (sea breezes, a mild climate: the standard treatment) when he was twenty (though he lived until he was eighty-two). But Thomas, too, seems to have been prone to some sort of bronchial trouble. Soon the couple were travelling south for the winter, as so many did in those days, to France or to Italy. In summer—the seasonal heat of the Mediterranean being judged, on the very best authority, to be as dangerous as the chills of the northern winter—they chose their British holiday destinations with great care.

The Howard Place house deserved some of the blame. At that time the nearby Water of Leith offered, in addition to perpetual dampness, close proximity to sewage and the effluvia of local industry. Thus in 1853 the family moved to 1 Inverleith Terrace. The house was more handsome than its predecessor but turned out to be, if anything, even less congenial. Damp and mildew thrived, and the child did not. When well he was happy enough; he learned to speak early, and his mother recorded in her diary, in the summer of that year, that his favourite occupation was "making a church; he makes a pulpit with a chair and a stool; reads sitting, and then stands up and sings, by turns." But it was here, nevertheless, that the long purgatory of R.L.S.'s childhood began.

In *Memoirs of Himself*, written in San Francisco in 1880, Stevenson was explicit:

> I was an only child and, it may be in consequence, both intelligent and sickly. I have three powerful impressions of my childhood: my sufferings when I was sick, my delights in convalescence at my grandfather's manse of Colinton, near Edinburgh, and the unnatural activity of my mind after I was in bed at night.

First came a prolonged attack of croup (a croaking cough associated with inflammation of the larynx and trachea; perhaps noncharacteristic diphtheria) when he was twenty-nine months old. The laboured breathing of a sick infant is haunting, and it is easy to visualise the plump,

befrocked, curly-headed child of the first photographs disappearing as the
familiar, skeletal Louis began to emerge. Each of the nine following years
brought its woes in turn, dressed as fevers, sweating dreams, and endless
days in bed. Tuberculosis seems unlikely: in those days it would have
killed him, though he may have inherited a susceptibility to the disease.
But the combination of chilly Georgian interiors, Edinburgh's weather,
and an extraordinary lack of resistance banished the child to the Land of
Counterpane, susceptible to any ailment around. Illnesses which a more
robust infant would have shrugged off laid him low. Many of the barefoot
Edinburgh street urchins, ill-clad and ill-fed, coped with worse conditions
than mere draughtiness in a fine big house. Yet the move when he was
six to spacious Heriot Row, with its windows turned south to catch the
sun, did nothing to help: Smout's introduction to the new house was an
attack of "gastric fever" that almost killed him. To all intents and purposes
the boy was an invalid.

He had acquired a nurse, and no ordinary one. Alison Cunningham,
"Cummy" to the child and to the man who dedicated *A Child's Garden
of Verses* to her, was twenty-nine when she entered the Stevensons' service
at Howard Place. There had been other nurses—one was dismissed for
drinking in a pub while in charge of the baby—but Cummy was an extraordinary character, one worthy of her legend, whose influence did
Louis immense good and no little harm.

At least as devout as Thomas Stevenson, she had been brought up in
the Fife fishing village of Torryburn to distrust popery, speak up for herself (her habit of gesticulation was noted by many who met her), and
stand no nonsense. But the child, nursed through "a hacking, exhausting
cough" time and again, and "praying for sleep or morning from the bottom of my shaken little body," loved her. She looked after him—"more
patient than I can suppose of an angel"—from the age of eighteen months
until he was grown, and outlived him by nineteen years, dying revered
and conceited in Edinburgh, aged ninety-one. Which is to say that she
controlled his life, particularly the life of his mind, throughout his form-
ative years. Even at the end he was writing her affectionate letters. "My
parents and Cummy brought me up on the Shorter Catechism, porridge,
and the Covenanters," said Louis, saying the least of it.

After the death of R.L.S., Cummy allowed herself to be raised on a pedestal of Stevensonians, Still living, she was turned into a character, a little carping Victorian icon, and rendered less than real. Photographed in old age, she looked like "Whistler's Mother." But she was real enough in Louis's childhood, an abiding presence who insinuated herself even into his dreams. One legend had it that she had even given up the chance to marry because of her devotion to Louis. Lord Guthrie, in his memoir, recalled how she seized him by the arm

> . . . when I asked her about her alleged refusal to marry a man, to whom she was said to have been devotedly attached, on account of her resolution not to leave Louis. She scornfully replied, 'Devoted to that man! Fiddlesticks!'

Guthrie thought her "combination of devout piety and fondness for fun . . . a commoner one in Presbyterian Scotland than the playwrights and novelists would lead the world to believe . . . she was a Puritan of Puritans in religion and morals, but she was no ascetic." Contrary to the legend, however, it was, according to the judge (himself a later tenant of Swanston), "a common mistake to suppose that she was 'fond of children' in the ordinary sense of the phrase."

> The boys of the Taylor household , which succeeded the Stevensons in the tenancy of Swanston Cottage in 1880, have told me there was no love lost between them, residing in the Cottage, and Cummy, keeping house for the 'Waterman,' her brother James Cunningham, in the Gatehouse, after she had left the Stevensons' service.

It is a revealing anecdote of the woman whose own bed was kept in Louis's night nursery until he was almost ten years old. Cummy's name later became a cooing byword for selfless love and devotion to children, yet she did not find all children appealing. Youth had left her by the time of Guthrie's story, of course, but the saint of the legend seems to have departed with it.

In Steveson's childhood she was the sure centre of a turbulent, enclosed world. Cummy sang him ballads and psalms, read to him from the Bible and Bunyan (particularly during the long, still Edinburgh Sabbath), and told him "blood-curdling tales of the Covenanters and their strug-

gles." Just as important, particularly because Cummy read well and without affectation, she gave him a link with the Scots tongue, which
was then dying out in the better parts of the city, especially in the
New Town.

It was not all high seriousness. On Saturdays there was *Cassell's Illustrated Family Paper.*

> . . . we would study the windows of the stationer and try to fish out of
> subsequent woodcuts and their legends the further adventures of our
> favourites . . . Each new Saturday I would go from one news vendor's win-
> dow to another, till I was master of the weekly gallery and had thoroughly
> digested 'The Baronet Unasked,' 'So and So approaching the Mysterious
> House,' 'The Discovery of the Dead Body in the Blue Marl Pit,' 'Dr Vargas
> Removing the Senseless Body of Fair Lilias' . . .
>
> *Popular Authors*, 1888

It is hard to say which of the pair enjoyed these "penny-papers" more.
But Cummy, more than anyone, could claim to have aroused the mind
which later produced *Treasure Island*. Its obvious sources aside, the roots of
that novel are in those cheap publications, if anywhere. It has certainly
been suggested—by E. B. Simpson in *Robert Louis Stevenson's Edinburgh*,
published in 1913—that Stevenson's earliest fiction was dictated to his
nurse before the end of 1854, though no manuscript evidence survives to
support the claim. It hardly matters.

Less sentimentally, Cummy might also be accused of having fed the
vulnerable, hyperactive imagination of a child prone to nightmares and often deprived, because of illness, of the company of his peers. It may even
be said that the nurse was culpable in peopling his terrifying dreams. In
addition to her Calvinist bigotry—not discouraged in a household whose
head later became the author of *Christianity Confirmed by Jewish and Hea-
then Testimony and the Deductions from Physical Science*—Cummy was super-
stitious. Her idea of a constitutional was to take the child for a stroll
through Warriston Cemetery, a habit harmless enough in itself had she
not also filled his head with tales of body snatchers. His famous person-
ification of storm-swept Edinburgh nights, and their impression on him as
a child, have her mark.

... the horrible howl of the wind round the corner; the audible haunting of an incarnate anger about the house; the evil spirit that was abroad; and, above all, the shuddering silent pauses when the storm's heart stands dreadfully still for a moment. Oh how I hate a storm at night! ... I always heard it as a horseman riding past with his cloak above his head, and somehow always carried away, and riding past again, and being baffled yet once more, *ad infinitum*, all night long.

Scottish servants had a reputation for familiarity in those day. Regarded, and regarding themselves, as intregal parts of the household, they were often possessive of their charges, young or old. Cummy, at least, was in the habit towards the end of her life of referring to R.L.S. as "my laddie," even when she was demanding "something handsome" for the sale of autographed copies of *Kidnapped, Memories and Portraits, Travels with a Donkey*, and others of his works he had given her. It was a possessiveness verging on the desire to control. Of the mixture of sinister old tales, religious extremism, illness, and nightmare in the young Steveson's mind, James Pope Hennessey noted, acutely: "Psychologically it is . . . interesting to reflect upon the fact that Cummy was inducing a state of mental tumult which only she could claim."*

R.L.S.'s mother seems to have had little say in any of this; probably she saw nothing out of the ordinary; certainly she professed ignorance. In *Memoirs of Himself* Louis recalled his "high-strung religious ecstasies and terrors."

It is my nurse that I owe these last: my mother was shocked when, in days long after, she heard what I had suffered. I would not only lie awake to weep for Jesus, which I have done many a time, but I would fear to trust myself to slumber lest I was not accepted and should slip, ere I awake, into eternal ruin ... It is not a pleasant subject ... I shook my numskull over the spiritual welfare of my parents, because they gave dinner parties and played cards, things contemned in the religious biographies on which my mind was fed; and once, for a crowning point, I turned the tables on my nurse herself.

*Hennessey, J.P.: *Robert Louis Stevenson* (London, 1974); p. 30.

That night, while Cummy read from *Cassell's Family Paper*, he suffered "a pain in my side which frightened me: I began to see Hell pretty clear, and cast about for any sin of which this might be punishment." He found it in the story his nurse was reading and foreswore such "worldliness" instantly.

The interest of the anecdote lies in how little he blamed Cummy and the extent to which fear and illness were entangled. Plainly, the child thought sickness a punishment, and since he was sick more often than most, he must have thought himself more wicked than most. Cummy was part of the nightmare, yet in the confused moral universe of the child he loved her for it, just as the older Louis forgot and forgave.

It is no surprise, then, that the first work of the writer's which is preserved is "The History of Moses." Louis dictated the piece to his mother when he was six years old, towards Christmas 1856, just before the move to Heriot Row. His uncle, David Stevenson, had offered a prize—a Bible picture book, by one account; one pound, by that of R.L.S.—for a competition among Louis and his cousins. In her diary Mrs. Stevenson recorded: "It was begun on Nov. 23 and finished on Dec. 21st; he dictated every word himself on the Sunday evenings—the only help I gave him was occasionally to read aloud to him from the Bible to refresh his memory."

His mother was an able amanuensis. "There was a woman that had a child when all the babies were to be drowned and she was a good woman and she asked God how she could save her baby and God told her to make a basket of rushes and put it in the water, hiding it in the rushes," said the child before pausing for breath. He "contributed the illustrations in a very free style," showing some of the "Israelites going out [*sic*] Egypt" smoking pipes and "cheering the desert miles," together with a precise description of one of the plagues: "After that he sent swarms of flies which buzzed about in the most horrible manner." Louis won the prize.

Imagination, imprisoned in this theological theatre, was all the child had. Religion became his entertainment and he became a miniature fanatic, lecturing the adults on their failings. Otherwise Cummy told him her tales; his father made up stories; he amused himself with drawings, with toy soldiers on the counterpane, and with "Skelt's Juvenile Drama," the makings of a model theatre purchased from a stationer's in Leith Walk. Through it all his parents worried and prayed, but Louis failed to respond to either treatment, even if his nurse (who must bear most of the blame) had given him an altogether unhealthy appreciation of sin. "I remember repeatedly . . . waking from a dream of Hell," he wrote in *Memoirs of Himself*, "clinging to the horizontal bar of the bed, with my knees and chin together, my soul shaken, my body convulsed with agony."

By his own account, his dreams were extraordinarily vivid, and he remained fascinated with them, mining them for material, to the end of his life. "A Chapter on Dreams," written late in 1887 for *Scribner's Magazine*, explored these experiences and their effect on him. The essentials of the vampire story "Olalla" and *The Strange Case of Dr. Jekyll and Mr. Hyde* came to him in dreams. In his essay Stevenson described "that strong sense of man's double being, which must at times come in and overwhelm the mind of every thinking creature . . ."

Freud would have said that his dreams represented repressed desires; Jung that they were "the collective unconscious" of all humankind. Others posit the psychological importance of dreams during R.E.M. (rapid eye movement) sleep, especially for those under stress. Others still mention "involuntary poetic activity" or a mysterious problem-resolving activity. But for Louis, in childhood, the distinction between dreams and waking reality was not always a clear one. In his day it might have been said that dreams came from God; he would have believed it. His early life, as he remembered it, had the quality of hallucination.

It is difficult to imagine the childhood that left such vivid, terrible memories decades later, or to understand why Stevenson always held his nurse in such high regard. He was aware, of course, that her influence had been both good and bad. But with his mother often ill, in bed, or both, and his father often away, she was all he had, and in her way she cared more for him than for anyone else in the world. Cummy, "second mother," was always there, especially in the night, that period forever associated in his mind, and often in his art, with disorientation and a world out of order.

I remember with particular distinctness, how she would lift me out of bed, and take me, rolled in blankets, to the window, whence I might look forth

into the blue night starred with street-lamps, and see where the gas still
burned behind the windows of other sick-rooms. These were feverish,
melancholy times; I cannot remember to have raised my head or seen the
moon or any of the heavenly bodies; my eyes were turned downward to
the broad lamplit streets and to where the trees of the garden rustled together all night in undecipherable blackness; yet the sight of the outer
world refreshed and cheered me; and the whole sorrow and burden of the
night was at an end with the arrival of the first of that long string of country carts that, in the dark hours of the morning, with the neighing of
horses, the cracking of whips, the shouts of drivers and a hundred other
wholesome noises, creaked, rolled and pounded past my window.

Memoirs of Himself

The sight of the outer world refreshed and cheered me. Louis's terrors were
indoors, where prayers and the devil, sickness and silence, lay. It had not
even mattered that night still prevailed outside: there was light, and the
"wholesome noises"—any noises—of the awakening world. His own
world was one of slow footfalls, flickering lights, frowning adults, and per-
dition waiting to claim him. A theology built on damnation was no con-
solation to a child who must have felt he was being made to suffer; the
belief of the adults around him that God, for reasons best known to Himself, had willed his condition could only have made the terror worse. *Outside* was the sole competing argument.

The invented tales with which Smout consoled himself, and the games
he played with his older cousin Bob, were other escapes. Bob—Robert
Alan Mowbray Stevenson—was the son of Louis's uncle Alan, and elder
by three years. He spent the winter of 1856–57 at Inverleith Terrace, for
reasons unknown, though the alleged "mental instability" of his father
may have had something to do with it. Alan Stevenson, another engineer,
was eleven years older than Thomas, and died at the age of fifty-eight.

Together the boys played with the model theatre or in kingdoms they
imagined for themselves ("Nosingtonia" for Bob, "Encyclopaedia" for
Louis). It was more important to Louis than anyone then realized. In the
essay "Child's Play," published in the *Cornhill Magazine* in 1878, he wrote:

In the child's world of dim sensation, play is all in all. 'Making believe' is
the gist of his whole life, and he cannot so much as take a walk except in
character . . . I remember, as though it were yesterday, the expansion of

spirit, the dignity and self-reliance, that came with a pair of mustachios in burnt cork, even when there was none to see. Children are even content to forego what we call the realities, and prefer the shadow to the substance.

\

All children do it, but through such devices Louis, choosing shadow before substance, began to rescue himself. Happiness was elsewhere, out of the house or in imagination. He had no real choice but to follow. If his own accounts are in any way accurate, it is not an exaggeration to suggest that the child must, at times, have been very near breakdown, his feverish mind confused and wandering, his fertile brain sown with sin and devil. As he wrote:

> We learn, as we grow older, a sort of courage under pain which marvellously lightens the endurance; we have made up our mind to its existence as a part of life; but the spirit of the child is filled with dismay and indignation, and these pangs of the mind are often little less intolerable than the physical distress that caused them.
>
> *Memoirs of Himself*

If the world of home meant him no harm, then or later, it harmed him just the same, keeping the Sabbath (when reading and play were banned) with all the dour, dutiful intensity of which the Presbyterian sect was capable. The Stevensons and Cummy thought the child pleasingly and precociously devout: disturbed would be the modern word. Even for its highly strung day, the childhood of R.L.S. was odd. He was surrounded by adults and was the centre of attention. Each of his elders had mental quirks, and each imbued him with a version of faith more remarkable for its rigour than its charity. As a three-year-old, according to his doting mother's diary, Louis was "distressed to hear that sheep and horses did not know about God" and said that someone should read the Bible to them. In "The Foreigner at Home," written in 1882, he suggested that

> Sabbath observance makes a series of grim and perhaps serviceable pauses in the tenor of Scottish boyhood—days of great stillness and solitude for the rebellious mind, when in the dearth of books and play, and in the intervals of studying the Shorter catechism, the intellect and senses prey upon and test each other . . . About the very cradle of the Scot there grows up a hum of metaphysical divinity.

Cummy was there to rock the cradle. She was no dragon—he would not have loved one—and she could dance as well as pray. Bit it is a mark of how deeply Calvinism penetrated his own psyche that even as an adult Stevenson could not distinguish between her love and the childhood she created for him. His childhood circumstances were very Scottish, typical of his class and his day. But he was not typical: the solitude of illness had seen to that. As it was, survival lay in the "outer world"—and in the products of his imagination. It says much for his own innate mental hygiene that he rid himself of so many of the assumptions and presumptions on which he was raised. At the very least, *A Child's Garden of Verses* seems an altogether darker production than some of us were once led to believe, a fantasy opposing the reality acknowledged elsewhere

> *O Mother, Lay your hand upon my brow!*
> *Out in the city, sounds begin,*
> *Thank the kind God, the carts come in.*
>
> "The Sick Child"

Formal education began late in his sixth year, and it was another trial. A proponent of the "university of life," his father affected to despise schools and schoolmasters. He had, too, a loathing for mathematics peculiar in an engineer. And since he himself had played truant often enough from the old High School, he cannot have been too surprised subsequently by Louis's unsatisfactory scholastic career. Nevertheless, Thomas accepted that the boy had to be educated.

Sent first to Canonmills School, he was, according to one former pupil's recollection of *another* former pupil's recollection, "the butt of the school from the oddity of his appearance." That peer, William Boss, did however claim to remember a solitary Stevenson one day making "a mute appeal . . . for sympathy" amid the playground bustle. The anecdote is plausible, no more: away from his cousins he was a lonely child who floundered in his efforts to adjust to the company of other children. With Bob or his Balfour cousins he took a leading part in games; with others he was less sure of himself, fearing ridicule or rejection. Later in life his charm—and his ego—would grow as though to balance this early inarticulate solitude, as though in defence, or as a riposte on behalf of the misunderstood. But in the days when he was most vulnerable he had few weapons with which to protect himself. When well, he enjoyed physical activity, but this frailness made him avoid sport, and reminded him (as if a coddled only child needed reminding) of his singularity.

Illness, always. He did not learn to read until he was seven, and in *Memoirs of Himself* he gave a malady credit even for that achievement:

> I learned to read when I was seven, looking over the pictures of the illus-
> trated papers while recovering from a gastric fever. It was thus done at a
> blow; all previous efforts to teach me having been defeated by my active
> idleness and remarkable inconsequence of mind.

After Canonmills he was despatched to a preparatory instituion in India Street, but attended for only a few weeks before sickness again claimed him. He returned briefly to the school in 1859. When he was almost eleven he was enrolled, together with two of his Balfour cousins, in a class of some five dozen boys, at the august Edinburgh Academy.

Grandfather Lewis had died shortly before at the old Colinton manse, and that event, together with his enrolment at the academy, closed the first, uniquely strange chapter of the boy's life. Colinton had been his proto-arcadia, with its garden touching the river, its church-yard, hedges, and trees, its intimations of escape. They called him Lou now, not Smout. "It was a place in time like no other," he wrote of Colinton in his essay "The Manse."

The house, filled with trophies brought from the Far East by his mother's adventurous brothers, was run by his aunt Jane, Miss Jane Whyte Balfour, "chief of our aunts," who had devoted herself to the white-haired and awesome Reverend Balfour even before his wife's death six years previously. "The little country manse was the centre of the world, and Aunt Jane represented Charity," Louis thought.

She had once been a vivacious beauty but a fall from a horse had left her partly deaf and with poor sight. She spoiled Lou, bought him wooden soldiers, and encouraged the war games which were to be his quaint hobby throughout his life (to the point where his wife could claim, amid civil unrest on Samoa, that he would rather have been a soldier than a writer). More important, the manse was usually overrun with cousins,

half a dozen and sometimes more, some local and some returned from India. There were games and adventures all day and every day, even if the
experiment of eating buttercups was not one which recommended itself
more than once. It was not the ideal convalescence—once, his overexer-
tions sent him back to bed for two days—but Colinton was the closest
thing Lou had to a normal childhood; it had none of the terrors, the dark
corners, and the nightmares underwritten by Scripture of Heriot Row.
Jane Whyte Balfour earned herself a grateful verse in the *Child's Garden*:

> Chief of our aunts—*not only I,*
> *But all your dozen of nurslings cry—*
> *What did the other children do?*
> *And what were childhood, wanting you?*

Paradise was again postponed with the Reverend Balfour's death, aged
eight-two in 1860, the breakup of the household, and Aunt Jane's departure for London. She returned to Colinton years later, and when Maggie
Stevenson came back to Edinburgh for the last time, the sisters set up
house together. As long-lived as most of the Belfours, Aunt Jane survived
until 1907. But for ten-year-old Louis only seaside holidays, to North
Berwick in East Lothian in particular, offered some compensation for
what he had lost.

The illnesses persisted: five weeks in the autumn of 1858 when he
could not even sit up in bed; in 1859 chickenpox followed by months of
invalidism; in 1861 whooping cough, followed by six weeks in bed. He
suffered all the usual childhood ailments, as many of his biographers have
said, but given the mortality rates of the day it is some sort of miracle that
his exhausted body survived the endless assaults. The effect of sickness on
his personality was equally powerful.

Again, one begins to suspect that the clinical atmosphere of the
Stevenson household gave him little chance to develop resistance: Lou was
treated as sick or teetering on the edge of the precipice even when illness
was not diagnosed. His parents continued to feel unwell; in 1862 and
1863 the family went abroad after his father was "threatened"—whether
the threat came to anything is, interestingly, not recorded—"with spitting
blood." His mother also suffered some unidentified ailment around this

time. They travelled first to the south of England and to Germany, though neither trip left a remembered mark on Lou. His recorded composition (for 1861) was "The Antiquities of Midlothian," a description of visits to Craigmillar Castle, on the eastern edge of Edinburgh, and Corstorphine Church in the west.

It is difficult to write about Stevenson's education, for he scarcely had one. In 1861, when he was almost eleven, he had joined the youngest class at Edinburgh Academy with the two Balfour cousins, both named Lewis, but he did not thrive and did not prosper in a year and half under the tutelage of Mr. D'Arcy Wentworth Thompson, a pedgogue with a literary bent. Illness had a good deal to do with it, but his parents, who thought nothing of plucking him from the classroom when the urge to travel took them, did not help. In 1862 the family was in London and the Isle of Wight; in 1863 they were in Menton for two months, followed by a tour of Italy, Austria, and Germany for a further three. On both occasions these excursions were mounted for the sake of his *parents'* health, not his. But Louis's educational needs seem to have occurred to no one. It is, if nothing else, a mark of how involved the elder Stevensons were with themselves. After the European tour, at any rate, Louis did not return to the academy.

Cummy must have felt the mistress of such a situation and such a household. The master was distant, often preoccupied with his own health, distracted with worry over his son but not much impressed by the need for formal education, and, in any case, often away on business. In the matter of a sick child, Tom was as ineffectual as a Victorian father was expected to be. During this period Mrs. Stevenson, meanwhile, gave a fair impersonation of the weak, coddled Victorian wife of cliché, with little more on her mind than her kangaroo vines and church bazaars. She seemed a woman made dependent by her husband's affection and only too happy to allow the nurse to do as she thought best.

It was a dubious proposition. Only once did Maggie Stevenson forbid Lou's exposure to the works of one of Cummy's Calvinist fanatics. Otherwise it was a household in which power was distributed in unusual ways. Surviving childhood—an experience which, paradoxically, toughened him as it weakened him—all Lou had to do was slip the leash, and he worked to that end as soon as he could claim to be adult. Nevertheless

Alison Cunningham can best be remembered as the first of a group of strong, mature women who were, in their several ways, to dominate R.L.S.

That his parents were devoted to one another is beyond doubt. That Lou felt himself to be part of a secondary and subordinate relationship is equally certain. "The children of lovers are orphans," he said later. As an only child he was accustomed to attention and probably unduly upset on the rare occasions when he did not receive it. What is less clear is the influence this estrangement had on him. Certainly it gave him a taste for mother figures, and for erotic intimacy—*solitude à deux*. It also gave him a reason to rebel, or at least to set himself apart from the society of which Tom and Maggie were a part. But also, one suspects, it made him idealise the relationship between man and woman, to expect more of it than the world was likely to offer. To the adult R.L.S., love was an intense, serious business.

The European trip of 1863 prepared him for the thrill of escape, hinting at the variety of alternatives to Edinburgh the world had to offer. For one thing, Cummy (now Maggie Stevenson's maid) objected vehemently to the flamboyant popery of the natives—"It is awful to see the dozens of priests going about," she told her scandalised diary, "and allowing such wickedness to go unchecked." But to see her so exposed, her omnipotence so easily negated, must have had its effect. Similarly Lou, more mature than his years, was treated to some extent like an adult for the first time during that long excursion. Perhaps as a way of appeasing his own conscience for taking the boy from school, Thomas tried to turn the jaunt into an educational trip. Louis was taken to the smoking room of a Nice hotel for example, there to be exposed to the habits of several exotic nationalities, and initiated by his father into an appreciation of art and architecture. Bessie Stevenson, daughter of R.L.S.'s uncle David, accompanied the family on the trip and said Louis was more like a boy of sixteen than twelve.

Another influence was the atmosphere of the south itself, the hot reek and pure light of Provence. The full extent of its impact was to be recorded after another, later illness, but the sense, recognised by others before and since, of being *at home* in an atmosphere as different from home as it was possible to imagine, was profound. "The Rhone is the River of Angels," he told a friend years later. "I have adored it since I was 12 and saw if first from the train." The weather was no longer an enemy; invalidism might be conquered; the society of Edinburgh, the given of his existence, was not the only possible way of life. The world, suddenly, was a welcoming place. He was out of the nursery.

Cummy left a record of the trip in a "diary" not published until 1926. In reality it was less a journal than a collection of letters written to her friend "Cashie," nurse to the children of David Stevenson. It is wonderfully revealing of Alison Cunningham—wide-eyed, often horrified, and thoroughly bigoted. Leaving Edinburgh on January 2, the party made their stately way through York, London, Dover, Amiens, Paris, Lyons, Marseilles, Toulon, Cannes, Nice, Mentone (as it was then known), San Remo, Voltri, Chiavari, Pisa, Naples, Rome, Siena, Bologna, Venice, Innsbruck, Munich, Nuremberg, Frankfurt, and Ghent until, when May was almost at an end, they returned to London.

Amiens, Tuesday, January 6

My Dear Cashie,

We have crossed the Channel, and are now on French ground (2 P.M.). My beloved Lew was very sick in crossing; his papa attended to him. Mrs Stevenson, Miss Bessie, and myself were all lying in the cabin, afraid to lift our heads. None of us were sea-sick but Lew.

We have come to a place called AMIENS (7 P.M.). How strange and foreign everything looks! The houses are so funny inside. No sitting-room in this Hotel! They have all gone to supper. I had something at the refreshment rooms on the road, so I am not going down for anything, but here comes Miss Stevenson with some wine to me.

Evidently Cummy knew her place, and it was a comfortable one. Her Calvinism did not prevent her form taking a glass of wine—in Paris she chose it before beer—but it banished any understanding of Catholic countries. At Lyons, only a week from home, she noted priests and nuns "in great numbers . . . They go with a slow, measured step, and are most dejected-looking, seemingly too good for this wicked world." At Cannes she went walking with a young Irish lady's maid and visited the cathedral.

The girl explained all to me, and when we were coming out, she kneeled down and prayed. After she rose, I asked her what water that was in a font at the door. 'Holy water,' she replied, dipped her finger in it and crossed her forehead. 'Is that what you call holy water?' I said, and put my finger to see if it was like other water. Of course it is, they say, but consecrated and made holy by the priests. Deluded mortals!

It is hard now to feel the same affection for Cummy that Louis and his early devotees did. A few years later, in a sketch entitled "Nurses," he criticised the institution of the nanny, but in 1863, in the Stevenson household, her vapourings went unremarked. At Nice she was unwell, feeling herself "a very weak body sometimes. O may I profit by the rod in whatever form it may appear! Have not been up the Alps yet . . ." Later she reported on heathenish behaviour at a town carnival:

Been at church all day to-day . . . only a cold, dead heart kept me from enjoying it.

Fearful doings here again to-day, people imitating a funeral, carrying a figure representing a body, I suppose . . . They laugh and go on in a shock-ing manner, and are all dressed in white. Others again were parading the streets to-day in all the different gay colours . . . Some of them have a kind of red false face and queer-looking hat, and a horn sticking right up in front of their forehead, they are frightful-looking objects. When I came out of church this afternoon, I saw a great crowd at the other side of the water, and went across the bridge to see what it could be. It turned out to be some of these foolish men going on at an awful rate . . . I turned away in disgust. Just after I left, I met a priest. I let him pass me, then I followed him to see if he would not try to put a stop to such wickedness on the Lord's day. When he came up to the crowd, he stood on tiptoe . . . to see what was going on. I was quite shocked to see him laughing with the rest instead of trying to put a stop to it. I could stand no longer, so turned my face homewards . . .

During the Victorian era the British abroad earned a reputation for ar-rogance and ignorance. It has been said, rightly, that only their servants excelled them. Cummy—self-righteously aghast at "worldly pleasure of every kind, operas too!"—was a match for them all. Her *Diary* is the per-fection of the unquestioning belief, the parochial small-mindedness, in which Stevenson was raised. His parents may have been more sophisticated, but their outlook was little different from that of their maid. It is usual to remark that society was different then, and somehow exempt from judgment. Cummy makes such charity difficult; her bigotry was timeless. Just the nurse for a malleable boy.

For him, school remained a trial. After the experiment with Edinburgh Academy he was sent to a boarding school called Spring Grove, at Isleworth, near London. Aunt Jane, having moved from Colinton, was already boarding several of Louis's cousins nearby, and presumably someone had concluded that their presence at the school would help the lonely and difficult child.

It did not, of course: like generations of other sensitive boys he was thoroughly unhappy, averse to his English schoolmates (the beginning, perhaps, of his Anglophobia) and to their strenuous games. His father, he said in a report to Heriot Row, was to "take comfort" from the fact that he had not played cricket. Louis lasted a term before writing a desperate letter home (as he had been instructed to do should such an emergency arise) saying he felt unwell. In "The Foreigner at Home," R.L.S. recalled that:

> The boy of the South seems more wholesome [than the Scot], but less thoughtful; he gives himself to games as to a business, striving to excel, but is not readily transported by imagination; the type remains with me as cleaner in mind and body, more active, fonder of eating, endowed with a lesser and a less romantic sense of life and of the future, and more immersed in present circumstances.

It would have been difficult in the extreme for any boy to have been more romantic and less "immersed in present circumstances" than Louis. Still, Thomas appeared to understand—for all his undoubted narrow-mindedness, the stereotype of the Victorian patriarch never quite fits— and he rescued the child, carrying him off to Menton once again, a gesture symbolic to the son if not the father. The family spent Christmas on the Riviera (a season extended, typically for the Stevensons at leisure, until May of 1864) and afterwards the decision was taken not to return the boy to the English school. It is not hard to understand why the dazzling south was, for Lou, synonymous with escape.

His next school was run by a Mr. Robert Thomson in Edinburgh's Frederick Street. It had fewer than twenty pupils and a good reputation for its modern methods. Even with his health somewhat improved, however—". . . not a delicate boy as I remember him," one fellow pupil recalled—Lou did not flourish there. He was "quite a good scholar," particularly able in Latin and Greek, but otherwise unremarkable. Institutional life did not suit him—he had his father's tacit agreement in this—but he did begin writing and editing schoolboy magazines (the *Schoolboy*, in 1863, and the *Sunbeam*—"an illustrated Miscellany of Fact, Fiction, and Fun, edited by R. L. Stevenson"—in 1866) singlehandedly. By his mid-teens he had attempted a couple of novels set in Covenanting days.

H. Bellyse Baildon, a fellow pupil and a turn-of-the-century writer on Stevenson, recalled that Mr. Thomson's charges covered a range of ages and intellects. Some, he wrote, "were sent there for reasons of health, and others because they had not made that progress with their studies which their fond parents had hoped. Others were there, I fancy, because the scheme of education upon which the proprietor . . . proceeded fell in with the views of our parents."

In the case of Louis, all three reasons were plausible. Mr. Thomson's establishment must have seemed like Thomas Stevenson's last hope. No homework was set: the pupils "learned, in the two or three hours of afternoon school, what we were expected to remember next day."

Baildon remembered that Louis put his leisure to use. "For even then he had a fixed idea that literature was his calling, and a marvellously mature conception of the course of self-education through which he required to put himself in order to succeed." This sounds suspiciously like a statement made with the benefit of hindsight. Nevertheless, a man imagining the child anticipating the man, Baildon recalled:

Among other things we were encouraged to make verse translations, and for some reason or other, I specially well remember a passage of Ovid, which he rendered in Scott-like octosyllabics, and I in heroic couplets . . . But, even then, Stevenson showed impatience of the trammels of verse, and longed for the compass and ductility of prose.

Indeed. In any case, his parents persisted in disrupting an education which had never achieved continuity. In the spring of 1865 and 1866 he was with his mother at Torquay. Trips around Scotland filled the gaps between longer holidays. In the midst of it all he picked up what learning he could—from a French tutor in France (though on the second trip to Menton the gentleman did little but teach the boy card tricks), a German tutor in Torquay, a schoolmaster at Peebles. Tutors were also procured during his illnesses. All things considered, it was fortunate that, spoiled as he was, Louis had a good mind. Otherwise he would truly have become the parasitic buffoon many later took him to be.

Baildon remembered that at fourteen Lewis Stevenson, as schoolmates knew him, "was assuredly badly set up. His limbs were long, lean, and spidery, and his chest flat, so as almost to suggest some malnutrition such sharp corners did his joints make under his clothes. But in his face this was belied . . . The eyes were always genial . . ." He was reading Shakespeare, Scott, and Dumas (the last taste inspired by illustrated dessert plates he had come across in Nice). His health had improved somewhat, but in a household preoccupied to the point of obsession with illness, only an overnight transformation into a champion athlete would have stilled his parents' fears.

The hills, at least, engaged him. Colinton had given him the taste for the broad reaches of the Pentlands, where the wind whipped clouds and gorse alike and each day brought a promise of fresh horizons. The hills had history in them. They became the backdrop for his imagination.

Meanwhile, as he grew, wilful, skinny, and contrary, he found another escape. In place of the fantasies that had preserved him in childhood, he discovered a transfixing reality in the filthy wynds of the Old Town and the grubby exotica of the New Town's fringes. That, too, was another world, garish and bright, dark and romantic. He was beginning to write, not well but avidly, as though that was all he would ever want to do. It was, by any measure, all he could do.

3 1866–1870

The happiest lot on earth is to be born a Scotsman. You must pay for it in many ways, as for all other advantages on earth. You have to learn the Paraphrases and the Shorter Catechism; you generally take to drink; your youth, as far as I can find out, is a time of louder war against society, of more outcry and tears and turmoil, than if you had been born, for instance, in England. But somehow life is warmer and closer; the hearth burns more redly; the lights of home shine softer on the rainy street; the very names, endeared in verse and music, cling nearer round our hearts.

THE SILVERADO SQUATTERS

The Edinburgh of Stevenson's youth was a city divided, but the division was neither neat nor obvious. The physical bifurcation was no more complete then than it is now; the social gulf absolute only when it was insisted upon, and then for the sake of appearances, which were everything. The mass of the Old Town loomed over the New, safe behind the barrier of Princes Street and its gardens, but even in the barracks of the genteel, that "wilderness of the square-cut stone," there were patches of life altogether less respectable. The middle classes had not yet been entirely anglicised; their speech resembled the speech of the poor more than it does today; not all the schools to which they sent their children had yet begun unthinkingly to ape English institutions. And in the small place the city was (and remains), everything and everyone, high or low, was within walking distance.

Edinburgh's apparent spaciousness is something of an illusion, and in the 1860s and 1870s the classes touched on one another in several places.

To the west of Heriot Row was insalubrious Lothian Road ("O sweet Lothian Road / O dear Lothian Road," sang an older R.L.S.); to the east Leith Street; to the south the Old Town; and to the north the rowdy Port of Leith. But the haunts of the working class extruded, like calloused fingers, even into the New Town. Rose Street, tucked behind the Princes Street shops, was notorious for prostitution, and remained so until very recently. Jamaica Street, whose tiny pubs Stevenson was to frequent, was actually overlooked by the back rooms of Heriot Row. The physical barriers—the contrast between Old Edinburgh and that architectural assertion of a contrary spirit, the New—were real enough, substantiated by the city's unique topography and the accretions of history. But the true divide, cutting through streets and buildings, was one of class.

Looking at the New Town today, with its relatively low population densities and its abundance of offices, it is hard to imagine it as it was in Stevenson's youth. The big houses suggest a leisured calm; the wide streets imply gracious, ordered living. But the New Town then was a bustling place, with a population per acre greater than that of most modern housing estates. Today the main thoroughfares fall quiet after six P.M. In Stevenson's youth big families and hordes of domestic servants gave it a life, and a social mix, that it has long since lost. The heads of households were at the cutting edge of a rising commercial class, and money was being made. That, exhibited in the ownership of their Georgian piles, defined polite Edinburgh. Growing up in such an atmosphere defined R.L.S. in turn, if only by a complex process of exclusion.

Stevenson entered Edinburgh University when he was sixteen. By that time he had begun to establish some sort of intimacy with his father. He had been exploring Thomas's library for years, though it was to him "a spot of some austerity," crowded with religious and scientific texts. In reminiscences jotted down in 1873 and later published by Graham Balfour, his cousin and first biographer, Louis recalled that

> the proceedings of learned societies, some Latin divinity, cyclopaedias, physical science, and, above all, optics, held the chief place upon the shelves, and it was only in holes and corners that anything really legible existed as by accident. *The Parent's Assistant, Rob Roy, Waverley,* and *Guy Man-*

nering, the *Voyages of Captain Woodes Rogers*, Fuller's and Bunyan's *Holy Wars*, *Reflections of Robinson Crusoe*, *The Female Bluebeard*, G. Sand's *Mare au Diable* (how came it in that grave assembly!), Ainsworth's *Tower of London*, and four old volumes of *Punch*—these were the chief exceptions.

Little help there for the would-be author. Even the volume of Defoe admitted to the Heriot Row library was the sequel to the sequel of *Crusoe* devoted to moral questions exclusively. *Serious Reflections on the Life of Robinson Crusoe* is now, as one editor puts it, "deservedly forgotten." It was not neglected, it seems, by the self-improving Thomas Stevenson, who affected to prefer it to its racier parent.

He tried hard. Thomas did not cease to try. Whatever else can be said of him, there is no justice in claiming that he spared himself in an effort to make his son content. A just criticism would be that he, his wife, and Cummy had so lavished attention on the child they failed to foresee the sort of youth he would become as a result. Louis was hypersensitive—Baildon, his schoolmate, said he thought himself ugly; R.L.S. described himself as an ugly student—and highly strung. He was both precocious and infantile, happily cheeking his father in letters or arguing with him over the dinner table yet shedding floods of tears at the merest setback. He was strong willed, quick-tempered, sometimes petulant. He was clever and imaginative but, by his own account, idle. He was, in other words, an only child who had wanted for nothing, redeemed by cheerfulness and a good heart. Worse, in a youth supposedly destined to spend his life in the disciplined atmosphere of an engineer's office, Louis had never encountered a situation from which he could not escape. Illness would not have been his choice, but by being ill or unhappy or "difficult," he had avoided most of the rigours of formal education. The knowledge that any problem could be answered with a trip to the Riviera gave him an unusual perspective on life. Few had his problems or his advantages. Louis suffered, but he did so, as a rule, in comfortable surroundings.

True to the legend, R.L.S. bore his martyrdom with genuine humility. The horrors of his health would have crushed lesser men. As an adult he was often depressed and sometimes desperate. His relations with his father were to cause him genuine pain. Yet his optimism and his independence of mind can best be understood if we remember that someone, almost invariably his father, looked out for him until he was past the age when other men were raising families. His worries were not ordinary ones. If he needed money, it was provided. If he was ill, the best doctors were found. If travel was prescribed, no obstacle was insurmountable. If life became altogether too trying, the worst he had to face was a parental lecture in the comfort of the Heriot Row drawing room. And this went on, with his parents funding the behaviour of which they disapproved, until he was well into his thirties. Stevenson's struggles were real enough, but they should not be confused with the daily ordeals of the herd. It is small wonder that he turned out to be a lazy and conceited student who thought that working for a living was something other people did. Louis did not fail as a student—and he was to fail spectacularly—because of illness, any more than he failed as engineer or advocate. It never crossed his mind to attempt to succeed.

In the autumn of 1863 his father had taken him on a tour of Fife lighthouses—no doubt as in introduction, of sorts, to the family business. Lou was less impressed by the engineering than by the scenery, particularly Magus Muir, but he was aware, too, that this was the first time he and his father had been alone together "without the help of petticoats." His journey to independence continued in the summer of his first year at university, when he spent some time at Anstruther in Fife, dutifully studying harbour works in that "grey, grim, sea-beaten hole."

Later that season he and his father set off again, this time on the tour of the Scottish lights, which was part of his father's duties as Commissioner of Northern Lights. Lou, coddled for so long, enthused over the sea travel and the storms, though his father was downcast to see Wick harbour, which he had designed, wrecked beyond repair. In the Wick area, be it noted, the name Gunn was common, and there was more than one local named Ben.

Wick in 1868 offered Lou "one of the best things I got from my education as an engineer"—a descent in a diving suit—and the chance to behave as "the man that's in charge" during the rescue of a worker who had fallen into the harbour. "My hand shook so," he wrote to his father, "that I could not draw for some time after with the excitement."

They were to make other trips, in 1869 and 1870, during Lou's vacations, to the Pentland Firth and the Hebrides. For his father, this was the engineer's training Robert Stevenson had given him, but his boy wanted application, never mind attentiveness. The trips around wild Scotland fed the writer's imagination but bored the junior engineer. It was impossible to say when, or if, Thomas realised that he was wasting this time. His efforts were a triumph of hope over his experience.

In August of 1870 Louis spent three weeks on Earraid, off the isle of Mull. It was then being used as a base for the building of the lighthouse at Dhu Heartach, but it survived in Stevenson's mind to become the setting for "The Merry Men" and the scene of David Balfour's shipwreck. In "Memoirs of an Islet," written in 1887, Louis remembered

> The earth savour of the bog plants, the rude disorder of the boulders, the inimitable seaside brightness of the air, the brine and the iodine, the lap of the billows among the weedy reefs, the sudden springing up of a great run of dashing surf along the sea front of the isle, all that I saw and felt my predecessors must have seen and felt with scarce a difference. I steeped myself in open air and in past ages.

It was not enough. The life of an engineer had, it seemed to him then and in writing *Additional Memories and Portraits*, two opposing sides. On one, it would cure anyone "of any taste (if he ever had one) for the miserable life of the cities." Contrariwise,

> when it has done so, it carries him back and shuts him in an office . . . and with a memory full of ships, and seas, and perilous headlands, and the shining pharos, he must apply his long-sighted eyes to the petty niceties of drawing, or measure his inaccurate mind with several pages of consecutive figures. He is a wise youth, to be sure, who can balance one part of genuine life against two parts of drudgery, between four walls, and, for the sake of one, manfully accept the other.

David Angus, the brilliant young assistant who lifted this burden willingly from the longsighted Stevenson's shoulders, had much the same experience. Working for the firm meant being given "endless tracings to copy, calculations to make, and diagrams and plans to prepare." Everything—duplicating maps, reports, and letters—had to be done by hand, slowly and painstakingly.

Stevenson and Angus* would become friends, for a while, but whatever they had in common, it was not engineering. Angus (1855–1926), who spent most of his working life providing South America with a rail network, was to inspire Conan Doyle's novel *The Lost Continent*. He was all that Thomas might have hoped for in Louis: hardworking, upright, adventurous (he once had part of his ear shot off through a train window in Chile), a natural engineer who took mountains, jungles, and swamps in his stride. He built the Ailsa Craig lighthouse for the Stevensons and was the perfection of one brand of Victorian heroism, remaking the world with honest engineering. Louis had grown up with the romance of his father's and grandfather's trade, with the epic tale of the Bell Rock's construction and the expeditions amid the wildest landscapes Scotland had to offer. But the dusty realities of the office life, the hours and days spent reproducing a single dull diagram, seemed like a high price to pay for such adventures. He was no David Angus.

In Edinburgh he took to wandering around the streets and the nearby Pentland Hills, helped by the fact that in May of 1867 his father—perhaps seeking a substitute for the Colinton manse—had taken a summer cottage at Swanston. Lying on the eastern edge of the Pentlands, the cottage was more rural than the manse. I was to become, fictively, the home of the heroine of *St. Ives*, but in *Edinburgh: Picturesque Notes* he wrote that the property had been acquired by Edinburgh's magistrates to secure its water supply. "After they had built their water-house and laid their pipes, it occurred to them that the place was suitable for junketing . . . They brought crockets and gargoyles from old St. Giles', which they were then restoring, and disposed them on the gables and over the door and about the garden . . ."

The Stevensons were to rent Swanston Cottage for fourteen years. Angus was a visitor there, and used to tell his children how he and R.L.S. would go strolling in the evening, sometimes becoming so immersed in political debate that they found themselves walking all the way to Edin-

*See, generally, Mair, C.: *David Angus: The Life and Adventures of a Victorian Railway Engineer* (London, 1989).

burgh. At Swanston, Louis also added to his store of Lallans. There, each morning, were the moors and the hills, forever remembered, even in the far Pacific.

> Be it granted me to behold you again in dying
>   Hills of home! and to hear again the call;
> Hear about the graves of the martyrs the peewees crying,
> And hear no more at all.
>
> "To S.R. Crockett"

Stevenson was economical with such experiences. Swanston entered *St. Ives*; early East Lothian holidays resurfaced in *Catriona*; tramping out to Queensferry laid down a store of material for *Kidnapped*; the Pentlands beyond Swanston fed tales of the Covenanters into his imagination; trips north with his father gave him a surveyor's skill in recalling and describing natural features. Each detail would return later, when, as though of artistic necessity, he was somewhere else entirely.

Swanston Cottage became the Stevensons' summer home. In the early years it was a small place, with only one spare room. But for Louis the seeming vastness of the Pentland Hills before it was compensation. Swanston was good for his health and his imagination. He read Dumas there, explored the places where the Covenanters had camped, and grew to know the shepherds and the farmers. The road to the cottage took him past Hunters' Tryst and its inn, familiar to Walter Scott and Allan Ramsay. Beyond:

> The hills are close by across a valley: Kirk Yetton, with its long, upright scars visible as far as Fife, and Allermuir, the tallest on this side, with wood and tilled field running high upon their borders, and haunches all moulded glens and shelvings and variegated with heather and fern. The air comes briskly and sweetly off the hills . . .
>
> *Edinburgh: Picturesque Notes*

Swanston was important, too, for tuning his ear to the speech of the countryside, the old speech of the Lothians that was to give him his version of Scots. A little earlier there was, for example, the shepherd John

Todd, recalled in the essay "Pastoral" that first appeared in *Longman's Magazine* in 1887:

> He spoke in the richest dialect of Scots I every heard; the words in themselves were a pleasure and often a surprise to me, so that I often came back from one of our patrols with new acquisitions; and this vocabulary he would handle like a master, stalking a little before me, 'beard on shoulder,' the plaid hanging loosely about him, the yellow staff clapped under his arm, and guiding me uphill by that devious, tactical ascent which seems peculiar to men of his trade. I might count him with the best talkers; only that talking Scots and talking English seem incomparable acts.

Todd's speech survived, if nowhere else, in *Weir of Hermiston*, but there were many more like him around Swanston.

Back in town there was a different Lou. He was reading everything save, perhaps, the books he was supposed to read. He was writing steadily, sedulously—to use one of his own words later turned against him. Idle he may have seemed, and proclaimed himself to be, but: "I was always busy on my own private end, which was to learn to write . . . to anyone with senses there is always something worth describing." He stuffed himself with Hazlitt, Lamb, Wordsworth, Defoe, Hawthorne, Montaigne, and Whitman; Shakespeare, Scott, and Dumas were already familiars. His tastes were eclectic, as though he had an instinct finer than any teacher's for the works he needed to mould his talent. "I had vowed," he wrote, "to learn to write." Equally, he was feeding an appetite. His literary diet does not tell us so very much about the writer he was to become, but the voracity is revealing, that and the mixture of headlong narrative tempered with the pointed moralities of essayists. His fiction would reflect the depth of his training.

His father, proud but mindful of the fate that awaited most "professional" authors, did not, of course, regard Louis's ambition as the foundation for a suitable career. Victorian publishing had not reached its heyday, when mass literacy and cheap books meant the man of letters was working in a seller's market. Besides, Louis was enrolled at Edinburgh as a student of engineering, as family tradition demanded. There would be no opportunity for art. Nevertheless, by his sixteenth year he had already made his first, tentative appearance in print.

He had been scribbling away, addicted, at romances in the style of Scott. Now his father encouraged him to forgo such fictions and make use of the Covenanting history he had accumulated to mark the bicentenary of the bloody battle at Rullion Green. In November 1866, Thomas had one hundred copies of "The Pentland Rising: A Page of History, 1666" printed at his own expense and published anonymously by Andrew Elliot of Edinburgh. Aunt Jane Balfour recalled:

> I was at Heriot Row in 1866 from the 29th October to 23rd November, and Louis was busily altering the *Pentland Rising* then to please his father. He had made a story of it, and by so doing, had, in his father's opinion, spoiled it. It was printed not long after in a small edition, and Mr Stevenson very soon bought all the copies in, as far as was possible.

Making a story of it was not, it seems, looked on with favour. In any case, the youth of its author is all that makes the sixteen-page "slim green pamphlet" interesting. Desperately dull, derivative, suitably pious and stuffed with quotations from Defoe and others, it reads like an essay composed by an agile but unadventurous student somewhat older than Louis was. He did not think much of the work himself for very long, and in 1894, the essay "My First Book: 'Treasure Island,' " he noted "with amazement" that the "gentlemen of England" were prepared to pay "fancy prices" for what had become a collectors' item.

Louis was not much of a sportsman. He rode occasionally and skated at Duddingston Loch in the winter with his family and their friends. Golf bored him and he gave up on fishing in disgust. His imagination was caught only by the canoeing which his friends Charles Baxter and Walter Simpson had taken up. The latter became Stevenson's partner in one of these toys during the adventure of *An Inland Voyage*.

Not physical, then, certainly not competitive. Five foot ten inches tall or thereabouts, his face a thing of planes and angles, his hair lank, his fingers long, his chest turned inwards, the line of his torso like a question mark. Many saw charm in him, but glamour, if that is what it was, was only perceived later. The charm, too, was verbal rather than physical: he could almost talk the hind legs off a donkey—though not quite, as he was later to discover. Accounts of his chatter point to an excitable and nervous youth, someone trying to validate his half-formed opinions by expressing them as loudly as possible.

Like so many before and since, the young student discovered that a university education need not be time consuming. Each day meant a walk from Heriot Row up the hill to the old quadrangle. The journey took him through the populous, noisy, grubby, and, to those of a romantic disposition, glorious Old Town. Most days Lou found something better than lectures to detain him: Greyfriars Cemetery, where the Covenant was signed; Rutherford's bar in Drummond Street, known as "The Pump"; or a long walk to the distant villages of Corstorphine and Morningside that were fast becoming suburbs of the city. He began to know the town itself, collecting its types and its characters, disguising himself (once, shocking the family, as a rag-and-bone man), absorbing idioms, and shaping his own bits of verse and prose. He carried a notebook in his pocket at all times, and as Graham Balfour recorded, he always used the word "truant" when he spoke or wrote of his education.

It is possible that these diversions had as much to do with Stevenson's shyness as with boredom. He described himself as having been a "lean, idle, ugly, unpopular" student and obviously thought that he had not been able (or had never attempted) to fit in. Given his background, it would have been surprising, if, at first, he had. He was naturally gregarious but unskilled with people; as a child he had often been teased. Such types are swamped by university life. Yet while his parents imagined that he was submitting to the training that would one day earn him his rightful place in the family firm, he was avoiding classes with a marvellous scrupulousness and gaining what even he admitted was "the merest shadow of an education."

He had "taken out" classes in Latin and Greek but avoided them from the first. In "The Foreigner at Home," written in 1882 and published in *Memories and Portraits*, he contrasted his own experience with the "costumed, disciplined and drilled" worlds of Oxford and Cambridge:

> At an earlier age the Scottish lad begins the greatly different experience of crowded classrooms, of a gaunt quadrangle, of a bell hourly booming over the traffic of the city to recall him from the public house where he has

been lunching, or the streets where he has been wandering fancy-free. His college life has little of restraint, and nothing of necessary gentility. . . . Our tasks ended, we of the North go forth as freemen into the humming, lamplit city.

The young Louis took such offers of freedom at face value, and his "tasks" rarely occupied him until the lamps were lit, if he began them at all. He attended Greek classes so rarely that a knowledge of the language was to be forever beyond his grasp, somewhat to his adult chagrin. He preferred to spend his time compiling a "Book of Original Nonsense" and abandoned the course after the first session.

He cuts an odd figure, this youth. At one moment he can seem dreamy and lonely, wandering the streets with his notebook in hand, living in his head, or "retiring" to Swanston to sit alone on the hillside making "bad verses." At others he is the spirit of mischief, never without company, accepted as clever (if odd) by his comrades. The mix of gregariousness and solitude was typical Stevenson: throughout his life he loved company, even when writing. Every so often, however, he felt the need to take himself away. Edinburgh legends attach themselves to this period of his life, but few of the facts match them. He drifted, and every now and then he managed a few lines of verse amid the juvenile posturing that were not irredeemably "bad."

In 1869 Louis was elected to the Speculative Society, a snobbish literary and debating club of thirty members so adventurous and independent they allowed smoking on their premises. Intelligence was supposed to be the criterion for entry, but a good name, of which Stevenson was undoubtedly one, counted for more. Evening dress was insisted upon for the candle-lit meetings.

After early difficulties Stevenson (member 992) came to like the atmosphere of the Spec. He made no notable contribution aside from calling for the abolition of capital punishment (he failed to find as seconder) in anticipation of a scene in *Weir of Hermiston*. However, he did make several friends and began to develop the combative conversational style that was to dazzle many yet put him at odds with his own father. R.L.S. thought enough of that place, at least, to ask his old friend Guthrie to arrange for the admission of his stepson Lloyd to the society in 1886. He described it in *Memories and Portraits*:

> It is a body of some antiquity, and has counted among its members Scott, Jeffrey, Horner, Benjamin Constant, Robert Emmet, and many a legal and local celebrity besides. By an accident, variously explained, it has its rooms in the very buildings of the University of Edinburgh: a hall, Turkey-carpeted hung with pictures, looking, when lighted up with fire and candle, like some goodly dining room, a passage-like library, walled with books in their wire cages; and a corridor with a fireplace, benches, a table, many prints of famous members, and a mural tablet to the virtues of a former secretary. Here a member can warm himself and loaf and read; here, in defiance of the Senatus-consults, he can smoke.

Of the seven papers Louis was to give, the first was, typically an essay delivered on "The Influence of the Covenanting Persecution on the Scotch Mind" in March of 1870; two years later he was arguing that American literature compared favourably with English. But the real point of the Spec, loafing and reading apart, was that it exposed a youth who thought highly of himself to the scrutiny of his self-confident peers. He managed to be elected as one of the society's five presidents in 1872, but only just, coming bottom of the list with seven votes. By the time of his valedictory address in 1873, however, he was very much the varsity man, ". . . explaining to the other members that he is the cleverest person of his age and weight between this and California."

The invalid was absent at this time. Free of the Heriot Row infirmary, Louis had good health. So robust was he, indeed, that in 1870 he was bound over to keep the peace after being arrested during a traditional, riotous "town and gown" snowball fight. Marched up the Bridges between Old Town and New under police escort, he felt ashamed of himself. But when the party entered the High Street, public acclaim convinced him he was almost a hero.

Similarly, a trip around the Western Isles in the summer of that year had seen him writing home proclaiming he had "enjoyed [himself] amazingly." Undertaken as part of his engineering class, the voyage had taken him to Earraid, via Oban. He visited Tarbet, Ardishaig, Iona, Staffa, and

Portree. On board he met the artist Sam Bough and talked books, fell in with Miss Amy Sinclair (daughter of Sir Tollemache), for whom he made himself "as gallant as possible," and, when the ship called at Skye, was introduced to one of the central figures of his later life, Edmund Gosse.

Stevenson and Gosse (1845–1928), the son of the naturalist memorialised in "Father and Son," were not to meet again for seven years. But the future Librarian to the House of Lords and champion of Ibsen recalled the incident in an address to the first annual dinner of the Robert Louis Stevenson Club in Edinburgh in 1920:

> In the course of the voyage we entered a loch at midnight, and by the light of flickering torches, took on board a party of emigrants who were going to Glasgow *en route* for America. As they came on board an eerie sound of wailing rose in the stillness of the night, which pierced my heart; it was a most extraordinary sound. In the dark I saw that at my side was the young man from Portree, and we exchanged reflections on this extraordinary movement of human beings. I do not think we had any more conversation than that . . .

The voyage and the scenery were meat and drink to Louis. But it is revealing to realise that, a few colds aside, his health was good in these years. It began to collapse again only when domestic dramas put him under stress. Stevenson was weak in body, but psychology as much as a flawed physique worked to undermine him.

There was another side of his life in these years, and those who interpret Stevenson's character as a matter of dualities have found a good deal to say about it. Thin as a rake, says the legend, he led a rake's life. Dr. Jekyll after a fashion, they say, Mr. Hyde when his conscience relaxed. Others have affected to detect a great moral crisis in the soul of the Presbyterian youth as he indulged himself, an unjustified sinner. Traces of guilt are found and held up for inspection. But if Stevenson was depressed during this period—and he was, from time to time—youth is a likelier explanation than furtive fornication. In an age when nice girls didn't, young men had few choices in the matter.

In any case, much mythology has grown up around Stevenson's student days and his explorations of Edinburgh's less salubrious quarters. Even now, the legend of his whoring and drinking is widely accepted in the city that took at face value his claims of spiritual kinship with Robert Fergusson, the wild poet born a century before R.L.S., who died aged twenty-four. There are extant tales of romances, bastards, and exceptional virility, none substantiated.

Dissipation would have been difficult. He missed dinner at Heriot Row so rarely, he thought it worth mentioning when he did. Besides, "I was always kept poor in my youth, to my great indignation at the time, but since then with my complete approval," Stevenson wrote. "Twelve pounds a year was my allowance up to twenty-three . . . and although I amplified it by a very consistent embezzlement from my mother, I never had enough to be lavish. My monthly pound was usually spent before the evening of the day on which I received it . . ." Thomas Stevenson held the rein tight.

Nevertheless, until very recently there were tales believed widely of a blacksmith's daughter impregnated at Swanston, of Stevenson senior breaking up the romance, and other plot lines R.L.S. would have scorned. In some versions, there were two girls in the vicinity of the cottage. The more famous, otherwise known as "Claire," was the supposed subject (until a more plausible candidate was identified) of some early verse concerned with lost love and an unborn child. In other versions she became "Kate Drummond," a prostitute from the Highlands whom Louis wished to rescue.

All of this and more was demolished by J. C. Furnas in his 1952 biography, but the stories persist, perhaps because they satisfy a certain kind of Edinburgh mind. An individual claiming to be Stevenson's bastard turned up in the 1920s but his story did not survive scrutiny for long. Other old Edinburgh families harbour cautionary tales of drunkenness, wenching, and general bad behaviour, but firsthand evidence is not, of necessity, to be had.

If anything, the legend of the roistering R.L.S. is as much a tribute to the impact of his bohemian affectations on New Town society as it is to his virility. Even then, it is a bohemianism amplified with hindsight by middle-class gossips: his family said little at the time. Certainly he haunted brothels, of which there were many in Victorian Edinburgh, and indeed he wrote with affection of certain women who worked in them. One might even argue that his devotion to older women throughout his life can be explained by early encounters with experienced professionals. In the end, however, the attempt to paint Stevenson as a peculiarly successful seducer begins to look like another example of Edinburgh's resentment of its wayward son. There are none so prurient as Puritans. The worst that can be said was that his manner of dress was becoming eccentric.

Stevenson's adolescent pangs become illegitimate children; student curiosity (doubtless inflamed by too much Baudelaire) becomes legendary carnality. In reality, he may have become involved with a girl or two. It would be altogether more interesting if he had not. But the matching legend of his homosexuality cannot compete with that of his heterosexuality. (Nevertheless, in writing this book I was asked more than once if it was true that Stevenson was a pederast, and offered this information with complete assurance on several occasions. It said more about Edinburgh than any guidebook.)

Graham Balfour left one of the Samoan saint's papers unpublished. In it Stevenson described a "Mary H.," "a robust great-haunched, blue-eyed young woman, of admirable temper, and, if you will let me say so of a prostitute, extraordinary modesty." When respectable, she refused to acknowledge him in the street, and he did not think "that she thought of me otherwise than in the way of business." He met her years later, just before she emigrated to the United States, and recorded her talking of the past "in her sober, Scotch voice" and "her good honest loving hand as we said goodbye." If Mary was the model for the legends, their relationship seems to have been a small foundation on which to build so large an edifice. A habitual sentimentality about the past aside, Louis thought of himself as no more than trade. He was ever afterwards a defender of prostitutes, less for carnality's sake than charity's. In one letter he describes his conscience-stricken attempts to free himself from a relationship with a girl "to whom the postage even must have been a matter of parsimony . . ." Some slightly risqué verse—"A girl or two at play in a corner of waste-land/Tumbling and showing their legs and crying out to me loosely"—suggests little more than a young male trying and failing to be the louche bohemian. Colvin thought he had "strong appetites"; compared to Colvin, most men did. Louis, drunk on beer and the idea of himself, lost his virginity on some evening during these years. Many men did.

One tantalising fact remains among the myths. In 1877, when Louis had embarked on the affair with the woman who was to become his wife, he wrote to his friend W. E. Henley and made guarded mention of another "enchanting young lady whom you have seen, or rather from her inspiration . . . letters threatening exposure, etc . . ." This clear indication of blackmail, or at least attempted blackmail, does not sound like one of Louis's jokes. An enterprising whore may have decided there was money to be made from the gauche young man or his family, as indeed there was, though no one knows whether she had any success. It may have been this episode, serious or otherwise, that obliged R.L.S. to admit to his father that he was involved with a married woman. But that came later.

In the meantime his first friends at university were often entertained to respectable tea or amiable (if argumentative) dinner at Heriot Row beneath the watchful gaze of his parents. These young men came of New Town stock as respectable as his own: Charles Baxter, a lawyer's son; James Walter Ferrier, son of a St. Andrews professor; Walter Simpson, whose father discovered chloroform. They were boisterous but, at this point, harmless to themselves and to society. Baxter was always upstanding, loyal, and reliable, if with a taste for drink and anything risqué. Ferrier took to drink in serious style and died in his thirties of alcohol and tuberculosis. Simpson, whose father died in 1870, shared a flat with his brother and sister, providing both good company and a bolt-hole for Louis when the atmosphere at home became strained.

They were a pleasant-enough crew. Louis was inconsolable when Ferrier died, as much for the memory of the days that had died with him as for the man. Baxter became one of his enduring friends and was, for years, effectively his business manager. He and Louis, satirists of their society, invented characters for one another, two Holy Wullies called Johnstone (R.L.S.) and Thomson (Baxter), whose garrulous Scots shades would break into their correspondence for years to come. They also did honour to a landlord called Brash, a spectacularly obnoxious individual who inspired Louis to a series of sonnets, *Brasheana*.

He was wandering, though, as a later letter confessed:

Looking back upon it, I am surprised at the courage with which I first ventured alone into the societies in which I moved; I was the companion of seamen, chimney-weeps and thieves; my circle was being continually changed by the action of the police magistrate. I see now the little sanded kitchen, where Velvet Coat (for such was the name I went by) has spent days together, generally in silence and making sonnets in a penny version-book; and rough as the material may appear, I do not believe these days were among the least happy I have spent. I was distinctly petted and respected; the women were most gentle and kind to me; I might have left all my money for a month, and they would have returned every farthing of it.

This was not quite the life of a Scots Rimbaud, or a Fergusson, even if R.L.S. later believed the latter to be reborn in him and planned, at the very end of his life, to have the poet's monument, first erected by Burns, repaired at his own expense. Neither seer ended his nights of artistic rampage by returning to a good bourgeois bed in a good bourgeois household, even if Stevenson boasted in a letter to Sidney Colvin that he "never saw the [prostitute] yet that could resist me." His curiosity was as powerful as his sexuality, and if he lost his virginity to one of these amiable professionals, the adventure was probably launched (he was not so different from other men) just to find out what he was missing. Such an escapade was not so unusual then; R.L.S. was debauched on a part-time basis only. No doubt he knew all about the respectable middle-class Edinburgh men who kept the brothels in business. He was not insensible to scandal—and showed himself to be sensitive indeed to the feelings of women—but it is doubtful that he regarded his adventures in the "underworld" with the same quivering fascination as some of his later worshippers. Besides, the Velvet Coat of gamey legend had been purchased for him by the upright Thomas Stevenson. Middle-class attitudes magnified a modest rebellion, if the Edinburgh middle class thought about the Stevenson boy at all. Equally, if his parents knew of his scandalous behaviour, they do not seem to have done much about it. Whitman would have been mortified. Guthrie, in a vain attempt to separate the bohemian from the puritan, noted:

His extravagant revolt against some of the petty respectabilities of life; his exaggerated contempt for many of the conventionalities and restraints, and the manners and language, of so-called polite society; his indiscriminating thirst for novelty; his fondness, in season and out of season, for the bizarre and the gruesome, the grotesque and the uncanny; his childish inquisitiveness ... his strange relish of rough jests; his tolerance of Rabelaisian and so-called strong language; and his curious liking for queer company ...

He was curious, easily bored, and swore without inhibition: it is not much of a charge sheet. The sexual language of the day, such as it was, makes the truth hard to establish. What was said in pubs was not what was said between husband and wife. What was said in print was not what was said in letters. Euphemism was habitual and dominant. Even when Stevenson's letters carry an erotic charge, their language can seem an odd mixture of frankness and adolescent posturing. The only hard fact is that he was young.

If nothing else, these "bohemian" days did give Louis (member of the Edinburgh University Conservative Club) a sense of social injustice. He defended beggars and prostitutes, was ineptly kind to servants, took umbrage with the iron rule of class, and acquired a degree of contempt for New Town society. It was a foretaste of his behaviour is Samoa, but an inchoate, undergraduate version, the Tory playing with socialism.

More respectably, he had become friendly with Fleeming Jenkin, who in 1868 had become Edinburgh's first professor of engineering. Thomas Stevenson and Jenkin were acquainted, and on her arrival in the city Mrs. Jenkin called upon Maggie Stevenson. The professor's wife was much taken with Louis, and with his soft voice in particular. After meeting the youth while visiting Heriot Row, she told her husband that his student—or rather his occasional student, for Stevenson was no more attentive to this professor than to the others—was a Scots version of Heinrich Heine, no less. For whatever reason, it was around this time that Lou requested his mother to address him as "Robert Louis."

He had been given the name Lewis after his Balfour grandfather. Aspirations towards maturity aside, there is no convincing explanation of why he dropped the surname and amended the Christian one. A degree of Francophilia seems more plausible than the old tale of a local man called Lewis whose views on religion had upset Thomas Stevenson. Guthrie repeated the legend in his memoir:

Stevenson's change of name from Lewis, after his mother's father (a name shared with five cousins), to 'Louis' after nobody, the pronunciation remaining the same, took place, I have no doubt, with his entire approval, but it does not appear to have been directly his doing. There was in Edinburgh a certain Bailie David Lewis, an able and devout man, a useful citizen, and a disinterested philanthropist. But he was as one-sided a Radical and Dissenter as Thomas Stevenson was a Tory and Established Churchman. There was no personal animosity between them; I do not know that they ever met. But Bailie Lewis stood to Thomas Stevenson as the incarnation of everything dangerous in Church and State. His son must not be branded with the Mark of the Beast, and so, almost incredible as it sounds, in the case of a level-headed man like Mr Stevenson, 'Lewis' became 'Louis'!

Incredible indeed. It is hard to imagine R.L.S. altering his name to suit his father; it is harder still to imagine Thomas becoming quite so petty. If his father had ordered the change, why did "Lewis" request his mother to call him Louis? In any case, given that the spelling and not the pronunciation was altered, the change suggests the affectation of a tyro writer seeking a distinctive byline.

Writing preoccupied him increasingly, debauched or not. In later life he concluded that the years between twenty and twenty-three were the years for reading. He had access to the Advocates' Library and was immersing himself in Whitman and Herbert Spencer. A notebook for 1871–72 records that he was also studying Montaigne, Horace, Pepys, still more Shakespeare, Hazlitt, Burns, Sterne, Heine, Keats, and Fielding. What he wrote himself

> . . . was written consciously for practice. It was not so much that I wished to be an author (though I wished that too) as that I had vowed that I would learn to write. That was a proficiency that tempted me; and I practised to acquire it, as men learn to whittle, in a wager with myself. Description was the principal field of my exercise . . .
>
> *Memories and Portraits*

He tried to keep diaries but found them "a school of posturing and melancholy self-deception." Nevertheless, when he found a book that pleased him, he sat down and worked to master its style. "I was unsuccessful, and I knew it . . . but at least in these vain bouts I got some practice in rhythm, in harmony, in construction and the co-ordination of parts." In other words he was doing what thousands of would-be writers have done. But since Stevenson was candid about his apprenticeship, later critics turned his honesty against him. One passage bedevilled his reputation for years, and is worth quoting for that reason.

> I have thus played the sedulous ape to Hazlitt, to Lamb, to Wordsworth, to Sir Thomas Browne, to Defoe, to Hawthorne, to Montaigne, to Baudelaire and to Obermann. I remember one of these monkey-tricks, which was called 'The Vanity of Morals'; it was to have had a second part 'The Vanity of Knowledge'; but the second part was never attempted, and the first part was written (which is my reason for recalling it, ghost-like, from its ashes) no less than three times: first in the manner of Hazlitt, second in the manner of Ruskin, who had cast on me a passing spell, and third, in a laborious pasticcio of Sir Thomas Browne.

Some writers would have used such an episode to advertise their youthful seriousness; not Stevenson. Nevertheless, the habit of application, the needless rewriting until the *tone* of a passage was achieved, became a hallmark of his later work. He chose to begin—and it is not a bad tactic—as a craftsman before he contemplated becoming an artist.

Less serious was his involvement with the *Edinburgh University Magazine*, forerunner (and inspiration) to the long-running *Student* newspaper. Launched in the rooms of the Spec by three members who invited Louis to join them, it was, by his later account, a "grim fiasco," but at least he got his name in print:

> The magazine appeared, in a yellow cover which was the best part of it, for at least it was unassuming; it ran four months in undisturbed obscurity, and died without a gasp. The first number was edited by all four of us with prodigious bustle; the second fell principally into the hands of Ferrier and me; the third I edited alone; and it has long been a solemn question who it was edited the fourth. It would perhaps be still more difficult to say who read it. Poor yellow sheet, that looked so hopefully in the Livingstones' window! . . . And, shall I say, Poor Editors? I cannot pity myself, to whom it was all pure gain.

R.L.S. recorded that he had "sent a copy to the lady with whom my heart was at that time somewhat engaged," but she "passed over the gift and my cherished contributions in silence. I will not say that I was pleased at this . . ." The lady in question has not been identified, but one presumes she was not an unusually literate whore.

He began to visit the Jenkins at home (in which, as Furnas rightly argues, he would not have been acceptable if he was living up to his posthumous reputation for loose living) and began to participate in the amateur theatrical events of which the couple were fond. By all accounts he was not much of an actor. Nevertheless, he developed a particular admiration for the professor, identifying him as a man of the world and later composing an honest, unsentimental biography of his sometime mentor.

Jenkin was a man of many parts, most of them admirable: engineer, amateur playwright, amateur biologist, amateur philosopher, dancer, skater. Something of a know-all, a shade pompous, he was an individual to whom Louis could and did listen in a way he listened to few others. Jenkin opened up the life of the mind (or at least the *idea* of it) as no one else had. With knowledge came a degree of rigour and, perhaps most important, respect. The professor was strict when he had to be, indulgent when he could be. He accepted Lou's affectations as the price of youth and earned his undying gratitude. The tour of the Hebrides undertaken in 1870 as part of the professor's engineering course in "surveying, levelling etc" remained with him for life, and was mined repeatedly in his writing. In his memoir of Jenkin, published in 1888, R.L.S. described the young Jenkin but he could just as easily have been describing his young self:

> His thoroughness was not that of the patient scholar, but of an untrained woman with fits of passionate study; he had learned too much from dogma, given indeed by cherished lips; and precocious as he was in the use of the tools of the mind, he was truly backward in knowledge of life and of himself.

Nevertheless, to Thomas Stevenson, the relationship must have seemed, for once, entirely satisfactory. His difficult son, despite his all-too-evident intelligence, looked a poor prospect as the heir to a partnership with one of Edinburgh's most prosperous and distinguished firms. Lou's health was unreliable, his studies erratic, and his temper uncertain. His parents scarcely knew what to do with him and lived in hope that something, somehow, would turn up. A steadying hand, any steadying hand, was welcome. It was, though Thomas Stevenson did not yet know it, already too late.

Education accumulated with age, yet somehow Louis seemed stuck, casting around for a way forward. The idea of authorship was inchoate; it was hard to see how it might be given reality, yet there was nothing else he wanted to do. And as he matured in some ways—sexually, intellectually, artistically—he remained a boy in others, dreaming and doodling, casting himself in a series of performances, inventing an identity. He was not, in other words, so very different from many other young men. Only his single-mindedness in writing really distinguished him. Yet Velvet Coat remains one of the actors in the legend of R.L.S. and it was a legend to which he subscribed. Years later, in Samoa, Louis polished the myth with an elegaic poem:

> *Sing me a song of a lad that is gone.*
> *Say, could that lad be I?*
> *Merry of soul he sailed on a day*
> *Over the sea to Skye.*
>
> *Mull was astern, Rum on the port,*
> *Eigg on the starboard bow;*
> *Glory of youth glowed in his soul:*
> *Where is that glory now? . . .*
>
> *Billow and breeze, islands and seas,*
> *Mountains of rain and sun,*
> *All that was good, all that was fair,*
> *All that was me is gone.*

4 1871–1873

I think the spectacle of a whole life in which you have no part paralyses personal desire. You are content to become a mere spectator.

AN INLAND VOYAGE

In 1870 cousin Bob Stevenson returned to Edinburgh after graduating from Sidney Sussex College, Cambridge, fizzing with the idea that he could, and should, become a painter. The favourite playmate of Louis's childhood among his fifty-odd first cousins had become a tall, voluble, charming, eccentric, and enthusiastic adult. R.A.M. was touched with a little genius and a deal of his father's "instability" of mind; a protoaesthete bound, so most of his peers believed, for glory.

R.L.S.'s wife later thought that Bob "gave like putty." He was, said Fanny Van de Grift, "a physical, moral and mental coward. Louis was just the opposite. That was why Bob never came off." Nevertheless, the future Liverpool professor of fine arts, who was to share a Paris studio with Sargent and become a friend of Whistler's yet die unfulfilled in 1900 with only a couple of monographs to his name, burst upon Louis in 1870. Bob was full of himself and his future. Art was all, and convention its enemy. Louis Stevenson was dazzled. It was typical of Bob that he would recant within four years, writing to his cousin to admit: "We used to think we were like no one else about certain things, but that was a real phase too." At the time, however, Thomas Stevenson did not know how upsetting a youthful phase could be, and suspected nothing.

On 27 March 1871 Louis read before the Royal Scottish Society of

Arts his first contribution to the literature of his chosen profession. Regarded as "highly creditable," that paper, "On a New Form of Intermittent Light for Lighthouses," made appropriate mention of the author's grandfather, Robert Stevenson, and was awarded a five-pound silver medal. Thomas Stevenson was more than proud.

Twelve days later, during a walk at Cramond, Louis told his father that the engineer's life was not for him. Fleeming Jenkin had already made this plain when his student had applied for a certificate of attendance: "There may be doubtful cases; there is no doubt about yours. You have simple *not* attended my class." The news that Louis was spurning family tradition did not cause Thomas to ignite, or at least not definitively. In fact, he was curiously calm about it. You can imagine him shrouding his disappointment in silent depression, but in all likelihood the long hours at beaches and rivers struggling to enthuse his son had forewarned Thomas. His response was quick, clever, and typical. If engineering was impossible, then a career in the law, allowing leisure for literature, would serve as a compromise. Louis would become an advocate. It must have seemed, to one of them, ideal. But if the elder Stevenson thought that had settled matters, he was, once again, mistaken.

Shortly afterwards, during a holiday trip to Dunoon, Louis had his fortune told in the taproom of a hotel by a "Witch-Wife." She informed him, amid a good deal of mumbo jumbo, that he was to visit America, be "very happy," and be "much upon the sea." He was not impressed at the time. Much later, writing to Sidney Colvin from Honolulu, he thought about it again:

> It is a singular thing that as I was packing up old papers ere I left Skerryvore [his house at Bournemouth], I came on the prophecies of a drunken Highland sibyl, when I was seventeen. She said I was to be very happy, to visit America, and *to be much upon the sea*. It seems as if it were coming true with a vengeance.

Bohemia meant something to Louis, just as the word meant something then that ridicule has since destroyed. He did not need Bob Stevenson to convince him that its novelty carried the breath of life. Edinburgh (especially Edinburgh) was not bohemian, and if ever R.L.S. needed a reason to embrace the life, if not the work, of art, that fact alone was sufficient. Whitman, Baudelaire; France, America: *to break loose* . . .

Easier said than done; easier to pose, to fall into an alliance with glamorous cousin Bob and face down the little world of Edinburgh society with a joke, to play at counterculture, than risk work. But there was more to it than that. The young R.L.S. truly was appalled by the prospect of joining the family firm—his remarks on office life make that clear enough—and yet he was proud of his heritage. He wanted to write but found it hard to convince anyone, even himself, that such was a plausible ambition. He had developed, in eccentric stages, a mind of his own, and one antithetical to that of his father, though the degree of difference had yet to be revealed. Nevertheless, he had no desire to hurt the parent "of antique strain" with his blend of sternness and softness, the "man of many extremes, many faults of temper, and no very stable foothold for himself among life's troubles." Nevertheless, Louis was proving to be the chief among Thomas Stevenson's troubles.

Bob, by three years the elder, confirmed and supported his cousin's instincts. Louis thought he had "the most indefatigable, feverish mind I have ever known." They thought their elders hypocrites, and dull with it. Bob (Robert Alan Mowbray) Stevenson, happier in Paris than in Edinburgh, was sophisticated: he gave Louis an impetus his other cronies could not supply, though Louis hardly needed prodding. The affection between them was passionate, sometimes disconcertingly so. Writing from Menton in 1873 to Frances Sitwell, source of another infatuation, Stevenson revealed something of the depth of the relationship:

> In the interval my letters have come; none from you, but one from Bob, which both pained and pleased me. He cannot get on without me at all, he writes; he finds that I have been the whole world for him; that he only talked to other people in order that he might tell me afterwards about the conversation. Should I—I really don't know quite what to feel; I am so much astonished . . .

In the autumn of 1871 R.L.S. sat the preliminary examinations necessary for him to study law. A bout of illness in March of 1872 obliged him to spend a month recuperating at Dublane, but by May he had begun to

learn conveyancing with Skene, Edwards & Bilton WS, a firm of solici-
tors. His enthusiasm, such as it was, did not last, and in the course of a
year spent copying documents, he earned six pounds. For the first couple
of months Louis kept a journal:

Friday, May 10th.

—Office work—copying, at least—is the easiest of labour. There is just
enough mind-work necessary to keep you from thinking of anything else,
so that one simply ceases to be the reasoning being and feels *stodged* and
stupid about the head, a consummation devoutly to be wished for.

There were, of course, diversions:

Monday, May 12th (13th).

—In all day at the office. In the evening dined with Bob. Met X—, who
was quite drunk and spent nigh an hour in describing his wife's last
hours—an infliction which he hired us to support with sherry as *lib.* Splendid moonlight night. Bob walked out to Fairmilehead with me. We were
in a state of mind that only comes too seldom in a lifetime. We danced and
sang the whole way up the long hill, without sensible fatigue. I think there
was no actual conversation—at least none has remained in my memory: I
recollect nothing but 'profuse bursts of unpremeditated song'. . . . After we
parted company at the toll, I walked on counting my money, and I noticed
that the moon shone upon each individual shilling as I dropped it from one
hand to the other.

Wednesday, 22nd.

—At work all day at Court . . . In the evening I started in the rain alone,
and seeing a fellow in front, I whistled him to wait till I came up. He
proved to be a pit-worker from Mid-Calder, and—*faut de mieux*—I bribed
him by the promise of ale to keep me company as far as New Pentland
Inn . . . I heard from him that the *Internationale* was already on foot at Mid-
Calder, but was not making much progress. I acquitted myself as became
a child of the *Proprietariat*, and warned him, quite apostolically, against all
conversation with this abomination of Desolation. He seemed much impressed, and more wearied.

Respite from the office came at the end of July. Stevenson went to
Brussels with Walter Simpson to drink iced drinks and smoke "penny ci-
gars under great old trees." Simpson, who had inherited the baronetcy

from his father, Sir James, the pioneer of chloroform, was, Louis said later, "the eldest of my associates; yet he must have been of a more deliberate growth, for . . . I believe we were about equal in intellectual development . . ."

His was a slow fighting mind. You would see him, at times, wrestle for a minute at a time with a refractory jest, and perhaps fail to throw it at the end. I think his special character was a profound shyness, a shyness which was not so much exhibited in society as it ruled in his own dealings with himself . . . He was even ashamed of his own sincere desire to do the right.

Stevenson travelled on with his droll friend to Frankfurt, spending August learning German and attending the opera. His parents joined him at Baden-Baden, and they visited the Black Forest.

In Edinburgh, in September, was founded the L.J.R., a society of like-minded souls who were to meet weekly in a pub in Advocates' Close, just off the Royal Mile. In the event, it is thought they met only five times to discuss the principles of "Liberty, Justice and Reverence" over drinks while striving, allegedly, to "disregard everything our parents have taught us" and plotting the abolition of the House of Lords. Baxter, Ferrier, and a few others were involved, living dangerously and dressing eccentrically, none more than Louis. His hair was long, his jacket velveteen, his hat provoked the street arabs into howls of derisive laughter, and most telling of all, he was writing his "bad verses." He had also become acquainted with the works of Darwin and Herbert Spencer. Thomas did not see the funny side of it, and did not know the half of it.

In the winter of 1872 Louis fell ill again. His mother took him to recuperate at Great Malvern, where he moped and played billiards. Something clarified in his mind, perhaps provoked by another brush with death. He confessed to Baxter that he had given up lying: he was an agnostic. He was just twenty-two years old.

At the end of January 1873, Louis made his declaration to his father. Or as he recalled it to Baxter, "In the course of conversation, my father put me one or two questions as to belief, which I candidly answered."

Nothing could have been better calculated—and one wonders about the degree of calculation—to break the bond between the two men. Thomas had found a copy of the L.J.R.'s "constitution," and took it more seriously than its authors probably intended. Thomas's faith was absolute, and this was too much. However depressed he became from time to time, it was as a reaction to his own failings: doubt did not enter his equation. Lou's "atheism" was a blow impossible to bear, and if he had revealed it for dramatic effect, in the offhand way he affected, he underestimated its impact. Making a spiritual connection with Robert Fegusson was one thing ("born in the same city; both sickly, both pestered, one nearly to madness, one to the madhouse, with a damnatory creed"), living up to it another.

A less rigid man would have understood his son's rebellion better. Louis was of a generation stirred by the new intellectual mood that was abroad. Darwin, socialism, atheism: there was a logic to it all, a refreshing honesty, truths that the old shibboleths had obscured. Thomas, and he was not the only Victorian patriarch to react so, could not see it. The citadel of the Scottish Presbyterian Church was less open to attack than the Anglican Church, perhaps, but the last thing Thomas had expected was to see it undermined from within. In "Crabbed Age and Youth," written in the summer of 1877 when the storms had abated somewhat, Louis explained himself a little:

> I am no more abashed at having been a red-hot Socialist with a panacea of my own than at having been a sucking infant . . . For my part, I look back to the time when I was a Socialist with something like regret. I have convinced myself (for the moment) that we had better leave these great changes to what we call great blind forces: their blindness being so much more perspicacious than the little, perring, partial eyesight of men. I seem to see that my own scheme would not answer; and all the other schemes I ever heard propounded would depress some elements of goodness just as much as they encouraged others. Now I know that in thus turning Conservative with years, I am going through the normal cycle of change and travelling in the common orbit of men's opinions. I submit to this . . . but I do not acknowledge that it is necessarily a change for the better—I dare say it is deplorably for the worse. I have no choice in the business . . . I do not greatly pride myself on having outlived my belief in the fairy tales of Socialism.

The verse R.L.S. was composing in youth gives a clue to the thinking of the "red-hot Socialist." "White neck-clothed bigots" were being exposed, militarism confounded—though he had spoken against communism in a debate at the Spec. The next year he was writing to his father from France (at his father's expense, naturally) to rail against proposed income-tax cuts and anti–trade-union laws. Throughout his life he had an ambivalent attitude to the socialism of his day, sympathetic yet unconvinced. In the Pacific he was to see the destruction wrought by imperialism and commerce, and come to admire the communal life of the people, but he could never quite bring himself to break free of his background, just as he could never turn his Scottish nationalism into Nationalism. Guthrie recalled that as early as 1876 Stevenson projected a history of the Union between Scotland and England. It was intended to be a work

> which should discuss the success of that union as contrasted with the failure of the union of Great Britain and Ireland, although both were equally obnoxious to the majority of the lesser nations most directly concerned.

In the winter of 1880–81, R.L.S. was again to read widely on the subject but write nothing. His thinking on Scotland's relations with England was much affected by his views on the Irish Question, in which he supported the Crown, arguing that the alternative was bloodshed and chaos. Much later, aroused by widespread American support for Irish Home Rule but disgusted by terrorism, he did compose the "Confessions of a Unionist." *Scribner's Magazine* chose not to publish it.

His politics were ever complicated. As we know, he did not much like England and felt himself intensely Scottish, yet he later came to despise Gladstone (in part for "deserting" General Gordon at Khartoum), associate with rabid Tories, and oppose Irish agitation—accepting all the while that majorities in "the lesser nations," Scotland and Ireland, found the Union "obnoxious."

In "The Day After Tomorrow," published in the *Contemporary Review* in the spring of 1887, he wrote:

> We . . . all know what Parliament is, and we are all ashamed of it . . . There are great truths in Socialism, or no one . . . would be found to hold

it; and if it came, and did one-tenth part of what it offers, I for one should make it welcome. But if it is to come, we may as well have some notion of what it will be like . . . It will be made, or will grow, in a human parliament; and the one thing that will not very hugely change is human nature.

He spoke of the "ant-heap" and argued that "the rise of the communes is nonetheless the end of economic equality, just when we were told it was beginning." But all this was still to come.

Meanwhile, a chill descended on Heriot Row as Louis had the leisure to learn that honesty might not always be the best policy. His father hunted his library for arguments while his mother urged Lou to enter the theological equivalent of therapy in a church class for young men. "What a pleasant thing it is to have just *damned* the happiness of (probably) the only two people who care a damn about you in the world," Louis said in a letter to Baxter. The arguments and the rows went on, with Thomas at one point saying that his entire life had been rendered a failure. The "careless infidel" and "horrible atheist" began to contemplate an escape to Cambridge. "A little absence is the only chance," Louis told Baxter.

In a short story entitled "The Edifying Letters of the Rutherford Family" begun in 1876 that remained unpublished until 1982, R.L.S. turned the domestic storm into fiction. James Rutherford (Thomas) writes to a friend at Aberdeen University that William (Louis) "has several classes at the University this session; but I am more than doubtful whether he gives his mind to the business in hand. I am afraid he has an *excursive* and *discursive* mind, tending to nothing in particular. I see no signs of steady work, although much desultory reading . . . It is a terrible responsibility before God and one's own heart, to have the upbringing of an only child."

Later, in a subsequently deleted passage, William writes to "Charles Butler" (Baxter) and discusses their proposed society:

For the titles:- Liberty seems right—is the true blue, at least; youth's watchword, the gist of hope. Justice—which means the liberty of others—is quite as good. But where the devil, Butler, got ye Reverence? I will admit that 'L.J.R.' is a pleasant monogram to put upon our tankards. But what, in the name of Beelzebub, have we to do with Reverence? What is Reverence?

Such language had, of course, sent him into the purgatory from which he was struggling to escape. Elsewhere in the text there are some disrespectful remarks on religion and on William's deep desire to escape from the family home. It is some sort of testament to Stevenson's breadth of sympathy, however, that this incomplete piece of fiction makes an effort to comprehend the father figure, even to attempting to speak with his father's voice. James speaks for Thomas through the pen of his son, for example, when he says of the wayward William: "I have always laid myself out to be his *friend* rather than his *father* (perhaps wrongly) . . ." What Louis struggled to absorb in life—and the rows hurt him almost as much as they hurt Thomas—he found a way to explain in fiction. The "Edifying Letters" are slight, but given their origins, they say much for Stevenson's character.

In the meantime, his quarters on the top floor of Heriot Row were extended to allow him a study of his own. In July he was allowed to travel to Cockfield, near Bury St. Edmunds in Suffolk, to spend a long holiday with his cousin Maud, a granddaughter of the Reverend Lewis Balfour and an old friend from Colinton days, who had married the wealthy Reverend Churchill Babington, a Cambridge archaeology professor. Louis had first visited them in 1870. Now it was as though Thomas, if not admitting defeat after months of struggle and argument, had at least called a truce. His motives are not difficult to discern and do him credit. Louis had strayed into error, his soul was in peril. But he remained the Stevensons' only child. The traces of Smout were still discernible in him. The boy had faced death before and would doubtless face it again. If Louis could be plucked from him at any moment, Thomas did not want it to happen while they were estranged.

Here, as on many occasions, Thomas preferred to indulge his son rather than remain obedient to his duty as a Victorian parent. Lou's antics around the pubs, his failure to study, his impudence at table (for so some of the Stevensons' friends saw it), his decision to disavow the family's profession, and, last and worse of all, his lack of faith were each borne with a stoicism that even a modern parent can only admire. Even the "compromise" of Louis's reading for the bar was one likely to involve Thomas in years of expense. For all his rage and bewilderment, Thomas loved his son. If Lou had erred, there must be an explanation.

The Babingtons occupied a gracious Georgian rectory with an expanse of lawn and a moat at the bottom of the garden. Though welcomed, Louis thought Suffolk cold and the English strange. Not for the first time, he found Scotland's larger neighbour one of the few countries in which he did not feel at home. Its very social structure seemed to repel him, though he drew only vague conclusions from his alienation. One of the other visitors at the rectory turned out to be more than sufficient compensation.

Mrs. Frances Sitwell was a clergyman's wife who had parted from her husband. Her son, Bertie, was staying at Cockfield and had taken to R.L.S., just as the twenty-two-year-old took, to put mildly, to the thirty-four-year-old Mrs. Sitwell.

Their affair was never consummated, but Louis became thoroughly infatuated with this intelligent, vivacious woman, and was to remain so for two years. It was forgivable: she was a great beauty, as all agreed and as all photographs confirm. Her "official" admirer was Sidney Colvin, the newly appointed Slade Professor at Cambridge who was later to become Keeper of Prints and Drawings at the British Museum. Many men had fallen in love with her, but it was Colvin she finally married, though only after her husband's death, in 1903, when she was in her sixties.

This is not to say that she did not respond to Louis. Mrs. Sitwell's marriage had been an unhappy one, for reasons cloaked in Victorian euphemism ("uncongenial habits"). She had already seen one of her sons die and had been obliged to support herself with translation work, despite a respiratory weakness akin to Stevenson's. Prevented from marrying Colvin yet surrounded by admirers, usually youthful, she was happy enough and young enough to be flattered by Louis's attentions. She did not discourage him.

His confidence needed such a balm. Fanny took him seriously, listened to his tales of family woe, and was happy to walk and read poetry with him. As different as it was possible to be from the prostitutes who had provided him with his only sexual experiences, Fanny Sitwell was nevertheless yet another of those older women to whom Louis seemed to be drawn. Perhaps it is a trait in only sons raised by nannies, or perhaps such women—for his wife, of course, was another—reassured him. They had the confidence and experience the gangling young man so conspicuously lacked.

Mrs. Sitwell saw something in Louis, too. The Scots Heine had his usual effect. His cousin Maud had already shown her some work he had contributed to a short-lived university magazine. Now, dazzled by his talk, she summoned Colvin to confirm her intuition that the young Scot was something out of the ordinary.

In a volume of reminiscences, Colvin portrayed the student thus:

> . . . he comprised within himself, and would flash on you in the course of a single afternoon, all the different ages and half the different characters of man, the unfaded freshness of a child, the ardent outlook and adventurous daydreams of a boy, the steadfast courage of manhood, the quick sympathetic tenderness of a woman, and already, as early as the mid-twenties of his life, an almost uncanny share of the ripe life-wisdom of old age.

Be it noted that this paragon, this unearthly creature, was being recalled by Colvin long after R.L.S. was dead. Like many others, he allowed his sense of loss to turn his prose to treacle. Nevertheless, such a description goes some way to conveying the impact Louis had on many people. Charm is the most elusive thing, impossible to preserve in words or pictures. But Colvin spoke for many, and with more than mere hindsight or the need to render a special writer as a special person, when he composed his testimony. He saw something in Stevenson even before Stevenson had begun to prove himself. To some, such veneration is unbelievable, and R.L.S., vain though he could be, had no such high opinion of himself. But the gift for talk, the vehicle of his charm, was another kind of verbal dexterity. Arriving at the rectory from Cambridge, Colvin was soon convinced.

Louis was happier in Suffolk than he had meant to be. He had gone off to lick his several wounds only to discover that his suspicions were right: the world was a bigger and more welcoming place than Edinburgh suggested, even if this part of the world happened to be uncongenial England. Psychologically, Mrs. Sitwell released him. He had acquired a muse and earned the respect of a man as distinguished as the twenty-eight-year-old Colvin, who was to become his conduit to the literary world of London. But back in Edinburgh, as he discovered when he returned, the causes of his original unhappiness had yet to be cured.

> The mere return of Bob changed at once and for ever the course of my life; I can give you an idea of my relief only by saying that I was at last able to breathe. The miserable isolation in which I had languished was no more in season, and I began to be happy. To have no one to whom you can speak your thoughts is but a slight trial; for a month or two at a time, I can support it almost without regret; but to be young, to be daily making fresh discoveries and fabricating new theories of life . . . and not only not to have, but never to have had a confidant, is an astounding misery. I now understand it best by recognising my delight when that period was ended. . . . Laughter was at that time our principal affair, and I doubt if we could have had a better . . . it is also true that under all this mirth-making, there kept growing up and strengthening a serious, angry, and at length a downright hostile criticism of the life around us. This time we call, in looking back, the period of Jink.

The Jink, a word in their own language of slang and foreign tongues designed for the pursuit of "absurdity and consequent laughter," would return to haunt Louis. Thomas Stevenson had also detected the "hostile criticism of life" in his son. Casting around for a means to explain the transformation, he had found it in a bizarre quarter.

Around the end of August 1873 a cousin of Louis's had sent a letter to Thomas Stevenson from his deathbed. He found the prospect of death difficult, he suggested, if he could not warn Uncle Tom of Bob's dangerous influence on Louis. Bob was a moral "mildew," a blight. It was all that Thomas needed to hear. Everything was explained. He met Bob on the street and a furious row ensued.

Louis unburdened himself in one of his many letters to Mrs. Sitwell:

> There is now at least one person in the world who knows what I have had to face and what a tempest of emotions my father can raise when he is really excited. The war began with my father accusing Bob of having ruined his house and his son. Bob answered that he didn't know where I had found out that the Christian religion was not true but that he hadn't told

me. And I think from that point the conversation went off into emotion
and never touched shore again.

His father believed, and said, that Louis's views were "a childish imitation of Bob" and that he was ceasing to care for his own son. By
Stevenson's account he shook hands with his nephew, "wished him all
happiness" but prayed "that he should never see him between the eyes
again."

Oddly, this seemed to satisfy Thomas. Such was his blindness, he could
not credit the idea that his wilful son was capable of arriving at disturbing
notions on his own, or of picking them up from books and pub talk. No:
all that was necessary was for Bob, the agent of blight, to be "banished"
and Louis would recover. Soon, father and son began gingerly to resume
their walks together, with Louis striving to say nothing that would reopen
wounds. He had a "wearying, despairing, sick heart." Thomas, meanwhile, spoke openly of disowning him, and wondered at his own fear of
doing so. Lou toyed with idea of leaving home, but shrank at the thought.
Depressed, restless, uncertain, transfixed by the sexual current between
himself and Mrs. Sitwell which was being transmitted through an increasing number of letters, he was learning to live with the emotional chaos
that was to be his lot in life.

The correspondence grew apace. When, later, Colvin edited
Stevenson's letters, he chose to leave out many of those sent to Mrs.
Sitwell. Equally, Louis himself decided to burn most of those he received.
Both actions confirm that, for a time at least, her words were more ardent
than Colvin would have liked and Louis thought proper for preservation.
Perhaps she led him on, amused or aroused simply by the young man's
passions, without any intention of allowing him to make love to her. Or
perhaps her own feelings were genuine. The age difference between them
may not have mattered: she was six years older than Colvin, after all.
There is some evidence that Louis attempted to persuade her into a physical relationship during one of his trips to London and was rebuffed. His
"madonna," his "Consuelo," seems to have remained loyal to Colvin, and
one ambiguous reference to "S.C." in a letter from Louis appears to confirm as much. He renounced his physical passion, or at least accepted the
situation, and began to write to his friend as a matron rather than a mis-

tress, calling her "mother" rather than "madonna." Thus, in 1874: ". . . if you love me this letter shall be to you as a son's Christmas kiss."

It is not recorded what, or if, Maggie Stevenson knew of such language. We know she was discomfited to discover that Louis had a "second family" in London but not whether she objected to Fanny or Colvin. Certainly the pair were thought acceptable, though perhaps this was because the elder Stevensons did not care to investigate the irregular relationship between Mrs. Sitwell and S.C. Nevertheless, each of the older women in the life of Maggie Stevenson's son, from his nurse to Mrs. Sitwell to his eventual wife, seemed in some sense to supplant her. He competed with his father, and not just over religion, while finding something erotic in mother figures, be they whores, nurses, society ladies, or "trusty, dusky, vivid" Americans. Lou was the epitome of the only child of a Victorian middle-class family receiving his sexuality from the bosom of his mother. It is perhaps another reason why he had no children of his own.

In November of 1873 he and his father encountered Edward Strathearn Gordon, the Lord Advocate (the government's chief Scottish law officer), on a train journey. Thomas knew the man, as he knew most of the important figures in the Scottish capital, and they discussed Louis's plans to enter the law. The distinguished gentleman suggested, for reasons that are unclear, that Lou should become a barrister at the English bar.

Given his need to escape from home, and his evident desire to be as near to Mrs. Sitwell as possible, this was exactly what Louis wanted to hear. Colvin had already helped to place an essay, "On Roads," with the *Portfolio*, for which R.L.S. had received three pounds and eight shillings. If he was to further his literary ambitions, such good fortune had to be followed up, and that could best be done in London. For the first time in a year, the pieces of his life were beginning to fall into place.

There is a pattern to the career of R.L.S., a simple, melodramatic one, but true for all that: when things were going well, disaster was not far behind. Sometimes it can seem as though a rate of exchange was being applied to his life: everything had to be paid for. Equally, the setbacks usually turned out to be for the best, though that fact was rarely a comfort when disaster struck.

In London, almost inevitably and immediately, Louis became ill with a throat infection. Dr. Andrew Clarke took one look at his alarmingly scrawny patient—who had been losing weight, if such a thing were possible—and ruled that bar examinations were out of the question. Stevenson was put on a special diet while his parents were sent for.

When they arrived, Dr. Clarke told them that, given the poor general health of his patient and his family history, he feared consumption. Louis needed rest and a decent climate. Mrs. Stevenson suggested Torquay, but the doctor insisted on the South of France, and said, further, that Louis must go alone. Both of his parent affected dismay—though Thomas could well have been relieved—but Louis, with the prospect of the law postponed, was delighted. He wrote a farewell note to Frances Sitwell:

> I do look forward to the sun and I go with a great store of contentment— bah! what a mean word—of living happiness that I can scarce keep bottled down in my weather-beaten body. Do be happy.

Happiness: the word had reappeared, as though the name Menton, a place remembered from childhood, was enough to replenish his spirits. In early November his mother returned to London to see him off. The clouds rolled back. The sheer delight of escape was sufficient, even for a young man who was far from well, in body or in mind. He had been ordered south. And he had already lived half his life.

5 *1874–1875*

The promise is so great, and we are all so easily led away when hope and memory are both in one story, that I dare say the sick man is not very inconsolable when he receives sentence of banishment, and is inclined to regard his ill-health as not the least fortunate accident of his life. Nor is he immediately undeceived.

"ORDERED SOUTH"

*L*ouis travelled through Paris, Sens, and Avignon feeling sick and depressed, for all his declarations of happiness. An English doctor in Nice confirmed that he was not suffering from tuberculosis, but this hardly cheered him. He acquired a nervous facial tic, developed an uncharacteristic shyness with strangers, and went through a bout of disorientation that deprived him of the ability to speak French. The doctors allowed him opium to help him sleep, and promptly the invalid suffered hallucinations. He claimed to enjoy these fugues thoroughly, but unlike many of his contemporaries, he did not make a fad or a habit of the drug.

His physical health was wrecked, as usual, but his mental health was little better. He had, neither for the first time nor the last, all the unpredictable symptoms of a nervous breakdown. In sunlit places where numerous middle-class invalids were facing the prospect of death with forbearance, Lou continued to crack up.

It is usually presumed that physical illness impinged on the mental state of R.L.S., but the truth is that his mind frequently was under as much pressure as his body. He was as tightly strung as an overtuned piano. In November of 1873 he wrote to Fanny Sitwell from Avignon:

I am back again in the stage of thinking there is nothing the matter with me, which is a good sign; but I am wretchedly nervous. Anything like rudeness I am simply babyishly afraid of; and noises, and especially the sounds of certain voices, are the devil to me. A blind poet whom I found selling his immortal works in the streets of Sens captivated me with the remarkable equable strength and sweetness of his voice; and I listened a long while and bought some of the poems; and now this voice, after I had thus got it thoroughly into my head, proved false metal and a really bad and horrible voice at bottom. It haunted me some time, but I think I am done with it now.

Menton was favoured by the prosperous sick.* According to Thomas Carlyle, in a letter of 1867, there were about eight hundred British present there in that year, and half a dozen hotels (the Grande Bretagne, Victoria, de Londres, and D'Angleterre among them) to cater to their needs. In the book *Wintering at Mentone*, published in 1870, the publisher William Chambers wrote: "Menton is a dull, a very dull place; that is its reputation." In an attempt, perhaps, to live up to that reputation, the town had acquired a Presbyterian kirk by the end of the century. When Louis went there, Menton had little of the glamour it was subsequently to acquire.

His disjointed letter to Mrs. Sitwell in November of 1873 gives us the spectrum. He was sick, he was ill at ease, he was "driven forward by restlessness," but the France to which he always felt an allegiance touched him still:

Menton, November 12th.—My first enthusiasm was on rising at Orange and throwing open the shutters. Such a great living flood of sunshine poured in upon me, that I confess to having danced and expressed my satisfaction aloud; in the middle of which the boots came to the door with hot water, to my great confusion.

To-day has been one long delight, coming to a magnificent climax on my arrival here, I gave up my baggage to an hotel porter and set off to walk at once. I was somewhat confused as yet to my directions, for the station of course was new to me, and the hills had not sufficiently opened out to let me recognise the peaks. Suddenly, as I was going forward slowly in

*See, generally, Pemble, J.: *The Mediterranean Passion: Victorians and Edwardians in the South* (Oxford, 1987).

this confusion of mind, I was met by a great volley of odours out of the lemon and orange gardens, and the past linked on to the present, and in a moment, in the twinkling of an eye, the whole scene fell before me into order, and I was at home. I nearly danced again.

He wrote in sickness of what he was, with his past suddenly "linked on to the present," a continuum through which he moved. The bag of bones, instantly at home, felt like dancing. The "great volley of odours" that provoked his reaction is a quintessential moment.

He was there for his health. R.L.S. suffered from the recognised Victorian condition of "delicacy"—though his respiratory weakness went far beyond hypochondria—for which the recognised and universally popular treatment was the Mediterranean climate. As the historian John Pemble has recorded, not two decades after Stevenson had been ordered south, "Menton had become one of the principal British sanatoria abroad."*

Late in 1873 Louis concluded that the other guests at the Hôtel du Pavillon were bores, and he spent his first few days revisiting those parts of Menton he remembered from childhood. He confessed in a letter to Baxter that he was "weary and nervous," unable to read or write. Still, it was better than home:

> . . . you must not suppose me discontented. I am away in my own beautiful Riviera, and I am free now from the horrible worry and misery that was playing the devil with me at home.

Slowly, as the sun did its work and he began to relax, he started on the first piece of prose that was to win him real attention. It was hard going. "Ordered South" conveys some of the mood of dislocation and anxiety, of being stricken and weak amid so much natural beauty and vigour. It conveys, too, what was becoming Stevenson's habitual response to illness: he bore it, fought it, and tried to write through it. He learned from his skirmishes with mortality.

It was a characteristic that later won him much admiration, though few comprehended what it meant. Much of Stevenson's style is a sick man's response to the world: heightened, distanced, specific. "Ordered South"

*Ibid.

is an obvious example, given that it concerns convalescence. But read with understanding of the circumstances in which it was composed—by a mind in turmoil, sometimes hallucinating, groping after a style of its own—it acquires a strange vivacity and casts a shadow over the work that was to come. Much of Louis's prose had the clarity of fever and dream. The writer's business—ordering a world into coherence—acquired a new urgency in Stevenson, and it showed.

Nevertheless, he was soon telling Baxter that he was recovering more slowly than he had hoped. He felt guilty that he was not paying his way in the world and that his father was subsidising his convalescence. He strove, uncharacteristically, to keep his expenses to a minimum, and even resolved to get a job should Colvin, who was due to visit, advise that literature was not a paying proposition. This was a low ebb, even for Louis.

Shortly after his arrival he was again conveying his mood to Mrs. Sitwell in a letter:

> Being sent to the South is not much good unless you take your soul with you . . . and my soul is rarely with me here. I don't see much beauty. I have lost the key; I can only be placid and inert, and see the bright days go past uselessly one after another . . .

He believed he was dying, that he had aged prematurely ("I am a man of seventy . . .") and that his life, what was left of it, would be a brief glide into the abyss. This was melodrama, but the company of so many other invalids could not have helped a man of Stevenson's temperament. Louis rose above the moods of others as often as he rose above his own condition.

Shortly, however, his innate energy began to reassert itself. As was to happen again and again, the wheel of his physical fortunes turned and his spirits rose. He began to notice his surroundings, detecting glory in the leaves of the plane trees, in the moon rising over the Italian coast, and in the scent of violets. Louis had enjoyed his opium, though the style in which he wrote was "not quite equal to Kubla Khan." It was around this time that his essay "On Roads," inspired by his visit to Suffolk, appeared in the *Portfolio*, having been refused by the *Saturday Review*.

When Colvin arrived for the Christmas holidays, Stevenson moved to another hotel, the Mirabeau, in the East Bay. His motives were curiously modern and entirely understandable: the Pavillon was full of "horrid English." At the Mirabeau, French was spoken, and Louis was soon receiving praise for his accent. He was also entering a circle altogether more pleasing to a would-be cosmopolitan. Good company always seemed to rouse him, and the company he began to keep at the Mirabeau did more to raise his spirits than any amount of laudanum.

His excellent French was no barrier to the comedy of incomprehension that ensued. He began spending time with two noble sisters, Princess Zassetsky and Madame Garschine, from Georgia. Both were married, but had come to the Riviera sans husbands. They had a child apiece, though Louis was never entirely sure which mother claimed which child. The younger, a three-year-old girl, "a little polyglot button" who spoke six languages, fascinated R.L.S. But he knew nothing of Georgians, and they knew as much about Scots. The exotic had collided with the exotic. "The Eastern Question," as Louis called it, grew daily more complicated. "I am to them as some undiscovered animal. They do not seem to cultivate R.L.S.s in Muscovy."

The princess, the elder of the two, was said to have borne ten children and composed successful comedies. She certainly found Louis comic, and her extreme frankness disconcerted him. But discussions of Mill and Spencer were, surprisingly, possible, and agnosticism was confessed by all. The women had him photographed in an improbable cloak, held fancy-dress parties, and read his palm. It was fun, if disconcerting. But Madame alone was more disconcerting still.

Whether this still-handsome woman—yet again, it hardly needs be said, one much older than the twenty-three-year-old Scot; again a wife alienated from her husband—truly intended to seduce Louis is a question he could never answer. She flirted outrageously, and gave every indication of serious interest when he took tea at the villa the Georgians had rented (they came to the hotel only to eat). Revealingly, Louis wrote to Fanny Sitwell for advice. Could this woman of the world help him to interpret the behaviour of others of her kind? Was he being made to look a fool? Or was Madame serious? If the latter, it was a complication he did not seek but could not, it seems, bring himself to resist. When Madame

Garschine spent a day ill in bed, he was most upset. Perhaps he was fooling himself.

Louis was reading quantities of George Sand, a practice which could not have helped to ease the situation. He had also begun to work on articles devoted to his hero Walt Whitman and to Victor Hugo, though with little enthusiasm. In that area of his life, at least, his confidence had not returned. Colvin rated him highly; too highly, in Louis's self-lacerating opinion. Meanwhile, comprehension seems to have intruded into the business with the Georgian ladies. The "affair" cooled, and they, like so many before, began to take a maternal attitude towards him; the perfect substitute, to Louis, for passion. When they parted, he promised to visit them at home. Sadly for the biographer, this trip, so rich in promise, was never made. He had stumbled before these strange, enticing creatures, but he had not fallen. As Colvin rightly said, Louis was a "type-hunter."

In April of 1874 Lou went to Paris, with the halfhearted idea of studying Roman law at Göttingen. He also intended to visit Bob. His cousin introduced him to real bohemia, to a world of cafés, studios, and real artists. Lou was hooked, and would return to the scene time and again. But Paris in the spring of that year belied its reputation; the weather was sour and chilly, and all of the symptoms Louis had spent the winter curing returned. He ran a fever, suffered headaches and the renewed embarrassment of a facial tic. Rather than flee south, however, he decided to go home, calculating that, sick again, "I shall be a prince."

He was almost correct. His parents were relieved to find him sane— one of his pugnacious letters from Menton, defending his position at intemperate length, had convinced them that he had lost his reason—and prepared to be reasonable. His time away seems to have obliged Thomas to concede that Louis was no longer a boy, and required a decent allowance. Seven pounds a month was agreed, a sum Louis ran through as quickly as he had spent the shillings of his engineering days, but a small fortune in the slums of the Old Town. Again, one can only remark on the patience of the elder Stevenson. His son was not a child—the size of the allowance admitted as much—but still, at twenty-three, he showed no signs of fending for himself. Had there been siblings, or had he enjoyed better health, he would not, one feels, have been treated so leniently. In any case, the crisis of conscience over his financial dependency which had struck Louis in Menton seems not to have recurred.

He resumed his legal work, but his parents drew the line at allowing him to move to Göttingen. Lou's health was more precarious than it had been for years. The storms of childhood had been replaced by relative calm. If not robust, he had certainly kept sickness at bay. But the illnesses which bracketed his southern adventure were merely a preface to the years ahead, when every plan depended on a diagnosis. Soon after his return he was at Swanston, writing to Mrs. Sitwell to say how jolly he was, how nice his parents were, and how cold the weather was.

The summer was taken up with intermittent study of the law, theatricals with the Jenkins, some writing, and a good deal of travelling. Louis cruised in the Hebrides and canoed in the Forth with Walter Simpson. He holidayed with his parents in Wales and the West of England. He also became, much to his satisfaction, a member of the Savile Club, one of the newest and least hidebound of the London establishments. It was as though he was trying to rebuild his health as he built his career: in October he was walking in the Chilterns: London, the Savile, and Mrs. Sitwell called him often; but Edinburgh, and Swanston in particular, were their equals.

In lieu of foreign parts, the cottage was his bolt-hole. In May of 1874 he was working again on "Victor Hugo" and trying to simulate "jolliness." But he was depressed again. Happy enough to take his father's money, he nevertheless knew that, sooner or later, he would have to earn a living, and writing was the only trade that appealed. It was possible, in those days, to earn money as an essayist, and thus far that was the only form he had come near to mastering. But occasional magazine pieces would not keep him. The three pounds eight shillings he had made from "Roads" was less than half the amount his father was doling out to him each month. Besides, his erratic university career had ensured that he lacked the academic training to give his writing intellectual weight.

Louis had an aptitude for essays that was to do his subsequent reputation no good at all. Colvin had introduced him to Andrew Lang; he had met Gosse and W. E. Henley. All essayists, all leading lights in literary London, where a well-turned paragraph was prized. He had even joined the Savile Club. The pressure to achieve *something*, even as a "sedulous ape" to Hazlitt and the rest, obliged him to ignore his true gifts.

Henley he had met through Leslie Stephen, in February of 1875. Their relationship was to be one of the most important, and the most difficult, of Stevenson's life. Born in 1849, Henley, the son of a Gloucester bookseller, had developed tuberculosis at the age of twelve. It crippled him—one foot was later amputated—and, like Louis, exposed him to the threat of death for years. Later Lloyd Osbourne, Stevenson's stepson and an unblushing, devoted admirer of Henley, would describe W.E. thus:

> . . . a great, glowing, massive-shouldered fellow with a big red beard and a crutch; jovial, astoundingly clever, and with a laugh that rolled out like music. Never was there such another as William Ernest Henley; he had an unimaginable fire and vitality; he swept one off one's feet. There are no words that can describe the quality he had of exalting those about him . . . There is still a fellowship of those who proudly call themselves 'Henley's young men,' I hope it will not sound presumptuous to say I was the first . . . Even after all these years there is a surge in my heart as I recollect Henley; he shines through the mist with an effulgence; that magic voice rises out of the grave with its unforgotten cadences. He was the first man I had ever called by his surname; the first friend I have ever sought and won; he said the most flattering things of me behind my back . . .

Henley's habit of saying things behind the backs of others would later lead Osbourne's mother to very different conclusions, and cause R.L.S. something like grief, but Lloyd was right about his hero's impact. Henley, who lived until 1903, became an influential, often unpaid, literary impresario, selflessly working to place the manuscripts of those he thought talented or publishing them himself in one of the string of periodicals he edited. Hence the reference to "Henley's young men." He enjoyed collecting disciples, perhaps as insurance against his own want of ability. He was also oversensitive and self-important, prone to jealousy and easily slighted. He expected deference from those he aided. Louise gave it, but never unquestioningly.

Henley had little talent of his own. It is possible to say it now without a second thought. But in his heydey, in the late-Victorian seller's market for scribblers, he cut quite a figure. He was a New Imperialist, the bugle

boy of empire and the laureate of the public school. Sincerely—
shamelessly?—he fed Britannia's childishness. He composed, as one
historian of the empire records,* "an anthology of English poems 'com-
memorative of heroic action or illustrative of heroic sentiment,' and
summed up a nation's passionate pride of country in the ecstatic stanza":

> *Chosen daughter of the Lord,*
> *Spouse-in-Chief of the ancient Sword,*
> *There's the menace of the Word*
> *In the Song on your bugles blown.*
> *England—*
> *Out of heaven on your bugles blown!*

He was not, to be fair, invariably puerile. The four stanzas of "Invictus,"
perhaps his most famous poem, were a turn-of-the-century staple:

> *It matters not how strait the gate,*
> *How charged with punishments the scroll,*
> *I am the master of my fate:*
> *I am the captain of my soul.*

Similarly, he is still remembered (at least by Stevenson's biographers)
for his metrically tedious but apt verse portrait of his most famous
friend:

> *Thin-legged! thin-chested! slight unspeakably,*
> *Neat-footed and weak-fingered; in his face—*
> *Lean, large-boned, curved of beak, and touched with race,*
> *Broad-lipped, rich-tinted, mutable as the sea,*
> *The brown eyes radiant with vivacity . . .*

In time, Henley came to know them all, from Wilde to Bernard Shaw.
He once knocked Wilde over with his crutches, and Oscar remarked: "To
converse with him is a physical no less than an intellectual recreation." By
the end of his life Henley could claim to have discovered Yeats, Barrie,
and Kipling, and to have promoted Wells and Conrad. In Kipling he was

---

*Morris, J.: *Pax Britannica, Vol. II—The Climax of Empire* (London, 1968); p. 343.

to find his most suitable, if not his most malleable, protégé.* In 1889, when Edinburgh could still lay claim to being a publishing centre of sorts, some of Henley's friends set him up as editor of the *Scots Observer* with the aim of advancing yet another of the country's literary revivals. Hard as it now is to believe, the magazine "captured the taste of the younger literary set," Kipling not least among them, and it was in the *Observer*, early in 1890, that "Danny Deever," the first of the *Barrack-Room Ballads*, appeared, launching a career almost as important as Stevenson's. "The massive-shouldered fellow," less subtle in his politics than Kipling or R.L.S., was entitled to the credit.

In 1873 all that lay ahead. Henley had travelled to Edinburgh to consult the famous Professor Joseph Lister, whose skill seems to have spared his patient a second amputation. In the infirmary the young poet composed verse and wrote critical articles which Stephen published in the *Cornhill Magazine*. The editor, in the city in 1875 to give a lecture, decided to bring his two young contributors together. "He has taught himself two languages since he has been there," Louis wrote to Mrs. Sitwell. "I shall try to be of use to him." They became firm friends, though Stevenson could not guess of how much use he would subsequently be to Henley, and how little gratitude Henley would show, particularly after one too many whiskies. But it was in such company that his literary ambitions took their first form.

Stevenson and Henley were soon planning to collaborate—an arrangement Louis was always keen to attempt but one which was never worth the effort he put into it. His later, fruitless efforts to write plays with Henley resulted in the only substantial failures of his career, and destroyed the friendship to boot. At that time, however, both young men felt themselves in desperate need of money. The talk came, for the moment, to nothing. Louis had enough on his hands trying to earn a name as an essayist and reviewer among periodical editors.

R.L.S. the essayist completed most of his work by the age of thirty-five. Later efforts were those of the conjurer explaining his tricks. Often dismissed, the early pieces, from "Ordered South" ("not particularly well written," he thought) onward, are, nevertheless, the key to his style. If

*Carrington, C.: *Rudyard Kipling—His Life and Work* (London, 1955); pp. 197–202.

they are five-finger exercises distinguished by "lightness of touch," more "manner than matter," they are also, for the most part, rigorous efforts to refine his language, to achieve "those more exquisite refinements of proficiency and finish." His sentences are complex, too much so to many a modern ear. But they are made that way for the sake of clarity and precision, not effect. Stevenson was an instinctive grammarian: each sentence is given its load to carry. Most are hard to dismantle: the "decorative" parts prove integral. Equally, in the "biographical" pieces—on Burns, Thoreau, Villon, and the rest—R.L.S. (though he may not have know it) was developing a method of characterisation.

None of this was much comfort as he contemplated his future. If he thought about fiction at all at this stage—and there is some evidence of desultory attempts—he does not seem to have persisted. His father loved tales and melodrama. Was that an incentive, or the opposite of an incentive?

Essays, reviews, and some verse aside, the law was to be Louis's destiny. How or why Thomas believed this is something of a mystery. Lou did not pretend to be enamoured of this profession chosen by default. He was proud to pass his final exams for admission to the bar in July 1875, perhaps merely because he had at last succeeded at something, and a brass plaque was erected with all due ceremony at Heriot Row. But it was a faint hope that the advocate would ever practise, for all that the historical romance of the law somewhat appealed. Thomas must have know it, yet he nevertheless gave Louis a thousand pounds, a huge sum, to set him on his feet. The trials of R.L.S., and there were many, did not include starvation.

His essays, meanwhile, gained attention. "Whitman, Hugo, Knox" and "Ordered South" (published in *Macmillan's Magazine* in May 1874) were well received. A piece on Burns was rejected by the *Encyclopaedia Britannica*, mostly because Lou had suffered a relapse into Calvinism and upbraided the poet for his loose living. He worked on, still lonely, still uncertain. "I am still selfish and peevish and a spoiled child," he wrote. The putative affair with Fanny had ended before it began, apparently at her request. Unable to break with her, Louis had tried to settle for the role of dutiful son. It did not always work. Early in 1875 he had written to Fanny, his confusion plain in several respects: "It is not one bit like what I feel for my mother *here*. But I think it is what one *ought* to feel for a mother . . . That's a lie; nobody loves a mere mother as much as I love you, madonna."

His legal career went nowhere and his thousand pounds drained away. He lent (or gave) money to Henley, to Colvin, to Bob, to Bob's sister; other sums went to the wine merchant, to the bookseller. Some of it had been spent, too, on a visit to the artists' colonies at Barbizon, and to the forest of Fontainebleau and the Hotel Siron. Having refused two briefs and spent most of his father's money, Louis announced that, as a briefless advocate, he was retiring from the law.

6 1875–1876

One thing in life calls for another; there is a fitness in events and places.

"A GOSSIP ON ROMANCE"

H is health, yet again. The weather in the spring of 1875 and Louis's physical condition indicated foreign parts. His inclination, too, pointed abroad—to France, yet again.

Stevenson operated an entente cordiale all of his own, feeding on Villon, Hugo, Dumas, and Baudelaire. In this, as in most things, he was unsystematic but sincere. His love affair with France was deeper than recreational bohemianism and more passionate than the fashion of the day allowed. France's manners, mores, and habits of studied enjoyment struck chords in him during every visit. He was tied to Scotland, repelled (it is not too strong a word) by England—but he was drawn to France like a leaf drifting on a tide. It was not that he found no fault with the French, far from it, but he found in France a sense of freedom that touched every part of his life and art. French literature did not consume him to the point of becoming an obvious influence—his Scots English was not so malleable—but it left a trace, particularly in his syntax. Ambience was altogether more important; he was a sponge for that.

The country, its culture, and its people suggested to Louis that he was not entirely the lone eccentric Edinburgh thought him to be; neither was he necessarily the archetypal Victorian man of letters his London friends thought he should be. There were other choices available to him. It was small wonder that many people saw something "Frenchified" in his gestures and speech, though the former characteristic could equally be attributed to Cummy.

Stevenson's cosmopolitanism was real. Few writers, attuned to solitude and demanding routine, could have worked amid the continual upheavals to which his life was subjected; many would have found the culture shock of constant travel disastrous for their talent. Louis did not exactly thrive on change, but he sought it out as though as an antidote to some more profound malady. A lack of routine was his routine. He looked continually for fresh perspectives, feeding on novelty.

At this stage he was, in any case, a young man with an appetite for fun who had every incentive to leave home life behind. As usual the matter of sickness and travel was not a simple one. Stevenson's visit to France in the spring of 1875 was not made under duress—he could have gone elsewhere—but his poor health provided the occasion, just as his father provided the money. Given the choice in those days, Louis invariably chose France.

The Barbizon School had passed its zenith when he and Bob arrived at Fontainebleau. Corot, Théodore Rousseau, Millet, and Daubigny were no longer active. They had overcome neglect and won their battle to paint things in nature, as Millet said, "as if they had a necessary bond between themselves." But Rousseau was already dead and Millet was to die at Barbizon the year Louis first visited. The fields which had inspired the *Angelus* remained, but there were few notable artists left in the community. Nevertheless, the two Scots dressed the part, in peasant shirts and clogs, their exuberance sustained merely by the thought of "creative" life. Louis felt at home with artists, and toyed (ineptly) with a pencil throughout his life. But it was less the work going on around him (and that was fitful enough) that mattered than the society the workers provided. Louis had been profoundly lonely as a child: R.A.M. had liberated him. His friends at Fontainebleau finished the job.

Bob was already known to the multinational group at the Hotel Siron, and Louis was first welcomed more as the companion of a popular figure than as a personality in his own right. Nevertheless, he soon made an impact. He impressed Will Low, an American he had first met in Paris, with the vigour of his wit and conversation. As Low put it in a book of memoirs published after R.L.S. was dead, with the benefit of that hindsight which seemed to touch so many who had known Louis:

> It was not a handsome face until he spoke, and then I can hardly imagine that any could deny the appeal of the vivacious eyes, the humour or pathos of the mobile mouth, with its lurking suggestion of the great god Pan at times, or fail to realise that here was one so evidently touched with genius that the higher beauty of the soul was his.

A higher beauty, perhaps, but low habits. A good deal of carousing went on, as befitted a community of artists whiling away the summer at the edge of the Fontainebleau forest, and wine must have added a glow to the conversation which mere words alone could not have provided. The Siron group placed Louis second to Bob in their esteem, as R.L.S. himself tended to do, granting the elder cousin more than his share of wit and charm. Many knew Bob from Paris, where he kept a hospitable studio on the boulevard Saint Michel. The other Stevenson was new to most of them. But Low also saw fascination and charm in Louis, and also detected—just as Colvin had—a feminine quality.

It is not easy to judge exactly what was meant by this. Victorian men were unselfconscious in their expressions of "love" for one another; they gave free rein to their emotions, even dramatised them, and Louis was not alone in bursting into tears when passion (or a version thereof) gripped him. Such melodrama shaped the erotic atmosphere at the Siron. But many recollections of Stevenson also suggest that the slight, intense figure had a greater emotional range than most. With children he was childlike; with artists artistic; with women compliant; with officialdom sage or subversive by turns. He could play the waif (a habit of coddled childhood, perhaps) or the tribal elder, as he did on Samoa. He could be gentle or capable of an awesome temper. He had, it seems, the ability to put most sorts of people at their ease. It was charm, and he used it with some deliberation, even premeditation, in person and in his work.

Writing of Fontainebleau eight years later, Louis said:

> This purely artistic society is excellent for the young artist. The lads are mostly fools; they hold the latest orthodoxy in all its crudeness; they are at

that stage of education, for the most part, where a man is too much occupied with style to be aware of the necessity for any matter; and this,
above all for the Englishman, is excellent. To work grossly at the trade, to
forget sentiment, to think of his material and nothing else, is, for a while
at least the king's highway of progress.

This was choice indeed, coming from someone who had never done
a day's nonliterary work in his life; who by the time he wrote his memoir
had only once, briefly, held a job, and that the less-than-exacting post as
Fleeming Jenkin's secretary in Paris. If his career had ever depended on
understanding how the mass of people must live, R.L.S. would never have
found his way into print. But that was precisely the use of the Siron—an
inn rather than a "hotel," charging five francs a day for food and
lodging—to the young writer attempting both to reconcile his ambitions
with his home life and to escape from home. In Edinburgh his ambitions
made no real sense: a writing career was less improbable than impossible.
But at Barbizon, in fresh spring and lazy high summer, everything about
Louis seemed more plausible. His character, his leanings, even his dress,
passed without comment. He was no longer isolated; rather he was welcomed into a community, however fragile. In his essay on Fontainebleau
he noted that "the time comes when a man should cease prelusory gym-
nastic, stand up, put a violence upon his will, and for better or worse, begin the business of creation." It was around this time that he began to
think seriously about fiction. It was then, too, that another piece of the
puzzle of his life fell into place.

"Theoretically," he wrote of the Hotel Siron, "the house was open to all
comers; practically it was a kind of club." In effect this meant that any visitor who did not pass muster among the self-assured young artists, who
did not "appreciate the 'fine shades' of Barbizon etiquette," was excluded
or expelled by a variety of anti-social means. This stricture was normally
taken to include women, at least women of the more respectable sort.
      Returning to the colony in July of 1876, however, Louis discovered
that its annexe, near the river Loing at Grez, had by some accident allowed the opposite sex to intrude. Louis already knew Grez-sur-Loing,
having visited it with Bob, Low, and Walter Simpson with the intention

of canoeing on the river. Now he was told that Bob had gone to investigate the new arrivals. If the ladies proved unappealing or unresponsive to the "fine shades," Bob was to employ the usual tactics. Unfortunately, R.A.M. Stevenson seemed to have been taken prisoner: rather than expelling the intruders, he was making himself comfortable among them. Louis set out to assess the situation for himself and arrived at the Chevillon pension just as dinner was being served. His eyes lighted on Fanny Vandegrift (later Van de Grift) Osbourne.

Frances Matilda Vandegrift had been born in Indianapolis, Indiana, in March of 1840, the eldest of seven children. Her father, Joseph, was a lumber merchant, real-estate agent, and farmer originally from Philadelphia; her mother, Esther Keen, was a small woman of Swedish descent, who may (legend has it) have been married previously. When she was two years old, the child was baptised into the Presbyterian Church, doused in the White River before thousands of spectators. Dark-eyed, olive-skinned, and always tiny, she was called Fanny from the beginning.

Like Louis, she had her childhood filled with prayers and, from her grandmother, lurid bedtime tales. She liked to tell spooky stories herself, and learned to read early. In her biography of her sister, Nellie Van de Grift Sanchez described a bright child, good with her hands, who cared little for school. Seeking the obligatory pale Victorian prettiness beneath Fanny's dark skin, her grandmother scrubbed at her face and tried to keep her out of the sun. Eventually she gave up; Fanny became a tomboy and, by her teens, something of a dark beauty. Now, in France, she was a decade older than the young Scotsman, already equipped with children and, as it might have been said, "a history."

In December of 1857 she had married a blond, charming, feckless Southerner, one Samuel Osbourne, secretary to the governor of Indiana and not yet twenty-one when their first child, Isobel, known as Belle, was born. Some of Osbourne's family thought the bride "cold and distant," and Nellie agreed, but explained her sister's manner as shyness. Fanny and Sam, married young and in haste, were too involved with their bubbling, adolescent passion to care.

At the outbreak of the Civil War, Sam enlisted with the armies of the North and ended up a captain. Starved of action, he gave it up after six months, and in the turbulent years following the war's end, headed for California, instructing Fanny to follow him. She had barely arrived (via Panama) when her husband set off again, this time for the silver mines of Nevada, and a mining camp named Austin.

Life there taught Fanny more of rough-and-ready reality than Louis would ever learn. One of only a handful of women in the district (at one memorable dance there were fifty eager males and only seven females), she became a useful and inventive cook, learned to roll and smoke her own cigarettes, and mastered pistol shooting. It was a wild life, surrounded as she was by young, wild men, of which her husband was one of the wildest. Invigorating and exciting though this frontier existence seemed, Sam made no money mining, and the family moved yet again, this time to Virginia City in Nevada, the lawless centre of a lawless region. It was a town of saloons, gambling halls, brothels, and gunplay: Louis could teach Fanny nothing about lost innocence. Neither, in her turn, could she teach Sam. Soon he was being unfaithful to her.

Luckless in his ventures, he set off on a gold-prospecting expedition into Indian Territory and failed to return or send word of his whereabouts. Perhaps relieved, Fanny took Isobel to San Francisco, where she heard that Sam's party had been massacred. He had, in fact, become separated from his companions and survived, but in the meantime Fanny regarded herself as a widow.

Clad in mourning, she found a job as a fitter in a dress shop (passing herself and her skin colour as French) and established a relationship with John Lloyd, a Welshman who had been friendly with the Osbournes at Austin and who was, with touching sincerity, infatuated with Fanny. No one knows how far the affair went. Lloyd was a bank clerk, poorly paid and with a clear sense of propriety; Fanny's position was sufficiently precarious to warrant caution. In 1868, in any case, Sam reappeared out of the burning desert blue. A son, Lloyd, was born, but Osbourne soon resumed his infidelities (while still inviting his Welsh rival to Sunday dinner) in his spare hours from his work as a court stenographer. Sam's mother believed Fanny's temper drove him to these dalliances, but this time the shamed wife responded by returning to her parents in Indiana. Nevertheless, by 1869 she was back with Osbourne, and a second son, the beautiful, golden-haired Hervey, was born.

That Fanny was a remarkable woman is beyond doubt: that she loved her wayward first husband seems clear from the great reluctance with which this impulsive woman approached the idea of divorce. If she was a self-dramatiser, as many have said, she had plenty of material to work with. If she was impressionable, overwrought, and sometimes even disturbed, the events of her busy life—"like a dazed rush on a railroad express"—often gave her cause. Free to go her own way, she could be selfish and petulant; tested, as she often was, she was brave and resolute. She had a greedy spirit and remains a hard figure to like, but she earned her place in Stevenson's affections.

The only thing symmetrical about her was in her features: her personality tended to the exaggeration of emotion and of her own importance, both larger than her tiny frame might have suggested. Nevertheless, she saw and endured tragedy. More, as a strong-willed individual she suffered the fate of all wives of famous men, and was consigned to Stevenson's shadow repeatedly, even as she tried to thrust herself into the limelight. In San Francisco she aspired to art, and later could never resist advising (or instructing) R.L.S. on his work.

In East Oakland, over the bay from San Francisco, while Louis was failing to come to terms with university life in Scotland, his future wife was turning her small, short hands to expert cooking, enthusiastic gardening, and developing a taste for pretty clothes, many of which she made herself. Her sister Cora had returned with her from Indiana and married one Sam Orr, a friend of Osbourne's and his partner in the venture that ended in the desert massacre. Around this time, too, Belle caught the eye of a young Californian artist, Joseph D. Strong, Jnr., who painted her portrait. Nothing came of the relationship at first, but Belle was allowed to withdraw from high school and enter design school. Less conventionally, her mother also enrolled.

Fanny was one of those for whom the life of the artist, its affectations, conceits, and freedoms, was as important as art itself. She could not help herself. The romance of bohemia—however either word was defined—appealed to her. *La vie de bohème* bolstered her self-esteem and allowed her independence from Sam, if only, "spiritually." Art would soon be the pretext for her most sincere attempt to be free of him before their divorce. Meanwhile, his ways went unmended; he made little effort to conceal his affairs, and Fanny began to create a separate life for herself. She became particularly close to Timothy Rearden, a bachelor lawyer with a literary bent who ran San Francisco's Mercantile Library and was a friend of John Lloyd. In 1874 he and Fanny began a correspondence which quickly became intimate.

Again, no one can say how far this affair went, or even if it was an affair in any physical sense, but once again the goose was showing herself willing to share the sauce reserved for the gander. Propriety may have inhibited her. Perhaps the prospect of Sam and a lover in the same town seemed too risky in those moralistic days when women's lives were circumscribed by convention and hypocrisy. Fanny continued to show Rearden affection but decided to put as much distance between herself and her husband as possible: she would go to Europe to study art.

In itself such an adventure would have been enough to give her a "reputation." Perhaps in an effort to quell talk, therefore, Fanny elected to take her children with her, and a female friend from San Francisco to act as governess. Equally it may have been that she was already considering a permanent separation and wished to keep her children by her. Antwerp was her chosen destination. She was thirty-five but looked young enough to be mistaken for her daughter's sister.

Sam wrote to say how much he was missing them all—and certainly his daughter bore him no ill will—but the presumption must be that with Fanny out of the way he resumed his sexual escapades. Her presence had not prevented him; why, once he had dried his tears, should her absence? It was certainly alleged that he installed a lady friend in the family home as soon as the brood were gone.

Writing to Rearden, however, Fanny confessed that "I didn't know I should miss him [Sam] as I do." She had thought "it would be sort of weight off his mind to have us gone once more." Nevertheless, she requested her special friend cheer her husband "up a bit." If Rearden and Sam were on terms to make such a thing possible, her delicacy and display of sympathy for her spouse were probably a wise tactic: Sam was paying for the expedition, after all. Her true feelings were better reflected by the fact that she wept with relief and trepidation when she arrived in Antwerp and realised she had made good her escape.

The coquettishness of the letters to Rearden cast refracted light on one part of Fanny's character. Her husband's infidelities were blatant. Yet she could tease her male friend by affecting sympathy for the forlorn adulterer while also dangling her continuing relationship with John Lloyd before him: "You ask if I write to John. Of course I do. And receive the kindest and best letters in return . . ." She was a woman scorned but not subdued. Distance made the game safe, but she played it enthusiastically. With a husband like Sam she could hardly be blamed. If she made a mistake, it was to believe that in those days men and women played by the same rules.

Her first setback in Europe was the discovery that the Academy in Antwerp did not accept women. In the meantime Hervey became ill with fever. After three months of penny-pinching and dull living the family moved on to Paris, where Fanny found a studio whose criteria for accepting female students rested on cash rather than talent.

She must have seemed an odd and unlikely student, this forceful thirty-five-year-old American lady who turned up at life classes with her pretty seventeen-year-old daughter (one who had already attracted a marriage proposal during the Atlantic crossing), this matron who also had a pair of sons, aged seven and three, yet no husband anywhere in sight. She was an able-enough student, imitative rather than original, but the praise she had won in San Francisco impressed no one in the art capital of the world. Fanny was satisfied just to be there. Poor though the little family was, the life satisfied her ego and implied a final rejection of the existence Sam had given her. It also amounted to a statement that she was a person in her own right. She had been married while Louis was still learning to read; her life had been full of incident when his had been a round of doctors; yet everything she had been had revolved around the unpredictable behaviour of a handsome, charming, worthless man. Paris belonged to Fanny, and to her alone.

It did not last. Adversity came like a revenge. Hervey had never been a strong child. In the spring of 1876, when he was four, he fell seriously ill and was diagnosed as suffering from "scrofulous tuberculosis." It was a hideous illness and a horrible death. At the end he suffered convulsions, his bones stuck through his skin, which oozed blood, and his eardrums were perforated. The child begged for his father, and Sam arrived from America in time to see his son die. Hervey was buried at Père Lachaise in a temporary grave, where his bones would lie for only five years before being dumped in the catacombs. It was all the family could afford.

The nightmare exhausted Fanny, and the guilt—had her madcap flight to Europe somehow led to Hervey's death? Had she been cruel to separate the child from his father?—may have played a part in almost unhinging her. Sam prepared to return to America alone while she replayed the events of the child's death obsessively in her letters to friends. Grief brought no reconciliation with her husband.

She was deathly pale and almost stopped speaking. Her memory, too, became erratic. There were hallucinations and, suddenly, flecks of grey in her hair. It was all, of course, entirely forgivable, but a foretaste of things to come. With the governess gone, Fanny, Belle, and Lloyd planned to go to Grez, in the tranquil countryside, where she was to attempt recuperation on the recommendation of an American sculptor named Pardessus she had met in Paris.

She was not herself; it is as difficult now as it must have been then to say who she thought she really was, this bereaved and near-deranged American woman in a strange city, whose youth was slipping from her, who had only her artistic pretensions, little money, two children, and a marriage barely worth the name. Fanny Vandegrift had an instinct for survival, a tenacity astounding in man or woman, far less a woman in the middle of the Victorian age, but the world was testing her to the utmost. If she came to mistrust fate and the human race, the habit probably began when her golden child was taken from her.

Grez was beautiful, the living was cheap, and other Americans were there. Besides, where else could she go? The artists would not find her or her brood odd while she tried to mend her heart. Ignorant of Barbizon protocols, of course, Fanny could not have guessed that even the avant-garde would find her a puzzle. She thought herself respectable, and was indeed something of a snob, but respectable women, even aspiring artists, did not hang around artists' colonies. In one of his letters to Louis, Bob Stevenson had said of life at Fontainebleau that "everyone keeps a woman now" and that "Latin Quarter life" had intruded on the rural idyll. What they must have made of Fanny hardly requires to be said. Nevertheless, grief and fatigue notwithstanding, she somehow fitted in, and soon became the centre of attention. Bob Stevenson in particular found her charming.

Will Low had warned R.L.S. about the women. "It's the beginning of the end!" he reported a shaken Louis as saying. Nevertheless, at dusk on a July evening, he crossed the garden to the Hotel Chevillon and, according to Lloyd Osbourne, vaulted through the window and into the dining room. He was trying to make an entrance, obviously, but he was equally obviously trying to make an impression on the ladies. "The whole company rose in an uproar of delight, mobbing the newcomer with outstretched hands and cries of greeting," Osbourne recalled. When the commotion subsided, Bob introduced Louis, who accepted a cup of coffee and sat down next to Fanny.

The affair had no sudden beginning. Within days R.L.S. had started back for Scotland, and was not to return to Grez until September. From Edinburgh he indicated to Henley at around this time that some other woman at home was threatening to make their relationship public. Whether this was an old relationship risen from the grave or a recent one is not known.

For the moment, with Sam gone and the whirl of life at the colony going on around her, Fanny had little reason to think much about the thin, ruddy-faced young man with the long, lank hair and meagre reddish moustache. His cousin was by far the more interesting of the pair. Besides, she was still playing the coquette, still toying with the affections of the men who paid court to her.

In one letter to Rearden—who seems to have been losing patience— she remarked how Bob had written to say she should write to Louis. He was only a cad, but his cousin was "said to be dying." Louis had also written in identical terms: "They tell me dear Bob is not long for this world." The mad Stevensons, "so sweet," thrilled her. As for Rearden, as for San Francisco, as for America: "You needn't, as I have before remarked, call me 'My dear.' I don't think I am coming home in the spring. Fanny MO."

Louis had had a busy time of it: "A Defence of Idlers"("which is really a defence of R.L.S"); *Virginibus Puerisque*; and "Charles of Orleans" had been completed and despatched to the periodicals. He stayed with

the Jenkins near Loch Carron in the West Highlands and then travelled to
Antwerp to rendezvous with the diffident Walter Simpson. Thomas
Stevenson, if not happy with events, was still footing the bills for a son
whose health was proving no bar to adventure. In the meantime, Louis's
letters to Mrs. Sitwell were fewer and less intimate.

In their canoes, the *Arethusa* and the *Cigarette*, Stevenson and Simpson
had paddled on the Scheldt from Antwerp; thence to Brussels; thence
from the French frontier by the Oise, before returning to the Loing. This
escapade, such as it was, became Louis's first published book, *An Inland
Voyage*. As such, it was the least auspicious start a writer could have con-
trived. Similar accounts had been published previously, in the *Cornhill* and
elsewhere. What possessed R.L.S. to believe that his own jaunt would
yield a book worthy of his debut is a mystery.

The journey lacked incident and the book, unpublished until 1878,
suffers the same want. Louis admitted as much in a letter:

> *Compiègne*, 9th Sept, 1876. [canoe voyage]
> I must say it has sometimes required a stout heart; and sometimes one
> could not help sympathising inwardly with the French folk who hold up
> their hands in astonishment over our pleasure journey. Indeed I do not
> know that I would have stuck to it as I have done, if it had not been for
> professional purposes . . .

It was as though, having begun the project and endured the "holiday,"
Louis was determined to get something for his pains. The reward, for
himself and his readers, was slight. Only the work's "epilogue," describing
how, alone and on foot, he was arrested at Chatillon-sur-Loire on suspicion of vagrancy, provided much hilarity.

> THE COMMISSARY (*taking a pen*) *Enfin, il faut en finir.* What
> is your name?
> THE ARETHUSA (*speaking with the swallowing vivacity of
> the English*) Robert-Louis-Stev'ns'n.
> THE COMMISSARY (*aghast*) He! Quoi!
> THE ARETHUSA (*perceiving and improving his advantage*) Rob'rt-
> Lou's-Stev'ns'n

THE COMMISSARY (*after several conflicts with his pen*)
Eh bien, il faut se passer du nom. Ça ne se'écrit pas. (Well, we must do without the name: it is unspellable.)

The piece is extraneous to the book proper. The rest is dull landscape sketches and dull character studies, as uninspiring as much of the weather the intrepid pair encountered. Nevertheless, arriving back at Grez from this less-than-epic journey, Stevenson could well have been anticipating some of his own concluding words from *An Inland Voyage*:

Now we were to return, like the voyager in the play, and see what rearrangements fortune had perfected the while in our surroundings; what surprises stood ready made for us at home; and whither and how far the world had voyaged in our absence.

7 *1876–1878*

*If it did nothing else, this sublime and ridiculous superstition, that the plea-
sure of the pair is somehow blessed to others, and everybody is made happier
in their happiness, would serve at least to keep love generous and great-
hearted. Nor is it quite a baseless superstition after all.*

"On Falling in Love"

Not at first sight, nor even second, at least not on her part. The
oddly garbed "Mad Bob"—a photograph shows him in a broad-
brimmed hat, with hooped stockings and a kerchief knotted around his
neck—was the one who invaded her field of vision. Bob, the self-
described "vulgar cad" and painter, was the one who had first caught
Fanny's eye, the one with whom she one day got lost in the woods, the
one she thought "the most beautiful creature I ever saw." R.A.M.
Stevenson could be as charming as his cousin when he chose, which was
often, and was more handsome in a conventional sense. He was bright,
kind, witty, and attentive—"exactly like one of Ouida's heroes," Fanny
told Rearden, adding that Bob was the best painter at Grez. Even after
Louis's dramatic arrival, it was his cousin who interested her.

Vain enough at the best of times, she needed the attention after all she
had been through. The young men were drawn to her pretty daughter
but were attentive to the mother nonetheless. The atmosphere was a tonic
to her, but innocent enough, however it might have seemed.

Louis reacted differently from the rest. Though many found her unusual looks attractive, Fanny was not straightforwardly beautiful. Dark,
yes, and exotic-looking with vivid, piercing eyes. But her American can-

dour, her intrinsic strength, her unusual looks, and perhaps most of all, her experience of the world drew R.L.S. to her almost immediately, though he did not yet call the emotion love. Had she known his history better, Fanny, who concealed a need to be cared for behind her exterior competence and vitality, would have known that she was, to Louis, one of a well-established type.

He was, in many important ways, still a boy. Illness had shredded his education and almost killed him, but it had also prolonged his adolescence, excusing him from the pressures of maturity. His life at this period was a series of vacations and jaunts interspersed with sickness and a little light essay writing. He was twenty-five, yet still being kept by his father, and not for any want of chances to earn his keep. The combination of illness and an extreme distaste for anything other than writing or travel had scotched that possibility twice.

There was, too, something childish in his charm from time to time. Even Fanny, who thought him the wittiest man she had ever met, was astonished by his habit of bursting into tears at what seemed to her the slightest pretext, and at his hysterical laughter (which he affected to "cure" by bending his fingers back until the pain brought him, so he indicated, to his senses). Bob Stevenson had explained this behavior by reference to his cousin's ill health, but as Fanny wrote of Louis in a letter home: "I like him very much but there are times when it is a little embarrassing to be in his company; and sometimes, I imagine, not altogether safe."

It should be said in mitigation that Louis was not alone in eccentricity or improvidence. Bob, too, could be lachrymose. He, too, preferred to wait for working life to find him; he too was prone to nervous collapse. Fanny boasted to Rearden that R.A.M. Stevenson "spent a large fortune at the rate of eight thousand pounds a year, and now he has only a hundred pounds a year left . . ." Eight thousand or a hundred, none of it was earned. Of the tribe of fifty first cousins, Bob was Louis's soul mate.

In a letter Belle called Louis "a nice looking ugly man"; to Fanny he was a "tall, gaunt Scotsman, with a face like Raphael," charming and dissipated and overeducated. In any case, he was as vulnerable to emotion as she. The Sitwell storm had passed, but the conditions that had produced it remained. Some biographers have wondered, almost wistfully, why

Louis was not attracted to the vivacious Belle rather than her difficult mother. Years later Fanny, emotionally disturbed, would become jealous of an innocent working partnership between the two. For the moment, perhaps because every other man around was drawn to the daughter, he showed no interest. If Fanny intrigued him, it was, more than likely, simply because she *was* a mother—free (up to a point), pretty, exotic, and American to boot.

There is no point in underplaying this. Fanny once said that she actually wanted to be a clinging vine and looked after. But Louis, for all his vigour, his insistence on freedom, and his temper, responded in a deep and basic way to older women. It is the key to his sexuality, if there is one. Perhaps they made him feel more mature than he was. They had always fed him, nursed him, and responded to his waifish charm and boyish enthusiasms. They, in turn, were not averse to the attentions of a younger man, Fanny least of all. His tastes were formed, even if his character was not. Later, on his second trip to America, the widow of General George Custer asked him, as so many were to ask, why the women in his books were so few and so weak. After an argument, he promised a real heroine in *The Master of Ballantrae*, but the result was a disappointment. His depiction of women was moulded by his conception of them. He did not live long enough to feel the need to change it, and only at the very end of his life did the gulf in years between himself and Fanny seem marked.

Life at Grez was as deliciously complicated as life in an artists' colony should be. Belle was in love with a rich Irish painter, Frank O'Meara, but found herself the centre of Bob's attentions. Louis, meanwhile, was drawn to Fanny, yet she, for the moment, preferred R.A.M. Stevenson. Mother and daughter appeared to compete. All very bohemian.

Back in Paris, in October, Fanny took an apartment in Montmartre to which the Stevenson cousins were frequent, almost daily, visitors. Bob had been his cousin's best advocate in his relationship with her. By January of 1877, 5 rue Douay had become Louis's forwarding address; Fanny was convinced he had tuberculosis; and she had decided not to return to America.

In Edinburgh, in November, Stevenson reviewed his situation in an essay, "On Falling in Love," which was to appear in the *Cornhill* in February of 1877 and later in the *Virginibus Puerisque* volume of 1881. Dealing with the only "event in life which really astonishes a man and startles him out of his prepared opinions," Louis was not autobiographical in the modern sense, but his analysis was penetrating. Suddenly, at least in prose, there was maturity:

> ... the ideal story is that of two people who go into love step for step, with a fluttered consciousness, like a pair of children venturing together into a dark room. From the first moment when they see each other, with a pang of curiosity, through stage after stage of growing pleasure and embarrassment, they can read the expression of their own trouble in each other's eyes. There is here no declaration properly so called; the feeling is so plainly shared, that as soon as the man knows what it is in his own heart, he is sure of what is in the woman's.

That "pang of curiosity" makes the passage, but if Louis was not writing out of experience, he was certainly preparing himself for it. Unless the essay had been on his mind for some time, it can only have been prompted by his relationship with Fanny. This was a man "practically incommoded by the generosity of his feelings" but aware that love is fleeting, scarcely eternal. No sooner has Cupid loosed his shafts than "the game dissolves and disappears into eternity from under his falling arrows; this one is gone ere he is struck; the other has but time to make one gesture and make one passionate cry . . . and they are all the things of a moment." But for Louis the game had just begun.

The pattern of 1876 was repeated the following year. Fanny spent the summer at Grez and Louis was there until July. At whatever point their physical relationship had begun, it was probably established by then. Stevenson later attested that he had fallen in love at first sight; if so, it was not reciprocated. But both he and Fanny were passionate people, neither had been involved sexually for some time (or at least no one has shown that they were), and they did not want for opportunity. The vehemence of her children's later denials seems ample proof that Fanny and R.L.S. had sex at Grez; Lloyd and Belle suppressed accounts of far more innocuous matters. Louis had been building up to an affair with *someone* for several years. Fanny's precarious social position was the only real inhibition. It was not an insuperable barrier, not for this pair.

For her part Belle Strong, infected with her mother's instinct for mythmakeing where Louis was involved, always insisted that the pair were not then lovers. But Belle herself, with her huge eyes and her neat figure, was at the centre of a tangle of relationships, involved with Frank O'Meara and adored by Bob Stevenson. After R.L.S. was gone, all of this was easy to forget. In any event, Louis and Fanny spent most of their time together until he returned to Scotland in midsummer. By September he was back in France, and his mail was once again being forwarded to Fanny's latest apartment.

She liked to think of herself as respectable, and insisted on proper behaviour throughout her life. Yet here she was, a married woman living in Paris with a young lover. It is not clear how Fanny reconciled her public stance with her private behaviour.

Her adultery could have proved a real obstacle to a divorce from Sam Osbourne, for example, and was scarcely acceptable outside Montmartre, but she went ahead anyway, with a man not so very much older than her daughter. Her age, and the thought of a "last chance," may have affected her, outweighing the risk of disgrace. Lonely and recently bereaved, she must have been flattered by Louis's passion. Equally, an affair was an opportunity for revenge for Sam's infidelities, an assertion of her independence and a confirmation that other men found her desirable. In one of her letters it is plain she had also got hold of the idea that the Stevensons were immensely wealthy. With two children to look after and no confidence in Sam's continuing support, that may well have been a factor. But most important of all was that she loved this skinny Scotsman who found American women so unusual and refreshing. Whatever else can be said of Fanny Matilda Vandegrift, that remains beyond question.

One can read too much into the psychology of illness and the psychology of Stevenson, ill or otherwise. Sometimes, even when the illness was all too real, the timing of its onset suited him admirably, as it had done prior to his escape to Menton. Thus it was that in the early winter of 1877 he contracted a severe eye infection and Fanny took him in. It set a pattern for their life together.

Unfortunately, her nursing was to no avail. Increasingly desperate, she telegraphed Bob to come and take his cousin home. But R.A.M. was himself ill in Edinburgh. When there was no response—and Fanny was at this

time in need of treatment herself, for an injured foot—she contacted
Colvin, bundled Louis up, and took him to London,

Fanny lodged with Mrs. Sitwell, in whom any feeling of rivalry was
long extinguished. She met Henley and Leslie Stephen and began to feel
her way into the London part of Louis's life. It went well: Colvin and Mrs.
Sitwell thought her charming. Fanny, perhaps insufficiently confident of
her relationship with Louis, treated his friends as hers, teaching them how
to roll cigarettes in their nonsmoking household. She was more barbed, or
more honest, when describing life in Bayswater in a letter to America:

> I was with very curious people in London, the leaders of the Purists, I was
> so out of place in their house that a corner was arranged, or disarranged,
> for me. They dishevelled my curls, tied up my head in a yellow silk hand-
> kerchief, wrapped me in yellow shawls and spread a tiger skin rug over my
> sofa, and another by me . . . It seemed most incongruous to have the sol-
> emn Mr Colvin, a professor at Cambridge, and the stately, beautiful Mrs
> Sitwell sit by me and talk in the most correct English about the progress
> of literature and the arts. I was rather afraid of them but they didn't seem
> to mind but occasionally came down to my level and petted me as one
> would stroke a kitten.

Fanny was never sure of these London people. Some she came to dislike intensely; others were supportable. Colvin thought her "vivid . . .
eager, devoted." Her eyes, he said years later, were "full of sex and mystery as they change from fire or fun to gloom or tenderness." Colvin and
Mrs. Sitwell were kind to her, but did Fanny no favours by allowing William Ernest Henley, the lame literary lion, into their household while she
was there.

The first meeting went well enough; later they were to become bitter
enemies. Henley—loud, bearded, gesticulating with his crutches—was
proprietorial of R.L.S. Fanny was becoming no less so. The clash was all
but inevitable—though Mrs. Sitwell's salon was neither the time nor the
place. Fanny was still finding her feet; she had not yet come to identify
Louis's London friends with assaults on his life.

Others of his friends objected to the metropolis, however, for other
reasons. Early in 1877 Louis had become involved with what Fleeming
Jenkin dismissed as "society journalism" and a magazine called *London*,

edited by Henley. It was an enterprise of little merit, organised with little competence. The editor was forever short of copy and forever calling on his friend R.L.S. to provide it while turning out yards of his own execrable verse to fill the many holes in its pages. As Louis admitted to Baxter in 1878: "I do write such damn rubbish in it . . ."

The periodical lasted barely two years and folded after its 114th issue. It was, like all of Stevenson's projects with Henley, largely a waste of his valuable time and energy. Nevertheless, it was for *London* that Louis produced his first convincing fiction. The insubstantial "Will o' the Mill" appeared in the *Cornhill* at the beginning of 1878, but it was *London* which accepted gratefully "The Suicide Club" and "The Rajah's Diamonds," both later to become part of *New Arabian Nights*.

The germ of the idea for "The Suicide Club" was Bob's. It appeared in the magazine as part of a series of linked tales entitled "Latter-Day Arabian Nights" (the title was changed for book publication in 1882) designed to imitate the *Thousand and One Nights*. This "blood-curdling humour," as one critic called it, was part satirical parody, part space-filler (Lloyd Osbourne recalled that Louis did not think much of the stories), and part technical exercise. There is one constant figure in the tales, Prince Florizel of Bohemia, whose antidote to the tedium of society life is to gain admission to various "strange societies." Hence the Suicide Club, that group of young gentlemen meeting to drink champagne and play cards as a way of deciding which of their number will give the ultimate answer to ennui.

It is odd to contrast the hysterical, lachrymose bohemian Louis sometimes affected to be at this time with the author who was poking merciless fun at the fey aesthetes and pessimists of the Suicide Club. Given his habits, his dress, and his attitude, he should have been the last person to be so tough-minded. But perhaps—for the tale often has a tone of scorn he usually reserved for himself—the satire was self-directed. Here, as later, he was offering a very Stevensonian response to the intellectual currents of his day. On the one hand there was mechanistic science, enemy of instinct, imagination, and happenstance. On the other hand there was the posturing of Swinburne, Wilde, and the rest. Significantly, Louis located himself outside this contest, artistically and, later, physically. Both positions were, somehow, beside the point. Or as the Prince concludes of the club's members:

'It does not seem to me', he thought, 'a matter for so much disturbance. If a man has made up his mind to kill himself, let him do it, in God's name, like a gentleman. This flutter and big talk is out of place.'

It was a small declaration of independence by the young author. Aesthetes bemoaning the cruelty of life were unlikely to impress one for whom life was a hard-won prize in a battle often repeated, for all his bohemianism. Parts of the tale, particularly in the second section, are sheerest melodrama—probably because of the speed of its production— and some of the satire is forced. But the thing was done, and tolerably well done. The "sedulous ape" had demonstrated that he had tricks of his own, or at least that he was practising a few. It was not noticed at the time, but Louis was already on his way to becoming the sort of writer his peers, and posterity, would find hard to place.

Fanny was involved in all this, presumably with Stevenson's encouragement. By her own account she chose writers for the magazine, accepted and rejected manuscripts, and offered criticisms whether or not they were sought. She also helped plan the *Arabian Nights*. Her relationship with Henley was reasonable, though she became irritated when he had taken too much whisky, which was often. Nonetheless, she seemed to enjoy her role as a woman of letters, and never doubted her fitness for it.

She and Louis spent their first Christmas apart, he with his parents in Edinburgh, she looking after Bob in Paris. The illness that had prevented R.A.M. from answering Fanny's appeal when Louis had been close to blindness with his eye infection seems to have been a nervous breakdown of sorts. Fanny, ever the nurse, helped to pull him through.

By January, Louis's affair was common knowledge among his friends. Soon afterwards he was writing to Henley describing himself as a "miserable widower" and saying how he hated "to go to bed where there is no dear head on the pillow . . ." Considering that he and Fanny had spent Christmas and New Year apart, sex must have begun sometime before. They, she in particular, would now live with the consequences.

By 1878 Stevenson's advance on his patrimony, the famous thousand pounds, was almost gone. That fact, and his own desire to make his relationship with Fanny an honest one, compelled Louis to share his secret with his parents. Their reaction hardly needs to be described: would their son never cease to shock? A lover, in Paris? An American woman—with children—seeking a divorce? Louis employed Colvin and Mrs. Sitwell to reassure Thomas. He himself tried to be vague. "We wish to be right with the world as far as we can," R.L.S. told Colvin in a letter, " 'tis a big venture . . ." It was, in every sense. But he showed just how ill fitted he was for it, and how much he was still prepared to depend on his father, by adding: "Three days from hence, I shall know where I am, and either be well off or quite a beggar." In February of 1878 Thomas came to Paris, at his son's request, to investigate the situation.

It seems to have gone well, or at least not as disastrously as Louis might have been inclined to expect. He was twenty-seven, still supported by his father and probably, in his turn, helping to support Fanny. Yet Thomas made less fuss than he could have. Perhaps he had now concluded that he would never be able to control his offspring. Perhaps he hoped that time, Fanny's marital position, and her intention to return to America would all cause the relationship to wither. In mitigation, however, it can be said that Thomas held advanced views on a woman's right to divorce. Nevertheless, there is no evidence that he met Fanny at this time. Louis left her to spend Easter at Heriot Row.

When he returned, "her nerves," R.L.S. informed Mrs. Sitwell, were "quite gone." She felt obliged to recross the Atlantic, she had little or no money, and Louis could no longer keep her. Their position was, for the moment, impossible. He was trying to raise cash from Baxter and Henley (evidence, perhaps, that Thomas's attitude to his son's love affair was not entirely benign), and by June of 1878 he had taken the position of secretary to Fleeming Jenkin, who was acting as a judge at the Exposition in Paris. Stevenson joined Fanny and her family at Grez whenever he could. Afterwards, the couple went to London. Sam's pittance had now dried up completely. In August, Fanny returned to California.

Louis accompanied the family to the boat train. As it pulled out, he walked away and did not look back. He already regarded himself as married to Fanny, and what must have come as a relief to his parents was a tragedy to him. His love was six thousand miles away. Though he did now know it, theirs would be a long separation. Other men would have reacted differently, absorbed the loss in another fashion. Louis went walking.

8 *1878–1879*

For my part, I travel not to go anywhere, but to go. I travel for travel's sake. The great affair is to move; to feel the needs and hitches of our life more nearly; to come down off this feather-bed of civilisation, and find the globe granite underfoot and strewn with cutting flints.

TRAVELS WITH A DONKEY IN THE CÉVENNES

Y ou can follow Stevenson's trail across the Cévennes without much difficulty; it is worth the effort. The hike and the book it produced amounted to a brief episode in his life, but one more illuminating of his character and his craft than most biographers allow. *Travels with a Donkey* is one of those works of R.L.S. easy to discount—"The book has that quality of ingratiating charm which Louis himself could switch on in person whenever he chose . . ."*—if you prefer not to examine why it has always been one of his most popular. Something emerges from the "travel writing" of the little volume which readers have always detected more easily than critics.

Granted, *Travels with a Donkey* has charm of a high, well-honed order and is full of that "sense of place" which is always acknowledged but never adequately explained. Yet the artful journal was written at a time when Louis had little cause to be either charming or optimistic. He stood at a crossroads, "a miserable widower," as he told Henley, and after this adventure everything in his life changed. As always, the circumstances in which he found himself, or placed himself, were crucial to his work. Sim-

*Hennessey, J. P.: *Robert Louis Stevenson* (London, 1974); p. 30.

ilarly, the adventure itself was more than a jaunt. Stevenson knew nothing about the high Cévennes: few people did, and he was no athlete, for all his nervous energy. To wonder how the place and the journey acted on the man and his art at this moment in his life is to begin to understand him a little more.

Within a month of Fanny's departure he was in le Monastier in the Cévenol hills. His first book, *An Inland Voyage*, had appeared earlier in the year, in an edition of 750 copies. It had not done well. Louis himself found it hard to praise, despite some decent reviews. "I read *Inland Voyage* the other day," he told his mother in a letter, "what rubbish these reviewers did talk! It is not badly written, thin, mildly cheery, and strained. *Selon moi.*" He still found fiction difficult, and prior to his departure for the Cévennes had fallen back into the habit of essay writing. He had earned twenty pounds for "Will o' the Mill" and forty-four pounds from the *London* magazine for the "Arabian Nights" tales. The first attempt to have the latter produced in book form had failed because of, according to Edmund Gosse, "their preposterous character."

Otherwise he had been submitting the pieces that were to reappear in *Virginibus Puerisque* three years later—"Aes Triplex" and "Child's Play" to the *Cornhill*, "A Plea for Gas Lamps," "Pan's Pipes," and "El Dorado" to *London*. Since Henley paid him only a little more than thirty shillings for these efforts, compared to the six guineas he got from *Cornhill*, one can only assume that Louis remained loyal in penury. During the summer Leslie Stephen had been urging him to attempt a novel and had held out the possibility of serialisation in *Cornhill*. His domestic affairs being what they were, Louis probably did not have the leisure for such a project, and no manuscript survives. Instead, he was writing the pieces which were to become his second book, *Edinburgh: Picturesque Notes*, and borrowing money from Charles Baxter.

The Cévennes project was, therefore, an attempt to make some cash from writing. But it was also a personal journey, a search for respite and escape. Stevenson travelled light, yet with many burdens, and alone.

Lord Guthrie tells us that in 1878 Louis took one advantage (probably the only real one) of the three hundred and fifty pounds his father had stumped up to allow him to become an advocate. In those days the Advocates' Library was one of only two copyright libraries in Britain which made its books available for borrowing (Cambridge University Library was the other). Bar fees went, in part, to support the institution, but in return there was accorded "the valuable privilege of borrowing 20 books at a time." R.L.S. needed no prompting. "The lists show," Guthrie writes, "that Stevenson borrowed in 1878 a large number of books relating to the Cévennes . . ."

Francophilia aside, it is hard to say precisely where the impulse came from, but a need to escape, to clear his head and settle his heart, was obviously one motive. Still, it was an odd choice of destination. The Cévennes region was wild, remote, and thinly populated, well off the usual tourist routes. Louis always responded to topography, but in this case he was responding to a region of which he, like most people, knew little. Other than as a place found with a pin stuck in a map, only the area's tortured history of religious struggle can explain why he chose to go there. From Monastier in September his letters went out, rehearsing the opening episode of the book that was to come. To his mother:

> You must not expect to hear from me for the next two weeks; for I am near starting. Donkey purchased—a love—price, 65 francs and a glass of brandy. My route is all pretty well laid out; I shall go near no town till I get to Alais. Remember, Poste Restante, Alais, Gard.

To Henley, suggesting, at least, that his appetite was unusually healthy:

> I hope to leave Monastier this day (Saturday) week; thenceforward Poste Restante, Alais, Gard, is my address. *Travels with a Donkey in the French Highlands.* I am no good to-day. I cannot work, nor even write letters. A colossal breakfast yesterday at Puy has, I think, done for me for ever; I certainly ate more than ever I ate before in my life—a big slice of melon, some ham and jelly, a *filet*, a helping of gudgeons [carplike fish], the breast and leg of a partridge, some green peas, eight crayfish, some Mont d'or cheese, a peach, and a handful of biscuits, macaroons, and things. It sounds Gargantuan; it cost three francs a head.

To Charles Baxter, before Louis got to know his wilful little donkey better:

> I go to Le Puy tomorrow to dispatch baggage, get cash, stand lunch to engineer, who has been very jolly and useful to me, and hope by five o'clock

on Saturday morning to be driving Modestine towards the Gévaudan. Modestine is my anesse; a darling, mouse-colour, about the size of a New-foundland dog (bigger, between you and me), the colour of a mouse, cost-ing 65 francs and a glass of brandy. Glad you sent on all the coin; was half afraid I might come to a stick in the mountains, donkey and all, which would have been the devil . . . Next address, Poste Restante, Alais, Gard. Give my servilities to the family. Health bad; spirits, I think, looking up.—
Ever yours,

R.L.S.

Along with his homemade sleeping bag, he took two changes of clothes; a "Scottish railway plaid"; a spirit lamp and cooking pan; a lan-tern and candles; a twenty-franc jackknife; a leather water flask, a blue-lined, eighty-page schoolboy's exercise book; blocks of chocolate; tins of bologna sausage; and, on his departure, a leg of mutton and a bottle of Beaujolais. He also packed an egg whisk for his morning egg-and-brandy nog and had a revolver, tobacco, and cigarette papers about his person.The only other items in his inventory were a few books, notably the French edition of Napoléon Peyrat's *Histoire des Pasteurs de Désert*.

Today the route itself has become part of the local tourist industry—a business R.L.S. would have deplored—and devotees hike, cycle, or pull the occasional picturesque reluctant donkey up the steep paths and across the high moorlands. The less energetic cheat, for it is possible to follow most of Stevenson's winding journey by car, even across the heights of Mont Lozère.

There are occasional signs on the way that the author's name is being exploited, albeit gently, but in le Monastier—his starting point in the Haute-Loire near le Puy, the "mere mountain *Poland*" where he pur-chased his troublesome companion—there is only a small monument and a rather dusty display of mementoes. The little town is quieter now than it was when Stevenson set off in September of 1878 after spending a month alone polishing *Edinburgh: Picturesque Notes*. Then it was the "chief place of a hilly canton"; today rural depopulation, the blight of the back country for a century and a half (not unlike that which afflicted the Scottish Highlands), continues to drain the life from what is now, in large part, a national park. On a hot summer's morning in le Monastier the view from the little café offers little more than a stray dog, a couple of old men in blue overalls deciding it is not too early for *pastis*, and a housewife bearing home her bread. Visitors are expected but not overwhelmed.

In an introductory passage dropped from the published edition of *Travels*, Louis explained something of the attraction of the region and its people:

> On the whole, this is a Scottish landscape, although not so noble as the best in Scotland; and by an odd coincidence, the population is, in its way, as Scottish as the country. They have abrupt, uncouth, Fifeshire manners, and accost you as if you were trespassing, with an 'Ou ést-ce que vous allez?' only translateable into the Lowland 'Whau'r ye gaun?' They keep the Scottish Sabbath . . . Again, this people is eager to proselytise; and the post-master's daughter used to argue with me by the half-hour about my heresy, until she grew quite flushed. I have heard the reverse process going on between a Scots woman and a French girl; and the arguments in the two cases were identical . . . Here, as in Scotland, many peasant families boast a son in holy orders. And here, also, the young men have a tendency to emigrate.

In the autumn of 1878 Stevenson was not yet twenty-eight. Marriage was intensely desired but, it seemed, impossible; Fanny was halfway across the world, in Monterey, awaiting her divorce, and he feared they would be parted forever. Or as Graham Balfour put it in his inimitable, Fanny-fearful style: "So there came the pain of parting without prospect of return, and he who was afterwards so long an exile from his friends, now suffered separation from his dearest by the breadth of a continent and an ocean."

Certainly he was depressed and uncertain: a small measure of renown as an essayist and a few short stories were not enough, nowhere near enough, to support him. His personal life was in chaos, a fact which affected the book he was to base on his recuperative hike. "It has good passages," R.L.S. wrote to Bob in April of 1879 as the volume was making its way through the presses:

> I can say no more. A chapter called The Monks, another A Camp in the Dark, a third A Night among the Pines. Each of these has, I think, some stuff in it in the way of writing. But lots of it is mere protestations to F., most of which I think you will understand. That is to me the main thread

of interest. Whether the damned public—But that's all one; I've got thirty quid for it, and should have had fifty.

It was Stevenson at his most practical and honest: some good stuff worth fifty quid. But the odd thing is that *Travels* is almost entirely free of anything resembling "protestations" to Fanny. In its original form, finally published in 1978 as *Cévennes Journal: Notes on a Journey Through the French Highlands* (and in France as *Journal de Route en Cévennes*) there are equally few signs of a soul in turmoil. How this came to be Stevenson's "main thread of interest" is not at first clear.

Fanny had gone first to Indiana, where her father had just died. Moving on to California, she took along her sister Nellie, later her adoring biographer. At East Oakland she found Sam making a comfortable living as a stenographer. The children were pleased to see him. Fanny, whose affection was exhausted, was not. Belle remembered "a perceptible chill between him and my mother." The freeze was to last for a year.

Yet the spring brought the hint, no more, of a thaw. Sam and Fanny appear to have made a last attempt of reconciliation. They went off alone to Monterey for a week before sending for the family. If Fanny had been a fool for Samuel Osbourne as a teenager, she learned no better as a grown woman. He installed the family in the tasteful wing of a Spanish house and immediately returned to San Francisco, ostensibly to work but in reality to resume a liaison with his latest ladylove. Lloyd remembered the house, if not the affair:

> Our home was a small, two-storied rose-embowered *adobe* cottage fronting on Alvarado Street; my mother rented it from two old Spanish ladies named Bonafacio, who lived in an upper part of it in a seclusion comparable to that of the Man in the Iron Mask. The only time they ever betrayed their existence was when the elder would scream at me in Spanish from an upper window to leave the calf alone. Our backyard pastured this promising young animal . . .

Sam bought them all horses to ride but his visits grew steadily fewer. By Lloyd's later account his mother must have confessed to her European adventure:

Once as I was studying my lessons in an adjoining room and felt that strangely disturbing quality in their subdued voices—reproaches on her side and a most affecting explanation on his side of his financial straits at the time of my little brother's death—I suddenly overheard my mother say, with an intensity that went through me like a knife, 'Oh, Sam, forgive me!'

It is just as possible, of course, that she was asking forgiveness for doubting his grief over Hervey as it is that she was confessing to indiscretions. Equally, the move to Monterey may have been part of an arrangement to which they had come. Sam did not want a divorce; Fanny did not want his affairs flaunted in her face. She was in no position to bargain, and Osbourne probably knew it. Cost aside, the arrangement suited him. He had failed to subsidise her in Europe, but now he was, for the time being at least, providing a home (conveniently distant) and taking care of the family's needs.

During that summer in the old Spanish capital, meanwhile, Belle fell in again with Joe Strong, the promising young painter who had made her portrait years before. Nellie, too, found herself in love with the handsome Adolfo Sanchez, scion of an old Spanish family but now saloon keeping in Monterey. Soon afterwards they announced their engagement. Belle and Joe hoped to follow suit but knew, by Belle's subsequent account, that an impoverished painter could not expect her mother's approval. The extraordinary Fanny, who had defied convention by living in sin in an artists' colony in France, had become Madame Propriety. The young couple eloped, with Sam's infuriating assistance.

All of this lay ahead when the heartbroken Louis set off. Yet *Travels*, and the trip which inspired it, seem an odd response to his tragedy. If anything the book, like the journey, was a therapeutic exercise. R.L.S. was positively jaunty when he wrote to Baxter on 17 September regarding the trip: "I shall soon go off on a voyage for which I think I shall buy a donkey, and out of which, if I do not make a book, may my right hand forget its cunning." Whatever misery he carried with him, and whatever loneliness he encoded in the text, the trip did him good. To Baxter, again, he later wrote: ". . . for the first time in a year I feel something like peace."

Only once does he slip, remarking that he was conscious of a "strange lack" while he slept alone beneath the stars: "For there is a fellowship more quiet even than solitude and which, rightly understood, is solitude made perfect. And to live out of doors with a woman a man loves is of all lives the most complete and free." Otherwise he made do with Modestine, the difficult donkey.

From le Monastier to St.-Jean-du-Gard was a circuitous ten-day trip for Stevenson, no small achievement considering the terrain and its antagonist. It was his first such journey alone. He had planned that Sir Walter Simpson should accompany him, but Sir Walter was a plodder who had been unable to keep pace with his friend on a previous hike. And as Richard Holmes has written,* Stevenson was in part involved in "a bet undertaken against himself, that he could survive on his own. His ill-health, his struggle against consumption, together with the real wildness of the Cévennes a hundred years ago made this trial a genuine enough affair."

In a brilliant essay Holmes also calls the journey "a pilgrimage"; later "an initiation," setting it against Stevenson's rift with his parents over religion and the decisions he faced over Fanny. All this seems a large burden to place on a little book which does not wear its charm lightly. Yet it has never been a mystery. In the dedication to Sidney Colvin, R.L.S. wrote: "Every book is, in an intimate sense, a circular letter to the friends of him who writes it. They alone take his meaning; they find private messages, assurances of love, and expressions of gratitude, dropped at every corner."

Louis made it explicit—"private messages"—that his bagatelle of a book contained secrets, and not for Fanny alone. Certainly the debate on religion, his defence of Protestantism amid the hospitality of a Catholic monastery, must have given satisfaction to his father after their explosive confrontations over religion. Equally Louis's praise for solitude seems odd coming from a man contemplating marriage, particularly when set beside the somewhat embarrassed description of the married couple with whom he was obliged to share a room at an inn—hence, perhaps, his single "protestation" to Fanny when he glories in the idea of *solitude à deux*.

The incidents of the book are emblematic, though none (we suppose)

*Holmes, R.: *Footsteps—Adventures of a Romantic Biographer* (London, 1985); pp.11–69.

are invented. Stevenson's childhood reading of Bunyan, and the solitary Sabbath games in which he played Christian, complete with little knapsack, echo occasionally in the pages of *Travels* as the confused young man sets out, like some Victorian hippy, to "find himself." The soul is allowed its valleys of the shadow and its bright mornings.

He was not so artless, though, that he would inflict any of this explicity on the "damned public," the "generous patron who defrays the postage . . ." "Hard upon October" he made first for the village of Goulet, detoured westward to le Bouchet, there to encounter the young couple. ("I kept my eyes to myself, and knew nothing of the woman except that she had beautiful arms.") He then turned south, through ancient Gévaudan, notorious a century before for a monstrous wolf which had terrorised the countryside.

Crossing the Allier by an old stone bridge (now destroyed) he came up through the pines to the Trappist monastery of Nôtre-Dame-des-Neiges, Our Lady of the Snows, where Lou's Protestant heritage asserted itself, however humorously, in the face of attempts at conversion. In the book he describes the monks as "full of holy cheerfulness," but in a poem recalling the visit, published in *Underwoods*, he calls them the "unsought volunteers of death." In matters of religion, consistency was not his god. He affected to find the prospect of the monastery terrifying but in fact there is more comedy in his description of it than in the rest of the book.

There are fewer monks today, but they do a good trade in wine and souvenirs. The hostel for contemplative visitors still operates, but the buildings in which R.L.S. slept were destroyed by fire in 1912. High above the world, the monastery and its inhabitants remain serene among the tourists.

The hiker moved on to l'Estampe, its streets thronged with sheep, before heading for Mont Lozère, the highest point in the Cévenol countryside. There he meant to make the main point of his expedition by testing his camping equipment and sleeping beneath the stars. It made for a famous passage;

> Night is a dead monotonous period under a roof; but in the open world it passes lightly, with its stars and dews and perfumes, and the hours are marked by changes in the face of Nature. What seems a kind of temporal

death to people choked between walls and curtains, is only a light and living slumber to the man who sleeps a-field. All night long he can hear Nature breathing deeply and freely; even as she takes her rest, she turns and
smiles; and there is one stirring hour unknown to those who dwell in
houses, when a wakeful influence goes abroad over the sleeping hemi-
sphere, and all the outdoor world are on their feet.

Mere charm, of course, but Louis was also placing himself in a singular
relationship to society even as he played the careless vagabond. He woke
while others slept, rested where they did not: he left people behind. Even
here, in a minor work, Stevenson is placing his hero (himself) outside of
the normal world. Personally, it was a small, temporary, and experimental
exile.

He climbed to the 1,700-metre summit of Lozère, the Pic de Finiels,
before descending to le Pont-de-Montvert in the valley of the Tarn. This
was, and remains, Protestant country, and if his book truly contained messages for those he loved, his passages on the "country of the Camisards"
were meant for his father. The Camisards were kin to his beloved Covenanters, though the lengthy account of them in *Travels* was added later,
from information gleaned in the Advocates' Library, to pad out his book
to publishable length. Nevertheless, it was another emblematic incident:
after the religious upheavals of home R.L.S. was defining himself as a
Protestant, for better or worse. His father would have heard that message.

Louis moved on to the valley of the Mimente, then as now one of the
most beautiful in the area, and to Cassagnas, "a cluster of black roofs."
Richard Holmes has found significance in the fact that the latter sections
of the book are "drained of colour." Others have found the area "un-
French." Perhaps, but in truth the regional architecture merely utilises the
dark native stone of the country. Florac, which Stevenson had already
passed through (noting with satisfaction that "Protestant and Catholic in-
termingled in a very easy manner" even if memories of religious wars remained "lively") is also a dark town.When the surrounding heights bring
forth one of their symphonic thunderstorms the sun can seem eclipsed,
and day seem like night.

Returning to the mountains for the last time, Stevenson exerted his
descriptive gift. "Peak upon peak, chain upon chain of hills ran surging

southward, channelled and sculptured by the winter streams, feathered from head to foot with chestnuts, and here and there breaking out into a coronal of cliffs." The chestnuts, once the staple food of the region and used in everything from flour to soup, are fewer now, neglected by the diminishing population and changing habits, their cultivation reserved for the delicious *marron glacé* and tinned purees. But the mountains remain as he described them, like a giant frozen wave waiting to tumble south, the mists burning from their summits on summer mornings. Whatever else he was, R.L.S., who scorned "realism" in fiction, was an able reporter. And, knowing of his "messages," it is hard to avoid detecting them:

> . . . it was a very solitary march all afternoon; and the evening began early underneath the trees. But I heard the voice of a woman singing some sad, old, endless ballad not far off. It seemed to be about love and a *bel amoureux*, her handsome sweetheart, and I wished I could have taken up the strain and answered her . . .

The last sections of the book seem rushed, as though the point of the journey had been achieved. In the upland village of St.-Germain-de-Calberte phylloxera, he noted, "was in the neighbourhood; and instead of wine we drank at dinner a more economical juice of the grape . . ." The last details are sketched, with a cursory effort at valediction. At last he arrived on the plain at St.-Jean-du-Gard. He sold the donkey for thirty francs fewer than he paid, with a tribute to her patience.

Writing to his son after the volume was published, Thomas Stevenson revealed, by his pomposity, much about the nature of their relationship. The book, he said, was "a very bright one," with a "stronger core of facts" than *An Inland Voyage*. Nevertheless,

> the book has the same faults as the *Inland Voyage* for there are some three or four irreverent uses of the name of God which offend me and must offend many others. They might have been omitted without the slightest damage to the interest or merit of the book. So much for your absurdity in not letting me see your proof sheets. The only other fault in the book is, I think, a superfluity in the way of description of scenery.

So much for "secret messages"; so much for fine writing. With readers like his father, it was not so hard to be a shocking bohemian.

Having returned via Alès, Lyons, Autun, and Paris, he was back in London by early November. He spent a few days in Colvin's rooms but told Henley in a letter: "I can only write ditch-water." He was attempting a short story, "Providence and the Guitar," inspired by some strolling players encountered at Grez, which was to appear in four instalments in *London* and to turn up later in *New Arabian Nights*. In the meantime he plugged away at his travel journal, filling it out with historical details of the Camisards and their struggles. Back in Edinburgh for Christmas he continued to work on the volume while he waited for news of Fanny. Henley spent a week with him at Swanston in mid-January and read the manuscript. *Travels with a Donkey in the Cévennes* was published in June of 1879, in an edition of 750. Steveson received thirty pounds for it and a two-shillings-a-copy royalty, to rise to four shillings when 700 had been sold.

The reviews were interesting. Even at this early date the argument between Stevenson and the literary community was beginning to take shape. A favourable piece in the *Fortnightly Review* noted: "Mr. Stevenson is a stylist who lays himself out for the mastery of style." The *Spectator* ("granny," as R.L.S. called it in a poem) attempted sarcasm. In certain circles, it said, "a man is not considered to have won his spurs until he has put pen to paper." The unsigned review went on: "It is no wonder, under these circumstances, that a young man who has a few holiday-weeks to fill thinks he cannot employ them better than by writing a book." Nevertheless, it was a "very readable volume."

Fraser's Magazine was more scathing. The book was a pretty one in which "nothing particular happens to the traveller; he has nothing much to tell us. But he tells us that nothing in detail . . ."

> He is a young man of letters, one of those who, standing on the very apex of culture and the nineteenth century, find nothing better to do than topple over and begin again on the other side; and he is at the same time, we presume, one of those darlings of fortune, who, having no natural hardships of their own, find a piquant gratification in inventing a few artificial ones . . . This is the last whim of exquisite youth.

Over the winter the darling of fortune had also begun work on one of his finest short stories, "The Pavilion on the Links," though it was to be almost a year before it was completed. The delay was due, perhaps, to the fact that he had begun the first of his more or less disastrous collaborations with Henley, in this instance a play based on the life of the infamous Edinburgh character Deacon Brodie. The character, an eighteenth-century businessman who turned to crime and lived the original double life, had long fascinated Louis. Outwardly law-abiding, he was a master criminal; honest by day, evil by night: the perfect, so we have learned, Stevensonian formula. Unfortunately the play, on which the pair worked intermittently for several years, was abysmal, as dire as anything being written in a forgetable era for the British stage. It turned up in Bradford in 1882 and reappeared over the decade in Aberdeen and London. It toured in America, but since the company was headed by a brother of Henley's who drank at least as much as Stevenson's collaborator, there was nothing in the production to mitigate the intrinsic defects of the work. R.L.S. later described it as "good, honest melodrama." Honest and melodramatic, perhaps.

It was attempted for money. Louis was struggling to save, trying not to spend the allowance his father gave him and cooking up schemes to get himself across the Atlantic. He told Henley that "£350 must be made and laid by ere I can breathe freely."

In October of 1879 there appeared in the *Cornhill* an essay entitled "Some Aspects of Robert Burns." Louis had already written one piece on the poet, which had been rejected by the *Encyclopaedia Britannica* because it failed to achieve the right note of uncritical admiration. Now Leslie Stephen, inspired by Professor John Campbell Shairp's study in the English [*sic*] Men of Letters series, asked Louis to prepare his own portrait. It is fair to say that it was not one calculated to please the Scots, whose refusal even now to face the facts about Burns imprisons "the Bard" in a ludicrous cult.

Stevenson must have been aware of it, and set about the icon with a will. He has been called a hypocrite for the assault, since he attacked Burns for his attitude to women while he himself was spurning the sanctity of marriage. But it was not the breaking of vows Louis objected to; rather the poet's selfishness. R.L.S. put a high value on the relationship between a man and a woman, and berated Burns because he "trifled with life." The essayist took issue with the idea that the poet had died of drink, pointing out that others have drunk more. "He died of being Robert Burns, and there is no levity in such a statement of the case; for shall we not, one and all, deserve a similar epitaph?"

He was elbowing Scotland's most revered literary figure from his pedestal. The essay is grossly intemperate—the flaws of Burns are magnified at the expense of his virtues—but it is interesting to observe Louis dealing with one of the literary trinity of which he was, in time, to become part. Scott he respected, though he had fun at the expense of his eminent fellow advocate. With Burns, it was as though Louis was attacking something feckless in the Scottish character, and perhaps in his own, attacking it while trying and failing to forgive it, admiring the art while deploring the man. Very Scottish.

> Burns was so full of his identity that it breaks forth on every page; and there is scarce an appropriate remark either in praise or blame of his own conduct, but he has put it himself into verse. Alas! for the tenor of these remarks! They are, indeed, his own pitiful apology for such a marred existence and talents so misused and stunted; and they seem to prove for ever how small a part is played by reason in the conduct of man's affairs.

Reason. Louis was about to give a convincing demonstration of his own thesis. His cyclical career—stalled, tension rising, then bursting into motion—was about go spinning again, though whether even he suspected it is doubtful.

In the summer of 1879 Louis's depression was such that his friends began to worry. He had been parted from Fanny for almost a year; his work was suffering; and his health, as ever, was faltering. Edmund Gosse, whom Louis had first met in the Hebrides in 1870, wondered in a letter to him how "the Great Exhilarator," of all people, could feel depressed. But he could: "I can do no work at all," said Louis to Colvin. "It all lies aside. I want—I want—a holiday; I want to be happy; I want the moon or the sun or something. I want the object of my affections badly . . ." What he got was something more than a holiday.

Fanny had been sending him letters, rambling things accounted wild and disordered by Colvin and the others who were hoping against hope that Louis's infatuation would pass. Things were going badly in Monterey, though the precise nature of the problem was unclear. With his wife back at his side Samuel Osbourne seems to have seen no need for another separation; he had seen none hitherto. It is just possible that the errant husband also felt no need to admit his own failings by agreeing to the humiliation of divorce. That would be Sam. To be fair to him, divorce was no small thing then, even in America.

Whatever the reason, at the end of July 1879 a telegram arrived for Louis at Swanston. No one knows what it said. Biographers have assumed it must have been a plea from Fanny so heartrending that Stevenson could wait no longer. It may have been something casual that had an equal, catalytic effect—though a telegram suggests urgency, and melodrama was ever Fanny's style. On this occasion she had reason. Sam Osbourne had her exactly where he wanted her: back home, raising the children, unable to demand a divorce and unable to control his sexual escapades. All the efforts to escape, all the bids for freedom, had put her right back where she started.

In any case, the contents of that scrap of paper, so few words, were sufficient cause for Louis to purchase an eight-guinea ticket at the Anchor Steamship Line's office in Edinburgh. Without telling his parents, who had expected him to join them at a spa, he took ship for New York.

9 *1879–1880*

Travel is of two kinds; and this voyage of mine across the ocean combined both. 'Out of my country and myself I go,' sings the old poet; and I was not only travelling out of my country in latitude and longitude, but out of myself in diet, associates, and consideration.

THE AMATEUR EMIGRANT

*H*is London friends had tried hard to dissuade him. They cared for him and, for their several self-important reasons, thought they knew what was best for him. Gosse told Louis straight that the enterprise was a "mere freak," but Stevenson's mood of intense determination and anxiety rendered him immune to sense. There were worried discussions and debates. In the end, clever Charles Baxter having arranged funds, Henley saw him off on the train to Glasgow and R.L.S. sailed from Greenock on 7 August 1879, aboard the S.S. *Devonia*. Only Baxter had his forwarding address, with instructions that it was to be given to no one.

It is still worth asking what possessed him. He had survived almost twelve months deprived of Fanny, yet suddenly, because of one telegram, he was again throwing his life (and his career) into utter confusion, risking his health and the wrath of his parents, to achieve—what? Without the text of that long-lost telegram no one can say, but something in it precipitated the crisis. He had probably been thinking of such a trip for months. With her divorce now on the way, Fanny may have demanded marriage, or at least a decision to force Sam's hand: it was not beyond her. Something she said, rendered more lunatic in telegraphese, may have led him to fear the worst—that she was sick, or doubting their relationship, or both. Perhaps it was merely his own, highly developed sense of the dramatic that demanded a resolution. It is possible—and all of this is speculation—that he had decided to convince her of his seriousness with a grand gesture.

Perhaps and perhaps: given the players, any of these plots is possible. You cannot help but conclude that it was all a great adventure for R.L.S., another occasion for flight and exile. Fate, or so he would have said, had taken a hand. Chance had made its play. What else could he do? In reality, he was simplifying his existence by making a choice. And you cannot help but admire him for shrugging aside the sage advice of Colvin, Henley, Gosse, and the rest, those supremely bourgeois litterateurs in the age of the supreme bourgeois. At least Louis was doing something. He did not—and this must have rankled—need any of them.

He wrote a letter to his father and enclosed it in an odd note to Colvin. To the latter he said: "The weather is threatening; I have a strange, rather horrible, sense of the sea before me, and can see no further into the future. I can say honestly I have at his moment neither a regret, a hope, a fear or an inclination . . ." He then said that he had made his will.

The contents of the letter to his father are unknown, but Thomas was desperate that Louis should return forthwith and spare him any further humiliation. It was, he said, a "sinful, mad business," to be laid at the door of Herbert Spencer for "unsettling a man's faith."

Typically, for all the emotional upheavel, Louis seems to have planned a book on emigration from the start. Just as typically, he survived the storms of passion to get saleable copy out of the experience. He was going to America after all; and America, with its intriguing new writers, its limitless expanse, and its vigorous people, had long fascinated him. "For many years," he wrote in *The Amateur Emigrant*, "America was to me a sort of promised land." He was to dedicate the volume to Bob, in a kind of hail-and-farewell to the past:

Our friendship was not only founded before we were born by a community of blood, but is in itself near as old as my life. It began with our early ages, and, like a history, has been continued to the present time. Although we may not be old in the world, we are old to each other, having so long

been intimates. We are now widely separated, a great sea and continent intervening; but memory, like care, mounts into iron ships and rides post behind the horseman.

Early in the book Louis makes it clear that he did not travel steerage
among the emigrants, as myth has suggested:

> I was not, in truth, a steerage passenger. Although anxious to see the worst
> of emigrant life, I had some work to finish on the voyage, and was advised
> to go by the second cabin, where at least I should have a table at com-
> mand.

The work in question was "The Story of a Lie," which Stevenson had
laid aside in the summer but which he now resolved to finish as a way of
paying for his expedition. Steerage would have cost him six guineas, but
the commission for his piece of fiction was worth fifty pounds. The extra
two guineas were worth it, he thought, for the sake of a small table on
which he could write, though the miseries of the crossing were not pro-
portionately diminished. The food was disgusting, and Louis was soon
avoiding most of the fare on offer, preferring to lose precious weight by
dining on porridge, soup, and bread.

> At breakfast, we had a choice between tea and coffee for beverage; a
> choice not easy to make, the two were so surprisingly alike . . . As a matter
> of fact, I have seen passengers, after many sips, still doubting which had
> been supplied them. In the way of eatables at the same meal we were glo-
> riously favoured; for in addition to porridge, which was common to all, we
> had Irish stew, sometimes a bit of fish, and sometimes rissoles. The dinner
> of soup, roast fresh beef, boiled salt junk, and potatoes, was, I believe, ex-
> actly common to the steerage and the second cabin; only I have heard it
> rumoured that our potatoes were of a superior brand . . . the bread, which
> was excellent, and the soup and porridge, which were both good, formed
> my whole diet throughout the voyage; so that except for the broken meat
> and the conveniences of a table I might as well have been in steerage out-
> right.

This went on for ten days. Shipboard comradeships emerged but Louis
did not fail to notice that his fellow pioneers were a poor lot, failures

rather than heroes, middle-aged rather than youthful, a mixture of English, Irish, Scots, Germans, Scandinavians, and, for some reason, one Russian. "We were a company of the rejected," Stevenson wrote, ". . . all who had been unable to prevail against circumstances in the one land, were now fleeing pitifully to another; and though one or two might still succeed, all had already failed."

It needs to be said that his circumstances were to a large extent self-created. Nevertheless, and irrespective of his tie to Fanny, he felt the need to leave. He seemed to sense that the career that was slowly and painfully unfolding for him as a respectable man of letters was as much of a trap as any other profession. Equally, the days before his departure had shown him to be isolated from family and friends. The break was dramatic, but it was as clean as he might have hoped.

The Scots were the most doleful passengers of the lot, coming as they did from a country where the one thing that "is not to be learned . . . is the way to be happy." Just before landing in New York, Louis wrote to Colvin:

> At least if I fail in my great purpose, I shall see some wild life in the West and visit both Florida and Labrador ere my return. But I don't yet know if I have the courage to stick with life without it. Man, I was sick, sick, sick of this last year.

The "it" over which Louis doubted his own courage is ambiguous. Did he mean a "wild life in the West" or life with Fanny? The latter, probably, but it is clear that even at this late stage his romantic dash to rescue his love from whatever afflicted her was done with no great confidence in the future.

The Amateur Emigrant did not appear as a book until after Louis was dead. Neither he nor his London friends thought much of it and Thomas objected to its proposed publication, probably because it showed his son in such demeaning circumstances and because it invoked painful memories of wilful desertion.

Yet the work is among the best of the easy Stevenson: honest, unflinching, and (by his standards) pared down. As useful as a social document as it is as literature, it is nonetheless an example of Louis's mixing with his fellow men, sharing their existence, good or ill, yet maintaining a precious distance. He observed it all even as he lived, animating the forgotten characters yet reserving for himself both an authorial voice and an authorial reserve. It is clear, for example, the he interrogated his fellow passengers in an effort to understand their reasons for emigrating.

> The difference between England and America to a working man was thus most humanly put to me by a fellow-passenger: 'In America,' said he, 'you get pies and puddings.' I do not hear enough, in economy books, of pies and puddings. A man lives in and for the delicacies, adornments, and accidental attributes of life ... Every detail of our existence, where it is worth while to cross the ocean after pie and pudding, is made alive and enthralling by the presence of genuine desire ... This is not the philosophical, but the human side of economics; it interests like a story ...

Perhaps it was harder to compose his usual grace notes in his little cabin while the ship rolled like a cradle in a gale and the odours of tobacco, bad food, and vomit filled the rank air. But Louis's prose acquired muscles and sinews in its Atlantic crossing. The romantic escapist, the enemy of fictional realism, confronted reality. It shows. He was a good journalist.

Meanwhile, he had completed "The Story of a Lie." Dick Naseby, the "type-hunter" (as Colvin had called R.L.S.), was a self-portrait, and the character's father was in essence Stevenson's father; the relationship between the two men is essentially that which existed between Thomas and Louis. It is a solid, unremarkable piece of fiction but a considerable advance on "The Edifying Letters of the Rutherford Family," Stevenson's previous attempt to analyse a fraught father-son relationship.

On 18 August, early in the morning, New York harbor came into view. It was raining heavily when Louis disembarked. With a man called Jones who had befriended him on board, he made for the Reunion House, a dollar-a-day rooming house. Then he busied himself at the bank, the post office, the bookseller, and publishers. Stevenson, who had "only lost a stone" and was suffering from uncontrollable itching, which an apothecary put down to a liver complaint, was in no great shape for the journey ahead, but he had accepted his mission. When he returned to his lodgings, he was soaked to the skin, and for some reason had chosen to burden himself with the "six fat volumes" of George Bancroft's *History of the United States*. Drenched, exhausted, half-starved, and kept from sleep by his maddening itch, Louis was demanding trouble. He found it in a letter which, as he told Henley, informed him that "F. has inflammation of the brain and I am across the continent tonight . . ."

At the ferry station he discovered there were four boatloads of emigrants making for one train. At the Jersey ferry there was chaos, as children and luggage were lost in the pushing, shoving throng desperate to make the crossing and catch the train westwards. It was a miserable scene. These were the huddled masses yearning to be free, and Stevenson had seen nothing like them before. He described it in "Across the Plains":

> The landing at Jersey City was done in a stampede. I had a fixed sense of calamity, and to judge by conduct, the same persuasion was common to us all. A panic selfishness, like that produced by fear, preside over the disorder of our landing. People pushed, and elbowed, and ran, their families following how they could. Children fell, and were picked up to be rewarded by a blow. One child, who had lost her parents, screamed steadily and with increasing shrillness, as though verging towards a fit; an official kept her by him, but no one else seemed so much as to remark her distress; and I am ashamed to say that I ran among the rest.

At the Emigrant House at Council Bluffs, Iowa, he waited with a hundred others to be "sorted and boxed." On the train families, single men, and Chinese were segregated. The seats were wooden and it was impossible to lie down without an elaborate arrangement of boards and straw cushions, the makings of which were sold by the conductor, and without the cooperation of fellow passengers. The carriages stank, and the stench grew steadily worse as the journey progressed, forcing a gasping Louis to seek fresh air on the rear platform.

Crossing the plains, he became seriously ill. He was feverish; could not eat; and could not sleep without laudanum. In his delirium, the empty landscape played on his mind. No one knew him; no one in the world knew where he was. He had hurled himself into the void, and if he had sought a "taste of America" this was the real, raw thing.

But what is to be said of the Nebraskan settler? His is a wall-paper with
a vengeance—one quarter of the universe laid bare in all its gauntness. His
eye must embrace at every glance the whole seeming concave of the visible
world; it quails before so vast an outlook, it is tortured by distance; yet
there is no rest or shelter till the man runs into his cabin, and can repose
his sight upon things near at hand. Hence, I am told, a sickness of the vision peculiar to these empty plains.

His London friends may not have thought much of such prose—
reacting, one suspects, as much to Louis's wilfulness as his reporting—but
it reveals the genuine sensitivity of R.L.S. to his surroundings. Under
stress, he verged on hallucination. Even when calm his vision was penetrating; he felt what he saw. The plains had made him long for the mountains, but these in turn provided another sort of test of his endurance.
"Hour after hour,"

it was the same unhomely and unkindly world about our onward path;
tumbled boulders, cliffs that drearily imitate the shape of monuments and
fortifications . . . not a tree, not a patch of sward, not one shapely or com-
manding mountain form; sage-brush, eternal sage-brush; over all, the same
weariful and gloomy colouring, greys warming into brown, greys darken-
ing towards black . . . The plains have a grandeur of their own; but here
there is nothing but a contorted smallness.

Whether through exhaustion or because he had been "poisoned in
some wayside eating-house," Louis fell "sick outright." The train became
"the one piece of life in all the deadly land; it was the one actor, the one
spectacle fit to be observed in this paralysis of man and nature." Louis
longed for it all to end.

He kept sufficient of his wits about him to observe his fellow passengers. An admirer of America and Americans, he nevertheless despised
them for despising others, particularly the Chinese. "Awhile ago it was
the Irish, now it is the Chinese that must go. Such is the cry . . . For my
own part, I could not look but with wonder and respect on the Chinese.
Their forefathers watched the stars before mine had begun to keep pigs."
He noted that, if nothing else, the Chinese workers paid more attention
to personal hygiene than the rest of the passengers.

Yet something was made of even this nightmare when a version of "Across the Plains" appeared in *Longman's Magazine* in 1883.

Thinner than ever, and shabbier than any bohemian ever dreamt possible. It was a scarecrow of a man rather than a knight-errant who arrived at last. Even young Lloyd, delighted to see "Luly," as he was, noticed how sick and emaciated Stevenson seemed. As he later recalled: "His clothes, no longer picturesque but merely shabby, hung loosely on his shrunken body; and there was about him an indescribable lessening of his alertness and self-confidence." Even the boy wished that his hero "had more sense."

Fanny's initial reaction was odd: it was she who had launched Louis on his mad journey, yet at first she seemed unprepared to resume their relationship. Perhaps the sight of Louis made her realise just how poor his prospects were. Perhaps a year apart had robbed their French liaison of its magic. She was still married to Sam, after all; he at least was still supporting her, and her family opposed divorce. Perhaps she had not considered the possible reactions of the old Mexican family with whom she was boarding. Or perhaps she had yet to recover from the emotional upheaval she had recently suffered.

She is the most difficult of women to explain. Had Louis misunderstood her telegram? It hardly seemed plausible. What *did* she want? Her longing for Stevenson was not such that it had prevented her from resuming her correspondence with Messrs. Lloyd and Rearden, now both respectable (and wealthy) men of business. Whatever her reasons, she had induced Louis to travel six thousand miles and now seemed to be rejecting him. At any rate, his presence was not convenient. For the first week after his arrival he was, unsurprisingly, utterly miserable.

He chose not to stay. As in the Cévennes, he reacted to inner turmoil by setting off on his own, this time with a horse and pack to the Carmel Valley. In the event, however, the trip was not restorative in the way the French jaunt had been. In fact, as aware as he was of his ravaged condition, and as depressed as he was, Louis seems deliberately to have exposed himself to the risk of death. He almost succeeded.

He collapsed miles from anywhere, and survived for three days drinking only coffee before an old hunter and an Indian found him and took him to the hunter's Angora goat ranch. His life was saved, but only just, and the rancher spent a fortnight nursing him back to something like health before he returned to Monterey.

There he found lodgings with a local doctor, later moving to Girardin's French House. He liked Monterey (the wild coastline nearby was to find its way into *Treasure Island*) and soon began to make friends, notably with the raffish restaurant keeper Jules Simoneau, formerly a merchant at Nantes. Louis visited Fanny, but discretion, or her indecision, ruled these meetings. She, too, was recuperating. Nevertheless, Louis's confidence in their relationship began to return. Having won her once, he seems to have won her a second time. Soon he was once again making a financial contribution to the household, though he could scarcely afford it.

His parents refused to allow him any money. His departure for America had wounded them more than he could have realised. Thomas was ashamed and furious; Maggie in a state of shock. They felt themselves to be ruined in Edinburgh society, though it is difficult to say who in Edinburgh could have known what Louis was up to. Nevertheless, their dismay at his behaviour was profound.

Colvin, Henley, and Gosse were also concerned about R.L.S. and his finances, though for different reasons. Whatever their variable merits, these men were snobs. They refused to see any merit in the work Louis had done while away—Colvin thought *The Amateur Emigrant* "quite unworthy of him"—and believed that poor artistic judgement, combined with an unsuitable marriage, would destroy him. If his work is no good, said Colvin with a mixture of concern and condescension, how is he to live?

The mother hens of London continued to cluck. They began to blame Fanny, the "Bedlamite," as Henley was to call her, forgetting that she, too, had respectable Californian friends like Rearden, who opposed the match (but was nevertheless loyal enough to file the suit for divorce on her behalf). Every letter Louis received—and he thought them few enough—urged him to come home. He replied that he would not desert his wife, forgetting that legal marriage was not yet his.

Finally it was clear that a "private divorce" would come through by the end of January 1880 at the latest. In the meantime, Louis worked assiduously at the French House on a variety of projects, completing "The Pavilion on the Links," one of the best of his stories, and despatching it to Henley (who placed it with Leslie Stephen at the *Cornhill*) before commencing to work simultaneously on *The Amateur Emigrant* and a novel entitled *A Vendetta in the West*. The latter has not survived, and Colvin thought Louis destroyed it before it was complete.

Having won Fanny back, Stevenson took Lloyd for a walk on the beach and told the boy that he was going to marry his mother. Perhaps the attitude of Belle and others in the family had left Louis worried about the child's reaction. He need not have feared. Lloyd's memory was clear enough:

> I could not have uttered a word to save my life. I was stricken dumb. The question of whether I were pleased or not did not enter my mind at all. I walked on in a kind of stupefaction, with an uncontrollable impulse to cry—yet I did not cry—and was possessed of an agonising feeling that I ought to speak, but I did not know how, nor what.
>
> But all I know is that at last my hand crept in Luly's . . .

With Louis's agreement Fanny and her brood went back to Oakland before the end of November while he remained at Monterey alone. In December he was suffering again, with pleurisy, just as the latest cable arrived from Edinburgh to say that his father was very ill. Louis refused to leave. A suspicion that he was being blackmailed aside, he had also come to enjoy Monterey. Simoneau extended him credit and, together with others of his crowd, scraped together two dollars a week to allow Crevole Bronson, editor of the weekly Monterey *Californian*, to pretend to take Stevenson on as a part-time contributor.

Louis's gift for making friends stood him in good stead at Monterey. None of Simoneau's crowd had much money themselves. To call the Frenchman a restaurateur was to stretch a point. He ran a cheap eating house selling good, simple French food. But he, Bronson, Dr. Heintz (with whom R.L.S. lodged for a while), the bartender Adolfo Sanchez, and some of Simoneau's boarders thought the Scotsman a decent sort. He had talked kindly to an alcoholic old Indian when few others would and thus made himself acceptable. Simoneau's French House was a home from home for Louis.

Towards the end of 1879, he moved to San Francisco and spent six months there. His own spirits were good, but his friends in London continued to fail to see the point of his exile. "You might expect that Louis will resent our criticism of his last three works," Henley told Colvin in a letter in February 1880, ". . . but I think it right that he should get them . . . Monterey will never produce anything worth a damn." Earlier he had said that it was "absolutely necessary that [Louis] should be brought to see that England and a quiet life are what he wants and must have . . ." It was foretaste of far worse impertinence.

If nothing else, the idea that R.L.S. would take to an ordered life in England, of all places, was absurd. But the conspiratorial tone of these remarks, never mind their arrogance, suggests that discussions about *what to do with Louis* were at an advanced stage. It was a pattern that was to continue even in later years, when Stevenson's fame was immense: his friends knew best. In California he did not allow it to obstruct him, but he did not pretend to like it. Had he known what was being said of Fanny, he would have liked it even less. Instead, these friends only made him feel intensely isolated. On Boxing Day of 1879 he told Colvin that he had spoken to no one save his landlady, landlord, and waiters for four days. "This is not a gay way to spend Christmas, is it?"

After many second thoughts, much argument, and a deal of prevarication on Sam's part, the divorce came through at last. Fanny was not regarded as a heroine by all, and there were those who believed that Osbourne, deserted for three years, had been more loyal than she had had any reason to expect. In any case, as soon as the divorce came through in January, he lost his job with the Bureau of Mines. The burden of supporting the family, not to mention the East Oakland cottage as well as his own lodgings, fell on the meagre shoulders of the penniless writer. Colvin offered to lend him money, but Louis, perhaps aware of the uses to which his friends might put such favours, refused. "This is a test," he replied. "I must support myself . . ."

Each morning he had a ten-cent breakfast before writing for three or four hours and taking a "copious" fifty-cent lunch. In the afternoon he walked, sometimes to meet Fanny but often just for the aimless pleasure of it. By half past four he would be back working at his quarters at 608

Bush Street. At six he went out for coffee before returning for more work in the evening.

Fanny became ill again, perhaps because of the upset of discovering that she was to regain none of the money she had brought into her failed marriage. She had dizzy spells and became, briefly, almost blind and partially deaf. The divorce was through, but she withheld the information from her family in Indiana: she was free but not yet free. Colvin, meanwhile, despite all Louis had said in his letters, despite his evident love and determination, was still counselling against the match, much to Stevenson's irritation. It was clear that the love of his life was now an obstacle to others he loved. Only Baxter, of all his friends at home, was constant and uncritical: his support, moral and financial, made everything possible. R.L.S. was still frail—indeed he composed his own epitaph at around this time—and a doctor diagnosed malaria. It was worse than that.

Suddenly "Bluidy Jack," more terrifying than any previous condition, made his debut: Louis began to bleed from the lungs, his mouth so full of blood he could not speak. Just as she had in Paris, Fanny took him in, believing he had tuberculosis. Diagnosis was not an exact science then, but the symptoms suggest she was right, at that moment at least. The prospective head of the household was not much of a prospect. But as so often before and afterwards, sickness proved a decisive event in Stevenson's life, welding him to Fanny once and for good.

It also provided a definitive image. Henceforth Louis would be the picture of the invalid author, scribbling in bed while he fought back against illness, sometimes bereft of speech, often bereft of strength, camped at death's door. Fanny, at least, knew what she was taking on.

He worked on an early version of *Prince Otto* while he recovered, with Fanny's sister Nellie acting as his amanuensis. His finances were in a dire condition and he had instructed Baxter to sell his books for the cash. Then, out of the blue, came a cable from Thomas: "Count on 250 pounds annually." Yet again the old man had relented in his test of wills with his son. Talk of R.L.S.'s being disinherited was forgotten, and he, who had expressed some reservations about inherited wealth, accepted with gratitude. This time his father might really have saved his life. All that Thomas asked was that there be a delay between Fanny's divorce and her marriage to Louis.

Sam Osbourne asked the same. All parties sought respectability. Louis, in between bouts of illness, was introduced to Fanny's San Francisco friends. Living with Fanny, four cats, and two dogs in Oakland, he composed some of the verses later collected in *Underwoods*, revised *The Amateur Emigrant*, and pressed on with *Otto*. Nellie recorded that he had now begun to show all his work to Fanny for her criticism. With his father's money he had his badly decayed teeth repaired or replaced. But he was sick, always sick, and Fanny begun to conclude that if he was to survive they had better marry and leave the foggy Californian coast. Louis bought the licence.

The marriage took place on 19 May 1880 at the San Francisco home of a Scottish Presbyterian named William Scott, who was the president of the local St. Andrew's Soceity. Dora Williams, a friend of Fanny's, was the only other person present. He was thirty; she forty. The bride described herself on the marriage certificate as a widow; the groom was said to hail from "Edinboro." Louis presented Dr. Scott with his copy of Thomas's "proof" of Christianity to mark the occasion. The wedding bands were silver; they could not afford gold. He gave her some of the verses he had been writing as a wedding gift.

So it began. After a few days the couple headed for the mountains, on the recommendation of Dora Williams and her husband Virgil. Louis was still frail, and the Napa Valley was thought an improvement on foggy San Francisco. A train took them to Calistoga; horses carried them to Mount St. Helena.

They tried the products of the local wine industry, then in its infancy, and decided, on the advice of a local Jewish shopkeeper, to stay at a disused mining camp some way up the mountain. The house was not much of a palace for "the King and Queen of Silverado," as the book to which it gave its name was to show.

> It consisted of three rooms, and was so plastered against the hill, that one room was right atop of another, that the upper floor was more than twice as large as the lower ... Not a window sash remained. The door of the lower room was smashed ... We entered that, and found a fair amount of rubbish ... The window, sashless of course, was choked with the green

and sweetly smelling foliage of a bay; and through a chink in the floor, a spray of poison-oak had shot up and was handsomely prospering in the interior. It was my first care to cut away that poison-oak, Fanny standing by at a respectful distance.

Stores were brought up by wagon while the couple tried to make the place habitable. Lloyd soon joined them, and a dog, a setter called Chuchu, was added to their company. Louis rested, read, gave his stepson his lessons, and wrote little. His weak health aside, it was the best start possible for a marriage born out of dislocation and upheaval.

Peace meant intimacy, and the couple, both burdened for so long by worries, seized the opportunity. Fanny, the erstwhile frontierswoman, came into her own and refused to let Louis exert himself. She cooked, made doors, collected firewood, and became, as she was to remain, as much nurse as wife. Ironically, she and Lloyd were stricken with mild diphtheria for a while, but otherwise things went well. Louis loved the mountains, and the mountains were kind to him in return. He even began to think, with that charity that made itself vulnerable to abuse, that he had been hard on his friends at home.

As the weeks passed and his health improved, his thoughts turned increasingly in that direction. His parents wanted to see their new daughter-in-law as soon as possible; life in California, pleasant though it was, could not go on forever; and he was strong enough to face the journey. In her first letter to Maggie Stevenson, Fanny wrote: "As to my dear boy's appearance, he improves every day in the most wonderful way." Her careful, calculated message, together with a photograph Fanny herself thought somewhat flattering, did much to raise her in the esteem of her husband's parents. At the end of July the party left the Napa Valley.

From San Francisco they travelled—first class this time—to New York via Chicago, and boarded the *City of Chester*. On 17 August, a year after he had launched himself on his mad expedition, Louis arrived at Liverpool with his new wife and her young son. Stepping ashore, he stepped out of one world and into another. It was the pattern of his life, and he was coming adept at it. Now and ever after, however, many of his decisions were to be made for him.

Colvin, fresh from the night mail train, came aboard from the tug to

greet them, as though to be first to examine Fanny. With his usual sense
of priorities, he wondered to Henley if they would ever get used to her.
He found Louis thinner than ever but in better shape than expected, with
new teeth filling out his cheeks. It had to be conceded that marriage
seemed to agree with him.

Thomas and Maggie Stevenson were waiting ashore, doubtless swal-
lowing their misgivings, ready to carry their wayward son back to Edinburgh and a prodigal's welcome at Heriot Row. Colvin told Henley that
those "old folks put a most brave and most kind face on it indeed," which
was both decent and waspish of him. If nothing else, the Stevensons' new
daughter-in-law certainly *seemed* respectable. Fanny, for her part, did her
very best to ensure they would retain that impression. She had much to
gain. Mr. and Mrs. Thomas Stevenson did not yet know that, with Belle
Strong pregnant, their boy's new wife was about to become a grandmother.

10 *1880–1884*

Happiness and goodness, according to canting moralists, stand in relation of effect and cause. There was never anything less proved or less probable: our happiness is never in our own hands . . .

"A CHRISTMAS SERMON"

M aggie Stevenson was barely ten years older than her new daughter-in-law. Colvin, with a touch of acid, had judged the Scotswoman "the fresher of the two" when comparing them at Liverpool. Fanny had reason to be weary.

She was touching middle age when she began this new chapter in her life with a thirty-year-old author of unproven worth. It was not that she doubted his talent—she thought him a genius and never wavered from that judgement—but she could have been forgiven for wondering what sort of contract she had entered into, she to whom life had not been kind, not simple, not easy. Louis was kindness itself, but neither simple nor easy to live with.

She could take credit for having saved his life and for helping his reconciliation with his parents. Her apparent competence, the ease with which she managed R.L.S., impressed people. But Fanny had several disguises, and wore them according to need or whim. With Thomas and Maggie Stevenson she worked hard to charm, and to make them realise she was not the adventuress they must have feared. Just as she reassured them, however, Heriot Row reassured her. The precarious structure of Louis's life turned out to rest on sound foundations of prosperity and taste. She took to it all with unfeigned delight, particularly when Louis was obliged to don some of the splendid clothes he had left hanging in his Edinburgh wardrobes, though she later felt guilty that she was taking so much from her husband's parents and giving so little. As things stood, she was giving them more than she realised.

"Fanny fitted into our household from the first," Maggie told her diary. Thomas, in particular, found her charming, perhaps because she agreed with almost everything he had to say. Fanny, for her part, thought Maggie Stevenson a more sympathetic and complex character than Mrs. Stevenson's own diaries and letters have suggested to posterity. The two women had Louis in common, however, and achieved more understanding over husband and son than a wife and a mother usually do.

Walter Simpson presented the couple with a wedding present in the unlikely form of a black Skye terrier, variously named Wattie, Woggs, Woggy, Wiggs, and, finally, Bogue. True to his breed, he was a stubborn, short-tempered beast who snarled and fought his way across Europe, soiling carpets and upsetting waiters as he went, for six years. If Thomas Stevenson was right in believing that dogs possess souls, Bogue was a demon incarnate. His mistress, the old man decided, was not.

Thomas, no fool, may even have concluded that his son would be better off in the hands of this older woman, who seemed to know what she was doing and what she wanted. If Louis would listen to her advice, it could only be an improvement. Thomas seems to have admired Fanny's evident strength, and the admiration was reciprocated. Fanny wrote to Dora Williams:

> The father is a most lovely old person. He is much better looking I feat than Louis will ever be, and is hustled about, according to the humour of his wife and son, in the most amusing way; occasionally he comes in with twinkling eyes and reports a comic verse of his own making with infinite gusto. Mrs. Stevenson is a much more complex creature, much more like Louis. She is adored by her husband who spoils her like a baby, both I can see, have spoiled Louis.

This was astute. Fanny would not make the same mistake with Louis, perhaps because she herself needed a little spoiling, or so she believed. For the moment, her forcefulness was an asset. Louis's uncle George Balfour told him: "I too married a besom and have never regretted it."

Professionally, however, he took no such light-hearted view of his nephew's condition. There was a brief stay at Heriot Row, followed by a trip with his parents to Strathpeffer in the Highlands which did R.L.S. no good, whatever Fanny professed to believe. He hated the hotel and, as usual, his fellow guests.

They returned to Edinburgh in the autumn and George Balfour's opinion that Louis should get out of the country again as quickly as possible. The city's weather was as unrelenting as ever. And for all that he had enjoyed his visit home, Stevenson was more than ambivalent about Heriot Row, Edinburgh, and Scotland. He needed no second bidding.

They thought of returning to Menton, but Uncle George advised otherwise. It was decided that Louis, Fanny, Lloyd, and the terrier they had acquired should travel to Davos in Switzerland, then *the* place for fashionable consumptives.

They went first to London, where Louis enjoyed himself hugely and expensively for a week at the Grosvenor Hotel among his Savile Club friends. Fanny knew they had reservations about her, Henley in particular. Most did not care for the simple fact of the American woman; others were put off by her manner. She in turn did not much like the way Louis carried on with his chums, partly because she feared for his health, partly because of jealousy and insecurity. Fiends disguised as friends, she was to call them. He, it seems, simply reveled in the company of old comrades after a year of relative isolation.

On this occasion, at least, there were no obvious ill feelings, only large bills. R.L.S. had not even crossed the Channel before he had run through forty-six pounds at the hotel and was writing to Edinburgh for more funds. In the event, he had to borrow ten pounds (or rather reclaim money he had already lent) from Colvin to get to Paris. Typically, he induced his father, through Baxter, to reimburse his friend.

For a fortnight they crept towards Davos "in the midst of wind, rain, coughing, and night sweats." Louis had entered the period of his life when Bluidy Jack was forever at his heels and the search for health seemed endless. Lloyd Osbourne, in one of thirteen papers he composed on Stevenson at various phases of his life, described the Swiss resort thus:

Davos in 1881 consisted of a small straggling town where nearly all the shops were kept by consumptives. It possessed a charity sanatorium and three large hotels, widely separated from one another, in which one could die quite comfortably. It was then the 'new Alpine cure' for tuberculosis; and its altitude, its pine-woods, and its glorious winter sunshine were supposed to work wonders. For five months of the year—'the season'—it was buried in snow, and rimmed about with dazzling white peaks. Snow, snow, snow; icicled trees; a frozen little river; a sense of glinting and sparkling desolation—such was the place we had come to.

An eight-hour sleigh ride to the Hotel Belvedere was the least of the price Louis had to pay. At the hotel on the Magic Mountain, under the orders of the noted Dr. Karl Ruedi, his smoking was restricted and he was fed quantities of milk, meat, and red wine, all regarded as beneficial. He exercised a little but tired easily. Perhaps as a consequence, he was hardly writing at all. Lloyd Osbourne identified the condition as a "mental inertia" unusual to Louis.

Stevenson did not enjoy Davos much; nor did he enjoy the "new Alpine cure" on the second occasion that he was compelled to submit to it. The Alps seemed oppressive; yet again the English guests at the hotel were not to his taste; and he was bored. Sunshine and open skies revived him, not this Swiss holding pen where the "dead were whisked away very unobtrusively." He was to be trapped there for six months (though Ruedi first advised eighteen), and even the "wild love-affairs, tempestuous jealousies, cliques and coteries" among fellow guests, made reckless, according to Lloyd, by the closeness of death, seem not to have intrigued him. Given that it was the longest period he had spent in one place in eight years, this was hardly surprising. The only real intellectual company he had was John Addington Symonds, the historian of the Renaissance and a fellow sufferer. They became friendly, after a struggle, but never close.

Meanwhile, his work remained stalled. He composed "The Morality of the Profession of Letters," among the least of his works, and a few short pieces describing his chilly surroundings. He began a novel, *The Squaw Man*, to amuse Lloyd, but it never got beyond three chapters. Louis was in a trough, still living, albeit with increasing reluctance, off his father; still struggling as a writer; still duelling with death.

Death's proximity was obvious. Near the end of Stevenson's time at Davos, Mrs. Sitwell's only remaining son, eighteen-year-old Bertie, a fellow patient, died of tuberculosis. Louis had been fond of the boy and shared his old love's grief. He wrote a poem, "Yet, O stricken heart, remember, O remember" and told Colvin that the death "helped to make me more conscious of the wolverine on my own shoulders." It was never again to leave him.

The only amusing episode occurred when a young woman, a religious fanatic, waylaid Lloyd and began to question him about his love for Jesus. Failing to elicit the desired reponse, she took to passing notes on the same theme to R.L.S. in the dining room. Louis was too polite to say anything, but another guest, a young man, jumped to the conclusion that Stevenson was deceiving Fanny. After a brief farce in which Fanny's ever-suspicious mind was put at rest, the young man was shown the crazed notes. Apologies all round.

In April of 1881 they began to travel slowly homewards. Lloyd, to whom R.L.S. was growing increasingly close, had been packed off to boarding school. Fanny and Louis went to Barbizon, no doubt for reasons of nostalgia, and to St.-Germain-en-Laye, where they again ran short of money and again had to depend on Thomas to get them home. R.L.S. had done little work—indeed, had not truly earned any of the recognition those initials of his would later achieve in such measure—but in a cottage in Scotland that summer a new artist emerged.

> Sooner or later, somehow, anyhow, I was bound to write a novel. It seems vain to ask why. Men are born with various manias: from my earliest childhood, it was mine to make a plaything of imaginary series of events; and as soon as I was able to write, I became a good friend to the papermakers.
>   "My First Book: 'Treasure Island' "

So he said much later, in an article published in the year that he died. Yet all his efforts at longer fiction before 1881 seem desultory, as though he lacked the intellectual energy for the form. He had mastered short stories, and had an admirable facility and descriptive gift, but he seemed not to understand what the novel required of him. The problem puzzled Louis, too, for years.

Anybody can write a short story—a bad one, I mean—who has industry and paper and time enough; but not every one may hope to write even a bad novel. It is the length that kills. The accepted novelist may take his novel up and put it down, spend days upon it in vain, and write not any more than he makes haste to blot. Not so the beginner. Human nature has certain rights; instinct—the instinct of self-preservation—forbids that any man (cheered and supported by the consciousness of no previous victory) should endure the miseries of unsuccessful literary toil beyond a period to be measured in weeks. There must be something for hope to feed upon . . . I remember I used to look, in those days, upon every three-volume novel with a sort of veneration.

The benefit of hindsight, when mastery was his, was not available to Louis in the "fated year" in which he and Fanny joined his mother at Kinnaird Cottage above Pitlochry in the Vale of Atholl. It was a simply furnished place, lit by oil lamps and lacking a bath, but it was divided into two flats and appealed to both couples. Louis had been determined to avoid a Highland hotel; his mother thought the cottage had a certain chaste charm. They stayed for two months before going on to Braemar, where Lloyd joined them. Thomas, as usual, commuted from his office in Edinburgh.

The Highland weather did its Highland worst, and that, as Fanny had noted at Strathpeffer, was a good deal. It poured. Louis was shut up in the house, staring into the fire. Yet here he began once again to work.

He and Fanny told one another ghost stories to pass the time, a practice that inspired his penetrating Scottish fable "Thrawn Janet." R.L.S. planned a book on the Camisards, cousins in God to his own Calvinists. He also began work on "The Merry Men," that sinister story of the sea exhibiting Stevenson's mastery of Scots prose. The weather worsened; Louis began to spit blood again, and could not speak because of chest pains. The party moved to Braemar on doctor's advice but found it even less congenial. Louis, to entertain Lloyd, began a new story.

On a chill September morning, by the cheek of a brisk fire, and the rain drumming on the window, I began *The Sea Cook,* for that was the original title. I have begun (and finished) a number of other books, but I cannot remember to have sat down to one of them with more complacency.

Lloyd and Louis agreed subsequently that the story was inspired by a watercolour map, but disagreed over who had painted it. R.L.S., who was fascinated by cartography, probably had the best claim. Lloyd, in any case, made something of a habit of trying to appropriate the best of any collaboration with Stevenson. For Louis, "the map was the most of the plot." His island, "like a fat dragon standing up," bore a host of piratical landmarks. Lloyd, Stevenson's twelve-year-old "touchstone" for gauging the taste of boys, took to the tale; Thomas, up from Edinburgh, soon joined in. The apple barrel was his inspiration, and it was he who drew up the inventory of Billy Bones's chest. The first fifteen chapters of the book poured out.

Inspired, as Louis admitted, by Defoe, Poe, Washington Irving, and Captain Marryat, this "story for boys," with "no need of psychology or fine writing," is a marvel both for its construction and its psychological insight. It is a fable out of time and society—one reason, perhaps, why it has endured. Thomas, at least, was enthralled by it, and in so entrancing his father Louis went some distance to healing the breach between them. It was, R.L.S. said, "something kindred to his own imagination; it was *his* kind of picturesque . . ."

Gosse and Colvin, who came to visit, listened to early chapters as Stevenson recited them each evening. One Alexander Hay Japp, who had been corresponding with Louis, also called, ostensibly to pursue a discussion on Thoreau, and suggested that the work be offered to a London periodical. In September, James Henderson, editor of *Young Folks' Magazine*, accepted the story but requested a change of title.

After fifteen days Stevenson's inspiration failed him. He was due to return to Davos and, with the incomplete work already sold, had every incentive to complete it. Fanny did not like the tale, finding it "tedious" (though she changed her mind, and rewrote history, later). She also opposed the novel's publication in book form, but Louis agreed and was astonished to be offered "a hundred jingling, tingling, golden-minted quid" for it.

The rest is known: the story, appearing in the first of seventeen installments under the pseudonym "Captain George North" in October 1881, did not do particularly well as a serial; Stevenson's smart friends deplored its publication in such a periodical ("let them write their damn master-pieces for themselves," he retorted); yet when it emerged between hardcovers and began slowly to grip the imagination of an audience for whom the brave new world of Victorian progress was unsatisfying or stultifying, all were confounded. Stevenson had arrived, though he himself did not know it at the time.

Louis brought so much of himself to *Treasure Island*, it is hard to speak of the book except in terms of his life. The story's movement chimes with his own existence. Its first chapters are all upheaval and departure, a setting forth in a year left unidentified to a place unknown. Personality, as Robert Kiely* has written, is equally dispensable: it barely figures "except as a costume or disguise which may be put on and off at will." The hero is fatherless, his friends strip themselves eagerly of their accustomed roles in life; the villains (Silver aside) are figures out of nightmare, simple evil. It was the world as Stevenson's imagination understood it.

Silver is apart from all of this. Sometimes kind, sometimes cruel, he is an untrustworthy surrogate father who places more faith in Jim than Jim gives to him. Stevenson took one-footed Henley as his physical model of "maimed strength and masterfulness," but he may also have been thinking of his difficult friend's chimerical personality and their own relationship. The identification sounds like a sly joke. In "My First Book," Louis put it thus:

> . . . I had an idea for John Silver from which I promised myself funds of entertainment; to take an admired friend of mine . . . to deprive him of all his finer qualities and higher graces of temperament, to leave him with nothing but his strength, his courage, his quickness, and his magnificent geniality, and to try to express these in terms of the culture of a raw tarpaulin.

In a novel with an otherwise simple moral plan, Silver is ambiguous. Sometimes it is as though R.L.S. were tempting us to admire this figure whose personalty swings like a pendulum, whose character metamorpho-

*Keily, R.: *Robert Louis Stevenson and the Fiction of Adventure* (Cambridge, Mass. 1964); pp. 61–105.

ses almost in an instant. The word "duality" is often used. But *who* Long John actually is seems less important than what, by contrast, he shows the others to be. A strong man, he brings out innate strength or weakness in others; a dishonest man, he tests their capacity for truth. And, of course, at the novel's end he escapes: such mercury cannot be caught, as though to show that our moral judgements are not adequate to human variety. John Silver remains a triumph.

There has been much discussion down the years of the supposed model for the island itself. R.L.S. admitted to Colvin in 1884 that the book "came out" of Charles Kingsley's *At Last,* from which he had filched the Dead Man's Chest, and from a *History of Notorious Pirates* (probably the volume he had requested from Henley in August 1881). Kingsley's island has been identified as Dead Chest Island, off Puerto Rico; others have claimed an island off Cuba, and Unst in the Shetland Islands. The Pacific coast at Monterey had an influence. Stevenson himself offered no clues, because he had none.

All this, of course, is nothing beside the technical achievement of the book's construction: there is no more spare flesh on *Treasure Island* than there was on its author. Its plot grows like a crystal. The "succession of defeats" Louis had endured with fiction ended when he was thirty-one, suddenly and completely.

He continued to sicken. Pressed by the twin problems of health and money, he hatched a bizarre scheme to have himself made professor of history and constitutional law at Edinburgh University. The job brought £250 a year and the only lectures required were in summer. He could earn a living and still live abroad in the winter.

Whatever possessed him possessed his father. Both seemed to believe that Louis, a failed student with a near-spurious claim to the title advocate, could be a plausible candidate for the post. More than a touch of middle-class arrogance entered into the affair: this was no lad o'pairts trying to get ahead by his own efforts. Father and son began to exploit their connections; testimonials were procured from London and Scotland, from professors, ministers, and men of letters. The university was undeceived. In the election held to guide the administration, Louis received nine votes, the winner eighty-two. He was back in Davos, living in the rented

Châlet am Stein and playing war games with Lloyd, when he heard the news.

They had again travelled via London, stopping at Weybridge to visit George Meredith, whom Louis had met previously. The older writer (1828–1909), fascinated by human relations and natural selection, was a constant source of encouragement to the young Scot, even if his influence on Stevenson's style was hardly beneficial. When Meredith published *The Egoist* in 1879, R.L.S. thought he saw a portrait of himself in the character of Sir Willoughby Patterne. "This is too bad of you," he told Meredith, "Willoughby is me!" The author replied: "No, my dear fellow, he is all of us."

In his day Meredith was thought one of the greatest of English novelists. But his style, rhetorical, limpid, and overwrought, was not what helped to make R.L.S. in his maturity. In Weybridge, however, Stevenson added more chapters to "The Sea Cook," but by the time it had begun to appear in *Young Folks*, he had managed to finish perhaps only nineteen chapters. When the early sections were at proof stage, Henderson suggested, and Louis agreed, that the title be changed to *Treasure Island*.

Rosaline Masson, in a 1920s biography of Stevenson, called this period "a record year for bad health and good work." It is an apt opposition; both Fanny and Louis became ill at Davos. For her, a gallstone was diagnosed. She was obliged to go to Berne to seek treatment and did not fully recover until February. Louis, meanwhile, resumed his friendship with John Addington Symonds, the neighbour with whom he took long walks. Symonds was the sort of comsumptive who had decided to settle permanently at Davos, and who was then working on his *History of the Italian Renaissance*. Louis found the man more interesting than his work.

His own was proceeding well, for the most part. The remainder of *Treasure Island* had flowed "like small talk" and was finished in November. Early in 1882 he had reworked his Silverado journals and was carrying out preparatory work on a projected biography of Hazlitt. His early enthusiasm for the latter project waned inexorably as he discovered that his literary hero had been an unappealing man; no manuscript survives. Work was also going ahead on the essays contained in *Talk and Talkers*, for which Symonds became a reluctant Opalstein. Louis had been busy, too, on *Prince Otto*, the historical novel about which it is impossible to say too little. But *The Silverado Squatters* proved as significant, in its way, as *Treasure Island*. It has an immediacy, and a sense of character, that *Otto* lacked utterly. The novel proved one thing about his talent; the nonfiction something something wholly, distinctively, other.

In the midst of all this, he and Lloyd were having almost as much fun with the boy's toy printing press—the "Davos Press"—as Louis was having with its adult equivalents. The press had been procured during their previous stay as a weapon against boredom (and if Louis was bored with Switzerland, one can only imagine how the boy felt), but in the winter of 1881–82, it went into full production. Louis wrote the verses and designed and made woodcuts to accompany them; Lloyd printed and contributed some prose of his own. As an adult Osbourne recalled:

> I had a small printing press, and used to earn a little money by printing the weekly concert programmes and other trifling commissions; and growing ambitious, I became a publisher. My first venture was *Black Canyon, or Life in the Far West*, a tiny booklet of eight pages, and both the spelling and the matter were entirely original; my second was *Not I, and Other Poems by R. L. Stevenson*, price sixpence. How thunderstruck we should have been to know that forty years afterwards these were to figure in imposing catalogues as STEVENSONIANA, EXCESSIVELY RARE, DAVOS PRESS, and to be priced at sixty or seventy guineas apiece!

R.L.S. wrote to Gosse of *Black Canyon,* priced sixpence: "I would send you the book but I declare I'm ruined. I got a penny a cut, and a halfpenny a set of verses from the flint-hearted publisher, and only one specimen cow, as I'm a sinner."

By the spring of 1882 Stevenson's health had improved sufficiently for him to leave Switzerland, much to his relief. Dr. Ruedi had said he could live in the South of France but the family went first to London, then Edinburgh, where an anecdote has him paying a farewell visit to Swanston Cottage, "standing as if in a dream . . . taking his last long look at the Hills of Home." As usual, Thomas had rented a house for the summer, but even in fine weather the Scottish countryside, first at Stobo Manse near Peebles, then at Kingussie, was enough to drive Louis southward after he began to haemorrhage once more. *Familiar Studies of Men and Books*, containing nine of his essays, had appeared in March; in August the

New Arabian Nights had a moderate success. In Scotland he had begun *The Treasure of Franchard*, using memories of Grez. But he had to get away.

Fanny, suffering the aftereffects of Davos, was still too ill to go with him. Accompanied by Bob Stevenson (newly married and employed but still footloose), Louis set off for France without her: it must have seemed like old times. As though as a warning against such temerity, he had no sooner reached Montpellier than he suffered an appalling hemorrhage, and Fanny rushed to meet him at Marseilles.

That his ill health should have returned so quickly did not deter Louis. He and Fanny began house hunting. They found a villa, the Campagne Defli, just outside the town at St. Marcel, in the dry Midi uplands, but the expected rejuvenation did not take place. He continued to haemorrhage. The place seemed a paradise at first, large and comfortable, but they lasted only from October until Christmas: Louis, after all his travelling, had expected to stay for years.

Though he did not yet know it, these were his last years in Europe. An outbreak of fever drove him to Nice while Fanny stayed behind to pack up. After four days she had not heard from him and was blithely informed by the police that he was probably dead. When she found Louis in Nice, her first letter to him had only just arrived.

Escaping from the Campagne Defli lease, they took at Hyères a tiny chalet designed for the Paris exhibition of 1878 and called la Solitude. Within a month Colvin had arrived to visit, and a French girl, Valentine Roch, had been engaged to lift some of the burden of housekeeping from Fanny. Louis was at work on *A Child's Garden of Verses*, and in May the hundred pounds he had been promised for *Treasure Island* arrived, lifting his spirits high. He began to believe that he might just be able to support himself, even if the constant house hunting at St. Marcel and Hyères had cost him more than he could afford.

Still the illnesses went on: an onslaught worse than anything Louis had suffered. Years later he told Colvin he had only been happy once and that was at Hyères. Yet there he coughed blood and suffered from sciatica and Egyptian ophthalmia while trying to complete *Prince Otto* and writing the poems for *A Child's Garden of Verses*. Here, too, while Louis was laid up, Fanny was instructed to go for a walk each day and return with a story to tell him. The result was *The Dynamiters*.

His efforts in these circumstances were remarkable, whatever one thinks of his legend. If R.L.S. clung to life, he also clung to his writing, as though it were a link to life. Without it, one feels, he would have succumbed. At la Solitude he completed *Prince Otto*, and worked on the poems that were to become *A Child's Garden of Verses*.

Otto is the most irritating of Stevenson's books, yet it was one he worked harder on than any save *Weir of Hermiston*. Some chapters were rewritten five times; for one he produced eight versions and Fanny a ninth. Yet it was a complete failure, in stark contrast to *Treasure Island*, even if George Bernard Shaw, for reasons best known to himself, thought it one of the best pieces of literature produced in a decade (according to his biographer, Michael Holroyd). Through *Otto*, R.L.S. learned that he could not, and should not, try to force his gift; that the easy style of *Treasure Island* was more valuable than the overwrought prose of a bizarre fairytale-cum-romance set in a mythical German state. Most authors learn the perils of overrevision; R.L.S. learned the hard way. Under the pernicious artistic influence of George Meredith, Louis became capable of writing tosh:

> That great Baron Gondremark, the excellent politician, remained for some little time upon his knees in a frame of mind which perhaps we are allowed to pity. His vanity, within his iron bosom, bled and raved. If he could have blotted all, if he could have withdrawn part, if he had not called her bride—with a roaring in his ears, he thus regretfully reviewed his declaration.

Nevertheless, observing Stevenson produce a bad book is somehow more revealing than observing him create a great one. Oddly, he knew the novel was flawed even as he composed it. In April of 1883 he wrote to Henley that "I have no idea whether or not *Otto* will be good. It is all pitched pretty high and stilted . . . I sometimes feel very weary; but the thing travels—and I like it when I am at it." The next month he was admitting that "some parts are false, and much of the rest is thin . . ."

It was as though he had abandoned his early habit of giving up on worthless books and was determined to press on no matter what. He had succeeded with books others thought slight and failed with things thought serious. Now he seemed determined to raise his style to heights of artistry, even if the effort was harmful to his art. He told Will Low that the book was "intended to stand firm upon a base of philosophy—or morals—as you please. It has been long gestated and is wrought with care." When it was published in 1885, the contrast with *Treasure Island* became clear. The critics were respectful but lukewarm.

Almost simultaneously, he began work on *The Black Arrow*, a decent enough tale intended as a serial for *Young Folks*—again under the pseudonym "Captain George North"—which Stevenson ruined by his inability to resist absurd medievalisms. Judging by their letters to the magazine, the young folks themselves seem to have liked it better than *Treasure Island*.

It has qualities, though Fanny hated it and Stevenson did not like it much. For one thing the novel manages to take the Middle Ages as its backdrop without, as was then customary, falling into the strong arms of Walter Scott. Several historians have, meanwhile, defended its plausibility. It has a moral content more sophisticated than some of its young readers might have expected, and the character of Gloucester is well done. But it is carelessly written (an interesting contrast with *Otto*'s composition) and was clearly intended as a potboiler. Towards the end of the writing, Louis himself had forgotten what had happened to several characters, and a proofreader had to remind him, when he sent off the last instalment, that he had neglected to account for the fourth black arrow. Later, when it was to be serialised in the United States, he was happy enough for the first five chapters to be dropped.

In the spring of 1883 Stevenson and Fanny went inland to Vichy, which Louis disliked, then to Clermont-Ferrand, then to the spa at Royat with its "more or less arsenical" waters, as Fanny called them, where R.L.S. worked on *The Black Arrow*.

All of her efforts were now directed at making Louis as safe from affliction as was possible. The battle never ceased, and it made a ruthless obsessive of Mrs. Stevenson. Even when her instincts were sound—guessing that colds are infectious long before medical science agreed, for example—she infuriated and humiliated unsuspecting visitors by preventing them from seeing Louis and making no apology for it. She was prepared to try anything, no matter how unproven, if it might help her husband. Fanny, as we know, did not cope well with emotional pressure, and the sufferings of her husband, not to mention the sheer horror of the haemorrhages soaking clothes and sheets, took their toll. Equally, however, there is a suspicion that she was eager to make herself indispensable. Louis belonged to her alone, and it gave her a kind of proprietorial satisfaction to eject competitors.

The hardest blow for R.L.S. came in September of 1883, with the news that James Walter Ferrier had died. The brilliant son of the philosophy professor, the charmer who had first invited Louis to join the college magazine team, had reaped the whirlwind of his own careless philosophy and succumbed to drink and tuberculosis. There had been no saving him from either affliction. Just before he died, he had suffered from delirium tremens and was the despair of his family.

Ferrier was, Louis admitted, the first friend he had lost. He bitterly regretted that he could not attend the funeral and found significance in the fact that death was no longer his personal opponent; its "trade winds" blew around all. Ferrier, he knew, was probably better off dead. Nevertheless, Louis could still feel his presence, and wrote to Henley:

Thinking over this wrecked and still brave life, I grow to think of him more and more with honour. Few have made such a plunge; but few, having lost health, hope and pride, would have made so fine a stand . . .

It was Stevenson's own legend writ plain: a fine, heroic stand in the face of the odds. To live as he had chosen to live, and as the dazed, drunken Ferrier pretended to live, took courage. To cast Edinburgh aside took courage; to live by one's beliefs took courage; to face death took every ounce of courage. R.L.S. understood grief—he was gentle and consoling when Fanny and Mrs. Sitwell lost their sons—but he clung tighter to his own invincible optimism when optimism seemed the least appropriate reaction. There are times when R.L.S.'s valour can seem the worst sort of giddy romance. His father, too, was failing, and irritated Louis with his deepening depressions. One letter to Thomas and Maggie is harsh beneath its playful surface: "Tell him [Thomas] that I give him up. I don't want no such parent . . . Up, Dullard! It is better service to enjoy a novel than to mump." He who could be so eloquent talking of sickness, death, and comrades fallen would have no truck with an old man who chose to "mump."

It was, for all that, a momentous season, with both *The Silverado Squatters* and *Treasure Island* going through the presses. By December, Louis was reporting an income for 1883 of £465.0.6d; a more-than-honourable achievement if his bills had not been so high and if he or Fanny or both had possessed any skill with money. But still his illnesses were as prolific as his imagination.

In January 1884, Baxter and Henley came to Hyères. The tiny house was overcrowded, and Louis took off with them to Nice. The trio had hardly departed when Stevenson was stricken with lung trouble and a kidney infection. So close was he to heaven's door that Bob Stevenson was summoned to be the man who would watch him die. Again, R.L.S. barely survived. He recovered for a while, and indeed seemed like his old self, but by the spring ailments came marching one after another into the tiny house: haemorrhages, sciatica, ophthalmia that made him "too blind to read." In May, he bled as he had never bled. Unable to speak, he pencilled a note for Fanny: "Don't be frightened—if this is death, it is an easy one." This from the house where he was happiest, or so he said. And after that, more images of Louis undefeated: lying in bed with his right hand strapped to his side (supposedly to prevent another haemorrhage) while with his left he composes lines for the *Child's Garden;* or lying near blind, without speech, and writing

> *Under the wide and starry sky*
> *Dig the grave and let me lie.*
> *Glad did I live and gladly die,*
> *And I laid me down with a will.*
>
> *This be the verse you grave for me:*
> *Here he lies where he longed to be;*
> *Home is the sailor, home from sea,*
> *And the hunter home from the hill.*

A London doctor despatched by Baxter and Henley offered the opinion that if Louis could be kept alive until he was forty, he would live to ninety, but life before forty would of necessity be the life of an invalid. His eating, drinking, laughing, talking, writing, and—in essence—living were to be controlled if he was to have a fighting chance. Much against his will, R.L.S. was induced to leave Hyères and return to Royat, and from there by stages to England. After la Solitude, in which he had been so happy, so sick, so hardworking, Stevenson found himself in Bournemouth, where Lloyd was at school and where he was to spend his last three years in Europe.

11 *1884–1885*

For nearly ten years my health had been declining; and for some while before I set forth upon my voyage, I believed I was come to the afterpiece of life, and had only the nurse and undertaker to expect.

"AN ISLAND LANDFALL"

Once lodged in Fanny's head, an idea was hard to shift. Having seen a matinee of *Deacon Brodie* in London, she convinced herself that plays were the easiest route to fame, fortune, and security. Henley and Louis had launched into the play in a fit of high spirits at Swanston in 1878; its very modest success in the capital with W.E.'s brother in the title role convinced Fanny that more should be produced. Henley, also keen to attach himself to Louis for all that he had become an important literary man in his own right, was at the outset her partner in this enterprise. It was a considerable waste of the time and precious energy of the man she lived to protect.

Louis was not exactly unemployed, after all. In the five years from his first book, *An Inland Voyage*, in 1878, he published eight volumes and worked on many other projects. The last things he needed were *Beau Austin* or the execrable *Admiral Guinea*, but these, finished by October, were his only publications for 1884.

It was Fanny and Henley at their worst. For two people so much at odds they had a good deal in common beyond, at the last, enmity. Strong-willed yet lacking self-esteem, pretending to art yet bereft of real talent (though both had judgement, another thing entirely), bombastic yet deeply insecure, they needed Louis, his name and his ability, to keep their scheme afloat. Such, revealingly, was their attitude to him that they would not take no for an answer. He, often quick to anger, was more tolerant than was good for him. In Bournemouth, Fanny immersed herself in *Admiral Guinea*; later she would cajole R.L.S. into a collaboration on *The Hanging Judge*.

Henley, meanwhile, was all for it, as he was for anything that might inflate his own reputation: he seems, here as elsewhere, a clod of a man. Together his friend and his wife, supposedly so keen on his well-being, dragged R.L.S. into the noisy, argumentative, strenuous business of collaborative playwriting. Both insisted they knew what was right for him. Working alone, however arduous, at least afforded Louis solitude. The business of the plays tested his natural gregariousness to the limit. Lloyd, contradicting his mother, described it thus in a preface:

> R.L.S. was no longer to plod along as he had been doing; Henley was to abandon his grinding and illpaid editorship; together they would combine to write plays—marvellous plays that would run for hundreds of nights and bring in thousands of pounds; plays that would revive the perishing drama, now hopelessly given over to imbeciles, who kept yachts and mistresses on money filched from the public; plays that would be billed on all the hoardings with the electrifying words: 'By Robert Louis Stevenson and William Ernest Henley.'
>
> R.L.S. entered enthusiastically into this collaboration, though, with his underlying Scottish caution, I doubt if he allowed himself to be wholly transported into Henley's fairyland. But he was stirred, nevertheless; shared to some degree, though reservedly, those ardent day-dreams of wealth; worked at the plays with extraordinary gusto and industry . . . disillusionment was slow in coming . . . The gorgeous dream was not so easily wafted away . . . Stevenson, I think, came soonest out of the spell . . . His ardour certainly declined; in the interval of Henley's absences he very gladly returned to his own work, and had, as a playwright, to be resuscitated by his unshaken collaborator, who was as confident and eager as ever.
>
> R.L.S. lost not only the last flicker of his youth in 'Wensleydale,' but I believe also any conviction that he might become a popular dramatist.

What to say of the dramas? The interested reader can at least take comfort from the fact that a biographer feels a duty to read them; no one else should. They are perhaps the least Stevensonian of the works to which

Louis's name is attached, and he produced some notably bad work on occasion. Their authors' ignorance of the stage is obvious; the dialogue is almost unrelievedly risible; the plots are hackneyed (Shakespeare stole plots,
why not . . .). *Brodie* is the worst sort of melodramatic amateur psychology; *Macaire* is Louis's love for French wit gone haywire; *Guinea* says
something about slavery, but not much. All swarm with dull prose, as
though woodworm had been loose on the rickety structure of Victorian
drama. Even R.L.S. called the team's efforts "Skeltery," in mock homage
to the model theatre that had fascinated him as a child. Later he maintained he had done it all for Henley's sake. He did not mention Fanny,
who seemed to have suffered more than most from the delusion common
to the spouses of the famous that a sexual and emotional affinity implies
artistic equality. In any case, a brief passage from Act III of *Macaire*, the
fourth play to be written, illustrates something of the problem:

> DUMONT, By the way, very remarkable thing: I found that
> key.
> MACAIRE, No!
> BERTRAND, O!
> DUMONT, Perhaps a still more remarkable thing: it was my
> key that had the twisted handle.
> MACAIRE, I told you so.
> DUMONT, Now, what we have to do is to get the cash-
> box, Hallo! what's that you're sitting on?
> BERTRAND, Nothing.
> MACAIRE, The table! I beg your pardon.
> DUMONT, Why, it's my cash-box!
> MACAIRE, So it is!
> DUMONT. It's very singular.
> MACAIRE. Diabolishly singular.

The "diabolishly singular" experiment was a disaster, a fiasco, and an
embarrassment. In March, Louis was writing to W.E.: ". . . I have come
unhesitatingly to the opinion that the stage is only a lottery . . ." Fanny,
the prime mover, hated having to face the facts. She blamed Henley, but
it did not end there. He, in turn, blamed her for breaking up the partner-

ship. Eager to coax Louis towards the footlights, his wife and his friend had tried to get along: it was a sham. Henley thought this mere woman an impediment to the creative process; Fanny concluded that the presence of the volcanic W.E. was killing her husband. A farce, in the end, and a risky one.

Later, in the autumn of 1885, Louis was to travel to Dorchester to see Thomas Hardy (who was merely polite about R.L.S.) only to collapse in delirium in a hotel at Exeter. The purpose of this suicidal mission? To seek Hardy's permission for a dramatisation of *The Mayor of Casterbridge.* The journey, like the whole episode of the plays, is somehow emblematic of the life Stevenson led at the house he called Skerryvore. Trivial matters gained vast importance; real work was done in the margins of a life punctuated by haemorrhages, social calls, crackpot schemes, and rows.

Fanny and Louis had gone first to Richmond, to consult doctors. Given a guardedly optimistic prognosis, they took lodgings on the West Cliff at Bournemouth. Then, in November, they rented Bonallie Towers, a furnished house among healthful pine trees in Branksome Park.

Louis survived the winter in reasonable shape. During the first two months he and Henley devoted themselves to their risible plays. Then, as though collaboration was some new drug, he worked on *New Arabian Nights* in harness with Fanny. At the end of October, John Singer Sargent arrived to paint the first of two portraits of Louis.

Sargent had been commissioned by Mr. and Mrs. Charles Fairchild, of Boston, Massachusetts, two rich fans of the unusual young writer. Louis thought the painter charming, but his first portrait, done late in 1884, was deemed a failure and a second attempt called for, by Fanny in particular. The better known of the two pictures, painted in the summer of 1885, is also the best image of Louis in motion: he seems like a long streak caught on the canvas, with Fanny relegated to a half figure dressed in a kind of sari on one side while her husband chatters and smokes and paces. Stevenson is astoundingly, terrifyingly thin, and Fanny did not much care for the picture. "I am but a cipher under the shadow," she told Sargent, revealing everything about her view of her marriage.

In November, Louis was commissioned by the *Pall Mall Gazette* to write a Christmas story. Unable to carry out the work—and therefore refusing to take the full forty pounds proposed—he offered the periodical "The Body Snatcher," a turgid, overcooked piece he had put together at Pitlochry in 1881, which was published without fuss, even if it was hardly a seasonal item. Henley thought R.L.S. foolish for being so pious about money. Louis replied with vigour: ". . . I will not take the £40. I took that as a fair price for my best work . . . I was not able to produce my best; and I will be damned if I steal with my eyes open." A pity he did not take the same line over the plays.

Thomas Stevenson, sixty-six and ageing fast, sinking into depressions and seeming to wander mentally, was desperate for his son to remain in Britain. He offered to buy a house for Fanny—a "wedding present"—and gave five hundred pounds to have it furnished. R.L.S. seems to have choked back his recurring complaints that he was still not paying his own way, while Fanny, so eager for her own household, accepted without a second thought. Or as she put it:

> . . . not without trepidation, at least on my part, we resolved to remain in-
> definitely in Bournemouth. As a reward for my acquiescence in this plan,
> and, I imagine, in the hope of making our stay more certainly permanent,
> my father-in-law presented me with a charming little house that we named
> Skerryvore.

The villa was on the Westbourne cliffs and called originally, with no originality, Sea View. Louis renamed it Skerryvore when they moved in at Easter, in memory of one of his family's greatest engineering achieve-ments. A ship's bell was placed in the garden.

In Samoa, Stevenson never spoke of the place. It was as though he had expunged the memory of imprisonment, despite having written some of his most famous works while living—like a "weevil in a biscuit"—at the house. He and Fanny had at first intended to stay in Bournemouth only a few weeks before returning to France, but were, in her version, pre-vailed upon by old Tom Stevenson to stay in Britain. That may have been one explanation: Bournemouth was also favoured by consumptives, and there had been a cholera outbreak at Hyères. Lloyd was also being edu-cated in the area and there were plans for him to go to Edinburgh Uni-versity to study science (the precedent of R.L.S. notwithstanding).

Fanny loved the house, in any case, calling it her "lovely luxurious little nest." After the years of upheaval it was understandable that she should want a place of her own where the door could be closed, Louis could be nursed, and she could begin to live like a woman of quality. She liked the constant stream of visitors less. Louis was making some money, but still not enough. His health was so poor that even France seemed to have lost its curative powers. Neither of them could face Davos again.

Yet it was as if Fanny had finally agreed with Colvin, Gosse, and Henley in seeking to establish a "quiet life" in England for her husband, by which he could become a proper man of letters. *Treasure Island* had given him a name among the critics, and even Henry James, with whom R.L.S. had a relationship of mutual respect and admiration dating back to 1879, found much to praise in it. Others were delighted that their friend and protégé was now so accessible. "Skerryvore," said Lloyd Osbourne,

> was an unusually attractive suburban house, set in an acre and a half of ground, and its previous owner—a retired naval captain—had been at no little expense to improve and add to it. Somehow it was so typical of an old sailor; it was so trim, so well-arranged, so much thought had been given to its many conveniences . . . The wanderers were now anchored; over their heads was their own roof-tree: they paid rates and taxes, and were called on by the vicar. Stevenson, in the word he hated most of all, had become the 'burgess' of his former jeers. Respectability, dullness, and similar villas encompassed him for miles in every direction.
>
> In his heart I doubt if he really ever liked 'Skerryvore'; he spoke of it with no regret; left it with no apparent pang. The Victorianism it exemplified was jarring to every feeling he possessed, though with his habitual philosophy he not only endured it, but even persuaded himself that he liked it.

Lloyd, devious though he could be, knew better than most. Fanny's protectiveness of Stevenson had by this time become an obsessive defence of her own status as wife, muse, manager, collaborator, and confidante. She liked Louis's friends less and less, and felt less and less compunction about saying so. Fanny may have loved Skerryvore, but for R.L.S., according to Lloyd, "those years . . . were gray indeed." He put it down to illness—"never was he so spectral, so emaciated, so unkempt and tragic a figure"—a thought which makes Fanny's obsession with the plays even less forgivable. Her son wrote of Stevenson that:

> There could be no pretence that he was not an invalid and a very sick man. He had horrifying haemorrhages; long spells when he was doomed to lie motionless on his bed lest the slightest movement should re-start the flow; when he would speak in whispers, and one sat beside him and tried to be entertaining—in the room he was only likely to leave in his coffin.
>
> How, thus handicapped, he wrote his books is one of the marvels of literature . . .

Fanny found reason for pretence. There is no escaping the thought that the plays promised her financial security should this "very sick man" succumb. True, the strain of caring for him was immense and her future without him unthinkable. But she had strange ideas about how best to keep him alive. Louis, for his part, wrote some whimsical verse to mark his own transformation into a man of property, with his coach house, lawn, pigeon house, shrubbery, drive, and kitchen garden:

> My house, I say. But hark to the sunny doves
> That make my roof the arena of their loves,
> That gyre about the gable all day long
> And fill the chimmneys with their murmurous song;
> Our house, they say; and mine, the cat declares,
> And spreads his golden fleece upon the chairs;
> And mine the dog, and rises stiff with wrath
> If any alien foot profane the path.

He was, he told Colvin, a "beastly householder," the sort on whom the vicar called. Yet still he worked, caught in a vice of sickness. Visitors came and went: Colvin, Henley, Bob and his sister Katharine, Shelley's now elderly son Percy, Miss Adelaide Boodle (a local who was more observant than she was wise, and left an account of life at Skerryvore), Sir Henry Taylor, late of the Foreign Office, and his wife. It was absurd, and Fanny, lover of "society" that she was, did not always like it. She was often rude to people she believed were tiring R.L.S.: visitors who had travelled far to see the writer sometimes found the door barred by the fierce little American woman. One visitor was different.

Louis and Henry James had thought little of one another at their first meeting. James judged *An Inland Voyage* charming but its author an inoffensive poseur. Louis, in turn, was far from awed by the Jamesian mode. In the autumn of 1884, however, the American had contributed a combative "manifesto" on fiction to *Longman's Magazine*. It praised *Treasure Island* but roused Louis's critical faculties. James had talked about the "art of fiction." Stevenson, in a reply entitled "A Humble Remonstrance," insisted on "the art of narrative." It was an acutely made distinction. The novel, he said, "is not a transcript of life . . . but a simplication of some side or point of life . . ."

It was a crucial debate for both men. In France, not many years before, Émile Zola (whom James had met and for whom Louis eventually arrived at a grudging respect) had scandalised the public with his "naturalism." But for Zola and his school the battle was both offensive and defensive: all serious practitioners were involved. One night at the novelist's house at Médan, to the west of Paris, some of the ladies present were talking about Prosper Mérimée.* "What a delightful story-teller!" said one. Joris-Karl Huysmans, a Zola disciple, was scornful: "A story-teller is a gentleman who, not knowing how to write, pretentiously recites twaddle." Huysmans himself old did not remain loyal to "ultrarealism" for long—an infatuation with devil worship saw to that—but by this account he might have been taking a swipe at the likes of Louis. R.L.S. could counterpunch.

James had been agitated by sentiments similar to Huysmans's in a lecture given by Walter Besant (author of numerous novels in partnership with James Rice and barely remembered today for his own *All Sorts and Conditions of Men*) in September of 1884. Besant had spoken up for the idea of a true-to-experience, "realistic" novel while trying to raise fiction to the status of the other arts. Rhetoric aside, he seemed to be talking about little more than accurate, if artistic, reporting.

James had replied that experience is an altogether more subtle thing than the enumerated facts; he spoke of sensibility, consciousness, and atmosphere. Novelists should not aim at reality, he argued, but at "the air of reality," if only because a novel is not, by definition, reality. It should

*Schom, A.: *Émile Zola* (London, 1987); p. 73. The anecdote is Maupassant's.

be an illusion, but a truthful one competing with life. One might have expected R.L.S. to agree. His own response was illuminating of his attitude to his craft and marked him out as a profound student of his art.

"Mr James," he wrote, was "the very type of deliberate artist, Mr Besant the impersonation of good nature."

> That such doctors should differ will excite no great surprise; but one point in which they seem to agree fills me, I confess, with wonder. For they are both content to talk about the 'art of fiction'; and Mr Besant . . . goes on to oppose this so-called 'art of fiction' to the 'art of poetry.'

"Fiction," as a definition, was both "too ample and too scanty." Homer, Wordsworth, Phidias, Hogarth, and Salvini (an acclaimed Italian actor of the period, noted for his Othello) all dealt in fiction. What James and Besant were talking about, whether they knew it or not, was the art of narrative. It was a crucial, characteristic argument. R.L.S., specific, exacting, narrowing the focus to get at the guts of the matter at hand, revealed as much about himself as he did about storytelling.

Presumably what Besant really meant was "the art of *fictitious* narrative *in prose.*" But why "in prose"? *"The Odyssey,"* said Louis, "appears to me the best of romances . . ." Chaucer contained "more of the matter and art of the modern English novel than the whole treasury of Mr Mudie." The choice of prose was stylistic, it did not make for a difference to the *fiction* of *The Pilgrim's Progress* crucial enough to distinguish it from *The Faery Queen*:

> A narrative called *Paradise Lost* was written in English verse by one John Milton; what was it then? It was next translated by Chateaubriand into French prose; and what was it then? Lastly, the French translation was, by some inspired compatriot of George Gilfillan (and of mine) turned bodily into an English novel; and, in the name of clearness, what was it then?

And why *fictitious*? "Boswell's *Life of Johnson* (a work of cunning and inimitable art) owes it success to the same technical manoeuvres as (let us say) *Tom Jones* . . ." James, meantime, had talked of the "sanctity of truth to the novelist" and of it competing with life. No art can. R.L.S. said:

"Life goes before us, infinite in complication . . ." Literature, so far as it imitates at all,

> . . . imitates not life but speech; not the facts of human destiny, but the emphasis and the suppressions with which the human actor tells of them. The real art that dealt with life directly was that of the first men who told their stories round the savage camp fire. Our art is occupied, and bound to be occupied, not so much in making stories true as in making them typical . . . Life is monstrous, infinite, illogical, abrupt and poignant; a work of art, in comparison is neat, finite, self-contained, rational, flowing and emasculate . . . A proposition of geometry does not compete with life; and a proposition of geometry is a fair and luminous parallel for a work of art. Both are reasonable, both untrue to the crude fact; both inhere in nature, neither represents it.

Louis was intervening in a fundamental debate and making a fundamental point. His reference to stories first told "round the savage camp fire" points to a conception of narrative that has helped his own works to endure long after Besant's. He did not outdo James, did not seek to, but after this episode the American understood what the Scotsman was about. He accepted and respected it, and wrote Louis a courteous letter to that effect. Henceforth, the two responded to one another like members of a guild, united in their belief in the essential purpose of good prose. James thought it "a luxury" to encounter someone "who *does* write . . ." He thanked R.L.S. for his article, and a friendship was formed. When James took his ailing sister to Bournemouth, it was only natural that he should call on the writer whom he admired so much. Soon he had his own special chair at Skerryvore, one of the pieces from Heriot Row, and his friendship became one of the most valuable of Louis's life. James even managed, with that delicacy for which he was famous, to keep Fanny on side: the Master indeed. Besides, they were two Americans abroad.

Adelaide Boodle was one of the few people who wrote about Stevenson who admired Fanny almost as much as she admired R.L.S. She was allowed into Skerryvore one day almost by accident, Valentine the maid having misunderstood the instruction that the couple were not at home. Miss Boodle arrived with her mother and caught Louis and Fanny un-

awares: he is his smoking jacket, she in a painter's apron, both still un-
packing their possessions. Once through the door, however, Adelaide was
not to be dislodged.

The Stevensons liked her, and she called frequently, developing an account of their domestic life that is both (unintentionally) amusing and invaluable. "There never was, and there never will be, another place like
Skerryvore," she wrote. Alone among the villas that had "laid waste all the
poetry of Bournemouth," the "little place took one's heart by storm."

Miss Boodle's heart had already been conquered, of course, by the time
she came to call. Nevertheless, Graham Balfour for one attested that Adelaide caught the tone and style of Fanny and *"Lou-us"* (as his wife pronounced it); she admitted that they had terrible rows; and confessed to
noticing the age difference between R.L.S. and his wife. She tried to
teach Louis the piano and ran errands for Fanny. Mostly, however, she
drank in the conversation of the sublime R.L.S.

Louis had been asked to give a course for young writers at the British
Museum (it never came off) and used Adelaide, who had her own ambitions in that direction, as a sounding board. She was enthralled. But Miss
Boodle's admiration for Fanny meant that she saw some of the darkness
at Skerryvore: the illness, the deteriorating relationship with Henley, the
occasional discord between husband and wife.

Adelaide thought Fanny heroic; others have been less kind. Most of
Stevenson's friends resented her and several of his biographers (this one
included) have found her hard to like. Yet he lived with her for fifteen
years, never straying, taking her part against all comers, even when she
was unhinged (as she was on Samoa) or merely in the wrong. For him it
was a great romantic love. It is less easy to say what it was for her.

Fanny thought he could die at any time and probably did not even
hope to have Louis for as many years as she did. They had no children.
Did the matter ever arise? Some have argued that neither Louis nor Fanny
sought parenthood, but that makes no sense set alongside Stevenson's enthusiasm for the family he inherited from Sam Osbourne, or at least the
idea of family. His relationship with Belle was tense until the last years at
Vailima, yet when she showed reluctance for the South Seas adventure he
almost begged her to join his tribe, saying that he wanted *family* around

him. It was as if he sought to become another Stevenson patriarch. Why no children of his own?

He was ill, of course, but not impotent: there were to be a couple of pregnancy "scares." Fanny was a little too old for another attempt at motherhood, of course, but not impossibly so. Their life was not ideal, of course, but Lloyd Osbourne did reasonably well as a child. The decision to avoid parenthood even after they were settled casts light on life at Skerryvore. There seemed always to be an underlying tension: bohemian bliss was gone, as Lloyd Osbourne suggested, and Louis was outgrowing the need for a mother figure. On Fanny's part the plays, the house itself, the undeclared war with her husband's friends, and her growing ambitions to write, all showed how much willpower the "cipher" could exert in her efforts to make the marriage a partnership of equals.

To say so misses all of her good qualities, her bravery in particular. But the nurse can resent the patient on whom all attention is lavished. Living only to care for Louis, Fanny was becoming greedy for attention herself.

12 *1885–1886*

*I think I see you, moving there by plain daylight, beholding with your nat-
ural eyes those places that have now become for your companion a part of the
scenery of dreams. How, in the intervals of present business, the past must
echo in your memory!*

KIDNAPPED: DEDICATION TO CHARLES BAXTER

D eath haunted Skerryvore, as James was well aware from his first
visit. Old Thomas was weak and wandering; his son was often at
death's door; in June of 1885 Fleeming Jenkin died; and towards the end
of the year Fanny's friend Virgil Williams passed away. The appearance of
the *The Strange Case of Dr. Jekyll and Mr. Hyde* in such an atmosphere
seems oddly apt. Lloyd Osbourne recalled its creation:

> One day he came down to luncheon in a very preoccupied frame of mind;
> hurried through his meal—an unheard-of thing for him to—and on leav-
> ing said he was working with extraordinary success on a new story that had
> come to him in a dream, and that he was not to be interrupted or dis-
> turbed even if the house caught fire.
>
> For three days a sort of hush descended on 'Skerryvore'; we all went
> about, servants and everybody, in a tiptoeing silence: passing Stevenson's
> door I would see him sitting up in bed, filling page after page, and appar-
> ently never pausing for a moment. At the end of three days the mysterious
> task was finished . . .

Fanny, in a note written for the same volume, gave her account of the
story's genesis. Henley had come to stay when the Stevensons first arrived

in Bournemouth "for the purpose of writing plays with my husband" (the project, by this account, was all Henley's doing). *Brodie* had been "no more than a *succès d'estimé*," she wrote, but R.L.S.'s friend had returned to visit them at Skerryvore with hopes of continuing the collaboration.

A link with the quintessential dual personality thus established, she recalled a bookcase and chest of drawers in Louis's Heriot Row nursery which the daytime cabinetmaker William Brodie (who was hanged for burglary in 1788) was reputed to have made. Cummy, "with her vivid Scotch imagination," had, Fanny said, told "her nursling" many romances about these articles of furniture and their creator. Years later, Louis had been impressed by a "French scientific journal on subconsciousness." That, Brodie, the play, "Markheim," a haemorrhage, and a "hectic fever" were the elements, she said, of a dream of *Jekyll and Hyde*. For good measure, she suggested that writing plays "in the almost overwhelming society of Mr Henley" had so exhausted Louis that he slept badly and dreamt well.

Plainly, the episode of the plays still rankled with Fanny even years later. By her account R.L.S. "had no particular liking for dramatic composition . . ."

> but Mr Henley possessed an extraordinary enthusiasm. I even found myself unwittingly drawn into the whirlpool. I remember being promised a ruby bracelet to be bought from the proceeds of the first performance, for a suggestion for *Admiral Guinea*.

This was Fanny at her most disingenuous. If she, usually so fiercely protective, had truly believed that Henley's "overwhelming society" was exhausting Louis, she would have done her utmost to end the play-writing sessions, or at the very least refused to have anything to do with them. Instead, she was making "suggestions." In fact, so involved was she that by the end of it she had *Admiral Guinea* almost by heart. One wonders, too, who specified rubies.

In any case all this was written years after a more serious and painful rift between Louis and his old friend, a rift of which she, however innocently, was the cause. Henley was the villain of Fanny's little drama. Nevertheless, "during the enforced cessation from dramatic collaboration," Louis was sleeping uneasily.

> My husband's cries of horror caused me to rouse him, much to his indignation. 'I was dreaming of a fine bogey tale,' he said reproachfully, following with a rapid sketch of *Jekyll and Hyde* up to the transformation scene, where I had awakened him.
>
> At daybreak he was working with feverish activity on the new book. In three days the first draft, containing thirty thousand words, was finished, only to be entirely destroyed and immediately rewritten from another point of view,—that of the allegory, which was palpable and had yet been missed, probably from haste, and the compelling influence of the dream. In another three days the book, except for a few minor corrections, was ready for the press. The amount of work this involved was appalling. That an invalid in my husband's condition of health should have been able to perform the manual labour alone, of putting sixty thousand words on paper in six days, seems almost incredible. He was suffering from continual haemorrhages, and was hardly allowed to speak, his conversation usually being carried on my means of slate and pencil.

Only one person at a time was allowed in the room, and then, on doctor's orders, for no more than fifteen minutes. It was Fanny's "ungracious task to stand guard . . ." She neglected, however, to mention that the rewriting of the parable had been at her behest. The appalling amount of work involved had been doubled by her vigorous objections to the first draft that Louis, struggling to hold on to the atmosphere of his dream, had produced in such a fever. Perhaps she feared to seem responsible for his subsequent relapse, or perhaps she felt that Lloyd, in his preface, had already said enough. One wonders if the two compared notes before composing their accounts. Given Fanny's attitude to Stevenson's memory, it is more than likely.

And yet, in the absence of Louis's first draft to contradict her, she seems to have been right. They had listened to a reading of the original. Lloyd, waiting "for my mother's outburst of enthusiasm . . . was thunderstruck at her backwardness."

> Her praise was constrained, the words seemed to come with difficulty; and then all at once she broke out with criticism. He had missed the point, she

said; had missed the allegory; had made it merely a story—a magnificent bit of sensationalism—when it should have been a masterpiece.

An odd scene. Here the author, knocking on death's door, interested only in a bit of sensationalism; here the wife, whose task in life was to keep her husband alive, is demanding masterpieces from a sick man whose efforts have cost him his last reserves of vitality. Fanny may have been honest; she was not, in this or in other episodes, very sensitive.

Stevenson was furious. Lloyd gives better accounts than most of his stepfather's capacity for anger—"whose very mien as he once raised a row about a corked bottle of wine had emptied half a restaurant"—but now Louis trembled, his voice "bitter and challenging," shouting Fanny down in a "fury of resentment." Lloyd had never seen him "so impassioned, so outraged." Such was the mood that the stepson left the room, returning later to find his mother alone, "pale and desolate."

Soon Louis returned. Lloyd and Fanny thought the row was to be resumed. Instead, R.L.S. addressed his wife. "You are right! I have absolutely missed the allegory, which, after all, is the whole point of it— the very essence of it." Then he astonished them both by throwing his manuscript in the fire. Lloyd thought at first he had done it out of pique, then concluded that Louis really had been convinced by Fanny's criticisms.

It is all very neat. Stevenson, who did not take kindly to criticism, whatever he claimed, stands revealed as a man of large heart capable of admitting he was wrong, and admitting it in the very terms his wife has used. Fanny becomes the honest woman whose literary judgement, of which she thought highly, is vindicated. In reality, she seems to have been genuinely horrified when he burned his manuscript. He may have been teaching her a sharp lesson.

Nevertheless, since R.L.S. did, in the end, agree, and did undertake the supreme effort of rewriting his piece from scratch, she is entitled to her version. He often took her advice but just as often ignored it. In this case, wrote Lloyd, "The culmination was the *Jekyll and Hyde* that everyone knows; that, translated into every European tongue and many Oriental, has given a new phrase to the world," It was despatched to the publisher six weeks later.

The roots of the allegory can be traced. Louis, dosed on tinctures, potions, and draughts, some of them disorientating, understood a little of the psychotropic effect of drugs. He spoke of it in early letters from Menton, when he was taking laudanum, the popular Victorian opiate, and again just before his death in 1894, when he resorted to the drug as a treatment for "collywobbles." It was a small dose, he told Colvin in one of his last letters from Samoa, "with the usual consequences of dry throat, intoxicated legs, partial madness and total imbecility . . ."

R.L.S. used this alcoholic tincture of opium, which normally contained a trace of morphine, for years, though with no sign of addiction. It was a commonplace remedy in those days, applied to coughs and to cancer, to toothaches, period pains, and hangovers, as well as to rabies, gangrene, and dysentery. It was, more importantly, often used as a treatment for respiratory illnesses. In any case, his experiences of mood-altering substances helped to furnish the transformation symbolism of the story.

Dreams, too, played their part. We know Louis's dreams to have been powerful; we know they stayed with him; we know that "his Brownies," the little workers of his imagination, could take credit for several of his stories. We know, the nightmare that gave him the essence of the story apart, that in childhood his dreams had made religion, the question of good and evil, almost a sinister thing.

The double has a long history in literature.* In the nineteenth century, when science and psychology contended with established religion, it became a common motif. The Romantics, dreamers and opium eaters, explored it. Hoffmann, Hogg, and Dostoevsky exploited it. Poe had employed it in *William Wilson* and Gautier in *Le Chevalier Double* ("Who in hell was he?" Louis asked Andrew Lang when the similarity was pointed out.) But doppelgangers and split personalties were devices used to explore issues of identity, sexuality, and morality.

James Hogg, whose *Confessions of a Justified Sinner* had appeared in 1824, was the countryman who preceded Louis into the mysterious territory of duality. Noting that a country as small as Scotland has contributed "two of the foremost masters of the double," one writer at least has observed that "though the ultimate reasons for the heightened Scottish

*See, generally, Herdman, J.: *The Double in Nineteenth Century Fiction* (London, 1990).

awareness of duality may lie deep in the national psyche and history, a proximate causation in the schematic polarities of Calvinist theology can scarcely be in doubt."

The point is well made. Louis had had firsthand experience of Victorian hypocrisy in Edinburgh; he had grown up in a divided city; he had often stepped out of the respectable New Town and into the disinhibited, amoral semi-underworld of the Old. He knew well enough that respectable "burgesses" haunted the brothels. He understood the emblematic nature of a figure like Deacon Brodie in his own city, and he knew how Calvinism divided the world into the elect and the damned. In the play, Brodie calls his nocturnal self "my maniac brother who has slipped his chain."

Stevenson also admired the works of the German E.T.A. Hoffmann, himself something of a dual personality, a lawyer by day and "a fantasist with a strong penchant for the freakish and weird" by night. Hoffmann's Gothic works—notably *The Devil's Elixirs*, published in 1824, the same year as Hogg's *Sinner*—set the boundaries for the literature of the double, and provided the props, with its transforming substances and personified conscience.

R.L.S. had made attempts at something like it before. A short story called "The Travelling Companion" had used the theme. Louis called it "an unpleasant tale" but submitted it for publication. In "A Chapter on Dreams" he recalled that it had been "returned by an editor on the plea that it was a work of genius and indecent." He burned the manuscript (an odd precedent to the *Jekyll* row) believing that it was not a work of genius and had been "supplanted" by the new story. In a letter to Colvin he called the tale "a foul, gross, bitter ugly daub . . ."

"Markheim," begun in 1884 and revised shortly before the dream that produced *Jekyll and Hyde*, again showed that Louis was fascinated by the theme of duality. In this brief story a murderer is confronted with his double and thus with his own embodied conscience, identified only as the visitor:

> Do I say that I follow sins? I follow virtues also; they differ not by the thickness of a nail, they are both scythes for the reaping angel of Death. Evil, for which I live, consists not in action but in character. The bad man

is dear to me; not the bad act, whose fruits, if we could follow them far enough down the hurtling cataract of the ages, might yet be found more blessed than those of the rarest virtues.

As part of the fiction, this passage is slight. But its meaning is the substrate of many of Stevenson's works. It explains his refusal to draw a moral *Jekyll and Hyde* and elsewhere; it stresses, as Louis did, character as the pivot both of morality and narrative. Actions, in fiction and in life, flowed from it. No ethical scheme was perfect; even bad deeds could have good results.

Jekyll and Hyde is at once more clear-cut and more subtle. Its London (much of it actually a disguised Edinburgh) is a place of good and evil, light and dark. Hyde, as the mark of the devil, arises from the subterranean depths of the psyche, prowls the darkness; Jekyll is a man of science, virtue, and light. Yet while Hyde is "pure" evil, Jekyll is human, an admixture of public virtues and private feelings, a touch of evil, a whiff of pride. In the first draft, according to Balfour, he was "bad all through," the transformation only "for the sake of a disguise." In the finished version he actually feels liberated, not enslaved, by the change:

This, too, was myself. It seemed natural and human. In my eyes it bore a livelier image of the spirit, it seemed more express and single, than the imperfect and divided countenance I had been hitherto accustomed to call mine.

G. K. Chesterton, in his 1927 book on Stevenson, pointed out that "The real stab of the story is not in the discovery that one man is two men; but in the discovery that the two men are one man." Fanny's insistence on allegory schematised the tale somewhat, but Louis's intention survived. Jekyll, as "himself," is the Victorian denial of human appetites and human realities. Hyde is a monster not because he is an alien creature but because he *is* Jekyll, with his repressions dissolved utterly, out of control. Stevenson seems to be saying that if man's aspects are not kept in balance, if psychological health is threatened by a denial of the "animal," the beast inevitably breaks loose. In a letter written to the American journalist and author John Paul Bocock late in 1887, R.L.S. insisted:

There is no harm in a voluptuary; and none, with my hand on my heart and in the sight of God, none—no harm whatever—in what prurient fools call 'immorality.' The harm was in Jekyll, because he was a hypocrite—not because he was fond of women; he says so himself; but people are so filled full of folly and inverted lust, that they can think of nothing but sexuality. The hypocrite let out the beast Hyde—who is no more sensual than another, but who is the essence of cruelty and malice, and selfishness and cowardice; and these are the diabolic in man—not this poor wish to have a woman, that they make such a cry about. I know, and I dare to say, you know as well as I, that good and bad, even to our human eyes, has no more connection with what is called dissipation than it has with flying kites.

For the contemporary audience it was simpler. The sensational novelty of the tale, the hook that caught on the public imagination, was physical transformation. Alluring toxins, drink or drugs, made men bestial. Walter Ferrier had been one such victim. After his death his mother had written Louis a hysterical letter, describing her son as one "of those degraded ones whose society on earth is shunned by the moral and the virtuous among Mankind." To many readers that was the Victorian nightmare, a parable of those "not themselves" because of vice, drugs, or alcohol. If this was Fanny's allegory, it worked. Louis made the nightmare hairy flesh in Edward Hyde.

After a brief delay, the story catapulted Stevenson to fame. Discussed, used in countless sermons (once at St. Paul's), its title soon proverbial, it sold out repeatedly. *Longman's Magazine* was offered it first and decided to produce a complete shilling edition rather than serialise the story. It was ready just before Christmas, but the bookshops, already stocked, turned it down. It was offered again after Christmas but moved slowly until an unsigned review appeared in *The Times*:

Nothing Mr Stevenson has written as yet has so strongly impressed us with the versatility of his very original genius as this sparsely-printed little shilling volume . . . Either the story was a flash of intuitive psychological research, dashed off in a burst of inspiration; or else it is the product of the most elaborate forethought, fitting together all the parts of an intricate and inscrutable puzzle. The proof is, that every connoisseur who reads the story once, must certainly read it twice.

That did it. In six months forty thousand copies were sold in Britain; by the end of the century (according to Graham Balfour) two hundred fifty thousand had been sold in the United States. Numerous articles, translations and stage versions followed. The story even achieved the honour of being parodied in *Punch*, in February of 1886:

> MR STUTTERSON, the lawyer, was a man of a rugged countenance, that was never lighted by a smile, not even when he saw a little old creature in clothes much too large for him, come round the corner of a street and trample a small boy nearly to death . . .
> 'Let us never refer to the subject again,' said Mr STUTTERSON.
> 'With all my heart,' replied the entire human race, escaping from his button-holing propensities.

Some critics, Rider Haggard among them, objected to aspects of the tale, notable the terms of Jekyll's will. Others found its appearance, as a shilling paperback, somewhat disconcerting. Henry James thought the agency of transformation too materialistic. John Addington Symonds, forever struggling with his homosexuality, wrote mournfully that the book had left "a deeply painful impression on my heart that I do not know how I am ever to turn to it again . . . Most of us at some epoch of our lives have been upon the verge of developing a Mr Hyde." F.W.H. Myers, the psychologist, psychic investigator, and essayist, wrote page after insistent page of letters to Louis detailing ways in which the book could be improved in a "final revision, the possible lack of which would be a real misfortune to English literature." The public, meanwhile, went on buying and reading.

Louis consolidated his success in the summer of that year when one of his most compelling narratives was serialised in *Young Folks*. *Kidnapped* says as much about Stevenson as any autobiography. In David Balfour and Alan Breck he gave substance to two sides of his own character, adventurer and rationalist, man of duty and man of passion. It was another instant success, and Stevenson was enjoying an extraordinary bout of creativity that would end only with his death.

Kidnapped, begun in March 1885 but "laid aside" until early in 1886, deserves to be remembered as one of Louis's most achieved, most complete novels. For it alone Skerryvore should have been spared the stray German bomb that claimed it during the Second World War. Like most of his best books it flowed easily once begun, and has a confident coherence. It unites the historical background which so fascinated Stevenson with characters alive *in* their period while never allowing mere facts to derail the narrative. This is not to say that R.L.S. does not try to be faithful to history, only that he never allows himself to be overwhelmed by it in this novel begun "partly as a lark, partly as a potboiler."

Again, however (and the writer Jenni Calder, for one, has made this identification), Louis was creating a fable just as he created the fable of *Jekyll*. It is one person's story—struggle, if you like—telling of how he maintained his footing on shifting moral ground. It is also superb adventure, paced and plotted, carried along by the spirit of the alter ego, Alan Breck. Few of Stevenson's books are better. And if, yet again, he deals obliquely with evil, his ethical reasoning was sound. *The Master of Ballantrae* is more direct, and its narrative drive suffers as a result. Life moved forward, but not to a moral plan. The pity is that R.L.S. accepted Colvin's suggestion that the novel should end in Edinburgh with the rest of the tale left for a sequel; had he carried on, he might have achieved the large-scale novel of which many thought him incapable. *Kidnapped* is not defective on that account, but an opportunity was missed. Louis rarely had the health or the will for a big book—though he dreamed of one often enough—and *Kidnapped* was probably his best chance.

Fanny claimed an inadvertent part in its creation. Louis and Henley had discarded *The Hanging Judge* from their list of proposed plays. She, ever eager to create and "emboldened by my husband's offer to give me any help needed," decided to write it herself. She chose, she said, to set it in "the period of 1700," of which she knew nothing. An order was placed with a London bookseller "to send us everything he could procure on Old Bailey trials." When the "great package" came, both she and R.L.S. became fascinated with its contents. Other books arrived with accounts of other trials. In one, Louis read:

The
TRIAL
of
JAMES STEWART
in Aucharn in Duror of Appin
FOR THE
Murder of COLIN CAMPBELL of Glenure, Esq.,
Factor for His Majesty on the forfeited
Estate of Ardshiel.

The fuse was lit. After the interruption of *Jekyll*, Louis wrote to his father: "I am at David again, and have just murdered James Stewart semi-historically . . ." James Henderson, of *Young Folks*, accepting the novel for serialisation, warned R.L.S. not to have "much broad Scotch in it . . ." It began to run in the magazine on 1 May and was published in book form in July 1886.

Another portion of the legend was accomplished: sick, with death all around him, R.L.S. still produced a novel strong, true, and wholly alive.

There was little comedy about life at Skerryvore, and what there was was black. One episode, as daft as any in the career of Stevenson, showed how much he despaired of the invalid's life, even to the point of seeking death.

In the winter of 1886–87 he was much agitated with the Irish Question, as he often was. He opposed Home Rule, partly because he loathed Gladstone, partly because of the violence of the campaign: ". . . populations should not be taught to gain public end by private crime . . ." When he read of how one unpopular farmer had been "mobbed"—with the farmer, Curtin, and a member of the mob being killed—he was outraged. The farm and the farmer's family were being boycotted as a result of the incident. Louis decided that he and *his* family would join the beleaguered farm community. He had influence in America, where much of the Irish Land League's financial support was raised. His gesture would publicise an injustice. And if he died in damp Ireland, what of it? He would die soon enough anyway. The purpose was to *brave crime*.

Fanny and Lloyd were astonished and horrified. Lloyd, for one, had no intention of risking his young life in such a fashion. Fanny thought it nonsense but agreed to stand by her husband. The idea was dropped after another death intruded. Yet it is clear that Louis, left to his own devices, would have exchanged his own miserable existence for a little brief, glorious action. There was even significance in that, however bizarre the circumstances.

Bournemouth changed Louis forever. The books he wrote there showed the alterations that his longest duel yet with death had made. Lloyd Osbourne remembered the aftermath of life in Fanny's "nest" and the effect it had on the thirty-five-year-old R.L.S.:

> He was never afterwards so boyish or so lighthearted; it was the final flare-up of his departing youth. The years that followed, however full they were of interest and achievement, were grayer; it was soberer and a more pre-occupied man that lived them. The happy-go-lucky Bohemian who had been rich if he could jingle ten pounds in his pocket, and who talked so cheerfully of touring France in a caravan, giving patriotic lectures with a magic lantern on 'The Incomparable Colonies of France'—with an ensuing collection in the lecturer's hat—was soon to discover that success had its penalties as well as its sweets. It was all inevitable, of course; such hard work could not escape its reward, and none of us can keep back the clock.

Thomas Stevenson could not. Spending as much as he did, Louis had not yet made his fortune. He still depended on his father, financially and in less obvious ways. As long as Thomas lived, he remained the dependent child. And in May of 1886 Thomas died.

The summons had been sudden, and by the time Louis arrived in Edinburgh his father did not know him. One doubts, in any case, that the old man would have been able to put his last thoughts into a few simple words. Uncle George ordered Louis, who had become ill, not to attend the funeral. He remained ill for the three weeks he was in Edinburgh, reacting to the loss of his father in some deep, mysterious way, as though to be a sick child again could somehow repair the bond that had once existed between them. Since it could not, he must perforce, at last, grow up.

That meant departure, as it always had and always would. Stevenson was one of those who seemed unconsciously to believe that he could leave his old self behind through physical movement. It was as though he were shedding a life as easily as a skin, stepping out of one world and into another, becoming a different man in the process. In some sense his dispute with his father continued long after the old man was dead, but that May provided a bleak punctuation mark in the dialogue. Louis was his own man.

His father had left him three thousand pounds. It was more than enough to put into action a scheme he had been hatching with Fanny to return to America. The cab ride from Heriot Row to Waverley Station after the funeral was a short one. Years later he was recalled as shouting farewell to his city while the cab horses trotted away from Heriot Row. Flora Masson, daughter of a famous Edinburgh professor, was a witness:

> An open cab, with a man and a woman in it, seated side by side and leaning back—the rest of the cab piled high with rather untidy luggage—came slowly towards us . . . As it passed us, out on the broad roadway . . . a slender, loose-garbed figure stood up in the cab and waved a wide-brimmed hat.
>
> 'Good-bye!' he called to us. 'Good-bye!'

Soon his train was gathering steam, rolling southwards beneath the arches of the bridge on which a disconsolate youth had once dreamed of escape from bleak Edinburgh, from studies, from parents who did not understand him, even from himself. He had hung there with the wind and smoke in his face, watching the departures, and praying he could join them. Exile called, pulled like a magnet. Now the symbols had acquired their own reality. Louis Stevenson would never return to his precipitous city.

II: *exile*

13 *1887–1888*

But revolution in this world succeeds to revolution.

"THE OLD PACIFIC CAPITAL"

F anny was upset to leave Skerryvore; Louis was more worried about what was to be done with his mother. It is cruel to say, but his father's death had made a man of him, or at least got the job under way. Responsibility, for which he had shown no great aptitude, was his. Maggie Stevenson was fifty-eight, small, round, and dressed invariably like Queen Victoria in one of her severe moods. Her son and his wife proposed to travel halfway around the world. What to do with the widow?

Perhaps she surprised even herself, she who had been wrapped in cotton wool by a doting husband, or perhaps there was simply nothing else for it. But if Louis was in some sense liberated, however unwillingly, by his father's death, Maggie Stevenson also became a different woman with her husband's passing. She would not have thought it herself, for her grief was deep, but with Thomas gone, the metal of her tough Balfour ancestors emerged; she seemed calmer, more eager, more confident. On 27 August 1887 when the Stevenson party set off from London aboard the S.S. *Ludgate Hill*, the party numbered five: Louis, Fanny, Lloyd, their maid Valentine—and the widow. Late in life she was to prove herself made of sterner stuff than she had ever given anyone reason to suspect.

Before the departure they had stayed at a hotel in Finsbury Circus where Louis had made his several farewells. Henry James had sent a case of champagne to the boat; Gosse—who had found Louis, though in mourning for his father, looking "extremely elegant and refined"—had been asked to witness his friend's will. The vagabond of the first Atlantic crossing had been replaced by a family man.

The sea was rough, and the voyage took eleven days, yet R.L.S., who had lately been so ill, responded in typical fashion to the prospect of release, writing to Bob that he had "forgotten what happiness was" until they were away. The same effect as always; and for the same reasons. Skerryvore had been Fanny's nest but it had been Louis's prison, a clinic that might have had bars on its windows for all the difference it would have made to him. He did not mind the storms; in fact he gloried in them. To everyone's surprise Maggie Stevenson also discovered sea legs. They call her "Mother Carey's chicken, the stormy petrel, etc" and claimed she had to be watched lest she was swept over the side or "took it into her head to climb the rigging." The widow even mastered the art of jumping in and out of hammocks.

New York, when they arrived on 7 September, amazed and delighted Louis. He had not conceived, locked away in Bournemouth fearing for his life, that his fame was so widespread. He had not anticipated that America's reaction to celebrity could be so open and wholehearted. Two pilots boarded the *Ludgate Hill*. One announced himself as Mr. Hyde; the other, who claimed to be more easygoing, was called Dr. Jekyll. Meanwhile, a stage version of the book was about to take the city by storm (Fanny and Maggie saw it, Louis did not) and the most determined newspaper reporters in the world were swarming all over the ship demanding a few words with the Scotch genius. To complete the party, Will Low was there to greet them, and rich Boston admirers of Stevenson, the Fairchilds, those friends of Sargent, had booked them a suite at the Victoria Hotel as their guests. A carriage—and eight reporters—awaited. The contrast with Louis's last mad, miserable trip to America could not have been more dizzying.

He tried to pretend that it was nothing, that the press was a nuisance, that their idea of an interview was not his. He tried to talk to the reporters about the scandal of copyright and pirate publishers, he boosted Henry James and was polite about politics. But it was a game: "What a silly thing is popularity!" the amateur celebrity told cousin Bob. Protest was pointless, and besides, whatever he said, he gave every appearance of enjoying himself.

His pleasure was increased as a succession of publishers began to offer him extraordinary amounts of money for articles. In the end, he surrendered to *Scribner's* and agreed to accept $3,500 for twelve articles a year. Roughly speaking, that meant about sixty pounds a month, over seven hundred pounds a year, a goodly sum then. Louis could never work out the exchange rate—". . . it is more than £500, but I cannot calculate more precisely." Meanwhile, both *Kidnapped* and *Treasure Island* were bringing in healthy royalties from authorised editions. Money worries seemed to be at an end, and though Stevenson claimed to the editor of *Scribner's* that Americans paid too much and that "these big sums demoralize me," he took the money without fuss. The year before he had earned only £109.

Yet New York—"a mixture of Chelsea, Liverpool and Paris," he said—tired him. He was discovering that America has a voracious appetite for celebrity. After London and Bournemouth, Fanny knew perfectly well that all this excitement could be lethal. They were invited to Newport, Rhode Island, to the Fairchild mansion. Admirers dogged them. Fan mail—for that is what it was—arrived by the sackload and the press interest did not slacken. They prepared to move.

Meanwhile the sculptor Augustus Saint-Gaudens began work on the medallion of Louis that was to become Fanny's favourite image of her husband. Her instinct was right: the Louis of popular imagination is there better preserved than in any photograph or painting. Showing him sitting up in bed writing, smoking, and wearing his old red poncho, the medallion was later reproduced for hanging in St. Giles Cathedral in Edinburgh, though for the good people of Auld Reekie the original cigarette was replaced with a discreet pen.

Charles Scribner continued to be an author's dream. In addition to the magazine deal, he offered a good price for *The Black Arrow*, paid royalties for books he had previously published (though he was not obliged to do so under copyright law as it then existed), and offered Louis a contract giving the publisher rights to all Stevenson's works in the United States. Louis was in a seller's market, and the initials R.L.S. were enough to close almost any deal. After the years of exhausting work, it was satisfying but, ironically, tiring.

The party travelled to Saranac in the Adirondacks, close to the Canadian border. Colorado had been their first choice, but the long journey was thought too risky for the invalid. Besides, the pine woods at Saranac Lake were supposed to protect the lungs of the infirm. Fanny and Lloyd set off first to make sure the place was suitable, and the rest joined them within a month.

There was a doctor there, of course, and another clinic. Dr. Edward Trudeau had himself suffered from tuberculosis and was developing new methods of diagnosis. He took Louis on and, after an examination, was encouraging about the patient's condition. R.L.S. saw the physician regularly throughout the winter, and remained reasonably well. Fanny, yet again, did not.

Saranac was bitterly cold in winter and the village tiny. The railway did not reach it. Louis thought the place resembled the Highlands (his mother identified traces of Perthshire) without apparently recalling how little Scotland had done for his health. They rented half of a frame house from a local guide named Baker, and Fanny, her pioneer lore put to work again, struggled to keep the house warm, caulking the doors and windows, even importing fur and buffalo robes. But when Valentine tried to wash the floor, the water froze as it was being applied. Even food was sometimes hard to come by.

In choosing *Scribner's* Louis had been modest by American standards. Their $3,500 was not so much set beside the $10,000 a year offered by Mr. Sam McClure, representing Joseph Pulitzer's *New York World*, and a Scots expatriate whose enthusiasm often overcame his discretion. Louis had been suspicious of the offer and refused. But McClure did not give up and, with Mr. E. L. Burlinghame of *Scribner's*, was to loom large in Stevenson's American career. For the moment he was content. He wrote a letter joking over his good fortune to William Archer, a critic who had written this first general assessment of Stevenson and his work in *Time*. Archer had said that in "our new school of stylists" Louis held "an indisputed place." But the piece had ended with the judgement: "It is sad to find a man of Mr Stevenson's genial talent posing as a wilfully blind leader of the blind." The article had troubled Louis more than any piece of criticism, and a lively correspondence ensued, concentrating on "style." "We shall fight it out on this line if it takes all summer," R.L.S. said. Typically, he had become friendly with Archer as a result. Now he wrote:

> I am a *bourgeois* now; I am to write a weekly paper for *Scribner's*, at a scale of payment which makes my teeth ache for shame and diffidence . . . I am, like to be a millionaire if this goes on, and be publicly hanged (on two counts, now, for this and for Skerryvore) at the social revolution: well, I would prefer that to dying in my bed; and it would be a godsend to my biographer, if ever I have one.

Baker's cottage was a small house, painted white with green shutters, a red tiled roof and an open fireplace. Louis had a small corner study. "From the next room," he told Henry James, "the bell of Lloyd's type-writer makes an agreeable music as it patters off (at a rate which aston-ishes this experienced novelist) the early chapters of a humorous romance . . ."

This was *The Wrong Box*—previously titled "A Game of Bluff"—the first of the collaborations between R.L.S. and his stepson. The little book full of "judicious levity," published by Scribner's in 1889, remains an odd-ity among Stevenson's works. A black comedy involving (an R.L.S. favourite) a mismanaged trust fund and a corpse that keeps on turning up unexpectedly, it was to attract the attention of Graham Greene, who wrote of it in the *Times Literary Supplement* in 1970.

Green recalled that just after the war—when he was probably con-templating his own biography of Stevenson—he was shown the proofs of the novel in Scribner's Rare Book Department in New York. The pub-lished version had appeared while Stevenson was in Samoa. It had been issued before Louis's many corrections and rewritings could be included. He was promised a corrected edition but, Greene said, it had never ap-peared.

He himself, as a director of Eyre and Spottiswoode, the London pub-lishers, had suggested the joint production of a new edition but had been rebuffed. "Did they fear in their canny way that it would reduce the value of the proofs in the Rare Book Department, or were they afraid that pub-lication might draw attention to their possession of the proofs, which normally belong to the author or his heirs?" Greene asked the *T.L.S.*, going on to enquire after the whereabouts of the proofs.

As it turned out, Scribner's had sold them to the collector Edwin J. Beinecke, to whom Stevenson scholars owe so much, and they lay in the library named after him at Yale. Correspondents disputed Greene's claim that an author or his estate necessarily own proofs. Ernest J. Mehew wrote of the meal described in Chapter XV and said that "a small group of people" met at the Athenaeum (a club Louis joined and just as quickly attempted to quit) in London "every three years or so to talk about *The Wrong Box* and to eat the meal described . . ." A corrected edition appeared at last in 1989, but not before a risible film version unconcerned with textual niceties had escaped in 1966.

Lloyd did the first draft, calling it "The Finsbury Tontine," and intended to finish it alone. Graham Balfour suggests that collaboration appealed to Louis because, since Lloyd was an American citizen, any work they produced would be copyrighted in the United States. Osbourne, equally, needed little encouragement to hitch his wagon to Stevenson's star. He had, after all, dropped out of university with the express intention of learning to be a writer under Louis's tutelage.

They started and abandoned several projects before Lloyd's typewriter began to patter in October, and by December the draft was complete. By Osbourne's own account he "always wrote the first draft, to break the ground . . ." Much rewriting ensued. So much, in fact, that authorship became, according to Lloyd, a matter of some vagueness: "After this how can anybody but Louis or myself pretend to know which of us wrote any given passage?"

It seems that Louis first offered only to revise the story for publication after McClure expressed an interest. Yet when R.L.S. began to work on it in March, he seems to have rewritten the piece almost entirely. The manuscript of "A Game of Bluff" was left with Scribner's in May 1888 when Stevenson set off for California and the Pacific. Of the 128 pages, 105 are in Louis's hand.

Its subsequent history was typical of the fate of his manuscripts when he was in the Pacific: revisions posted off, confusions and misunderstandings, publishers and friends who thought they knew best, the book published uncorrected. As Graham Greene discovered, and as *The Beach of*

Falesá was to prove, many of Stevenson's works from this date forward suffered from their author's absence.

The winter of 1887–88 was a nightmare of ice, snow, and a cold like none they had experienced. They had two thermometers around the place, one indoors and one out. The "Quarterly Reviewer," hung on the verandah, often registered minus forty degrees. But even in the sitting room the thermometer dubbed "Gosse" was often at freezing point. Louis's ears took a touch of frostbite, the mercury dropped far below zero, and Valentine awoke one morning to find that her handkerchief had been frozen stiff *beneath* her pillow. All through January the temperature continued to fall. A coat froze fast to a door, anything damp in the slightest became rock-hard. Food—usually bread and venison, cooked by a local—had to be thawed. Louis claimed to have seen a pot of soup boiling with a lump of ice still hard at its centre. The snow was piled to the top storey of the house. Even the ink froze. Life ought to have been miserable.

And yet Louis seemed not to suffer. He took walks (avoiding the locals), dressed in his preposterous furs (which he adored), and continued to smoke heavily. In Dr. Trudeau's opinion his tuberculosis was arrested in the deep freeze of Saranac. Stevenson had sought a "Hunter's Home" (though he had no desire to hunt), and the Adirondacks, those rugged broken hills and tree-furred skylines, seemed to provide it. He and the doctor did not get along especially well, however, partly because of temperament and partly because Trudeau did not approve of Louis's cigarettes. The man of science and the man of letters did not see eye to eye, especially on the subject of tobacco.

The reasons are obvious, but the addicted R.L.S. preferred not to see them. He was a heavy smoker all his adult life—"Cigarettes without intermission, except when coughing or kissing"—and in Davos had taken his treatment like a man save when Dr. Ruedi attempted to restrict him to three pipes a day to spare his poor lungs from his beloved hand-rolled smokes.

Health, the product of inactivity, naturally made him restless for action. He wrote approvingly to William Archer, who had sent a copy of a friend's novel, of the prose enclosed. Louis found *Cashel Byron's Profession* "full of promise" and "horrid fun." With an eye on the competition he asked after the age of this George Bernard Shaw. Henry James, meanwhile, provided Owen Wister with a letter of introduction to "dear Louis Stevenson," "If you like the gulch & the canyon," he informed the author of *The Virginian,* "you will like *her* . . ."

Another novel was under way, putting a temporary end to Louis's efforts to assist Lloyd with *The Wrong Box.* He was in "these times of parturition . . ." once again.

Received wisdom has it that *The Master of Ballantrae,* another study in duality, has a flawed ending, but that is to do less than justice to a bleak, strange, and complex "winter's tale" whose ending, if rushed, has the force of implacable necessity. Louis began it in December of 1887, commencing, as usual, with a list of chapters—his route map. Its inspiration was Captain Marryat's *The Phantom Ship,* itself written in the United States in the 1830s and a novel Stevenson had just finished rereading.

> I was walking one night in the veranda of a small house in which I lived, outside the hamlet of Saranac. It was winter; the night was very dark; the air extraordinary clear and cold, and sweet with the purity of forests . . . For the making of a story here were fine conditions. I was besides moved with the spirit of emulation, for I had just finished my third or fourth perusal of *The Phantom Ship.* 'Come,' I said to my engine, 'Let us make a tale, a story of many years and countries, of the sea and the land, savagery and civilisation; a story that shall have the same large features and may be treated in the same summary elliptic method as the book you have been reading and admiring.'

Neither for the first time nor the last Stevenson seems to have been seized with a desire to make a big book, to paint on a large canvas. Some, even among his friends, were already accusing him of want of ambition. *The Master* was another attempt at an answer, though, true to his instincts, it was a novelist like Marryat who set him off.

It was another attempt, too, to explore infectious evil. Its origins lay in a walking trip he had taken through Carrick and Galloway in the west of Scotland in 1876 which had brought him to a place named Ballantrae. The name had returned to him that dark, icy night at Saranac while he contemplated Marryat's reconstruction of the Flying Dutchman legend. A story he had conceived at Pitlochry in 1881 also came into play—that and the Jacobite uprising of 1745.

Two sons; two narrators; good and evil; light and dark; sustained symbolism. Stevenson is rarely so schematic, and for once he found it hard to pick the plot up again after, as was his habit, he "laid it aside" when the first fever of creation had subsided. Yet it is one of the most subtle of his books, one in which love and hate are both destructive, equal and opposite. *The Master* is an ethical hall of mirrors.

The novel was not to be completed until May of 1889, when he was in the Pacific, pressed by the demands of serialisation and "near to confessing defeat." As so often, a deadline induced "a few days of furious industry," and "the novel was, for good or evil, rushed to its last word."

At Saranac, in the meantime, he was fulfilling his obligations to *Scribner's*. He was given no guidance as to subject and seemed to relish the chance to return to the essay form. Certainly he produced some of his best—"The Lantern Bearers," "Random Memories," "A Chapter on Dreams," "A Christmas Sermon"—and seemed more direct in his didacticism, more sure of himself, than ever before. He was equally busy on a host of other projects—with Lloyd and with Fanny, who had resumed work on *The Hanging Judge* and felt free to squander Louis's time on it despite "much acrimony." Then there were the visitors.

Sam McClure, blond doyen of the yellow periodicals, was still pursuing R.L.S. He visited Saranac several times, full of enthusiasm for skating and publishing ventures alike. Discovering that Louis was contemplating a sequel to *Kidnapped*, he offered eight thousand dollars for the serial rights. Stevenson had asked for only eight hundred, but he had also forgotten that he had recently concluded a deal with Charles Scribner for *all* his American rights.

Disingenuous? Absentminded? This, after all, was the author who had forgotten to secure the American rights for *Jekyll*. Or was he simply overwhelmed by McClure's offer? Fanny was away when the deal was struck, but when she returned she made her feelings plain. Scribner's reaction was equally one of shock and understandable suspicion. Louis, in something like panic, handed the mess over to Charles Baxter to resolve.

McClure, prepared to offer almost anything to snare R.L.S., was not discouraged. During another visit, as the family shivered in the misery of an apparently endless winter, he encouraged Louis to imagine that a yacht could be chartered and an escape made. McClure recalled offering ("I was young and bold") to meet all expenses in exchange for copy. In *My Autobiography* he recalled: "He was always better at sea, he said, than anywhere else, and he wanted to fit up a yacht and take a long cruise and make his home at sea for a while." Louis was for it, Maggie Stevenson was for it, Lloyd was for it—and Fanny, no sailor, perforce agreed. The winter nights passed more easily as they pored over maps and almanacs and wondered which part of the globe to visit. McClure tried and failed to find a yacht on the East Coast. Fanny, setting off west to visit Nellie and Belle, was instructed to see what she could do in San Francisco.

She left in March. Without her, Louis began to seem depressed. Then a letter arrived from London, from Chiswick, dated 9 March 1888, which made him angrier than he had ever been in his life, and as depressed as he was ever likely to be. It tore him apart, left him sleepless and speechless. He told Baxter that the communication had made him wish he had died at Hyères. His "confidence in all affection" was shaken to the core.

A little over a year before, he and Fanny had been at Henley's house. Also present was one of Stevenson's many cousins, the intelligent and cultivated Katharine de Mattos, Bob Stevenson's sister. Her marriage had failed, and Henley and Louis had been helping her to write (Stevenson was also subsidising her, as his dying father had requested). It is fair to say she was closer to Henley than her cousin, and certainly closer to Henley's idea of what a Stevenson woman should be.

Katharine had worked up a story about a meeting on a train between a young man and a girl who, it transpired, had escaped from the madhouse. Fanny, accustomed to Louis's patience and incapable of failing to offer others the benefit of her judgement, urged that the character of the girl be a water sprite, a "nixie." Katharine demurred but Fanny persisted; Fanny—so transparent—offered to collaborate despite this polite rebuff. Katharine still seemed determined to keep hold of her little story. Henley then tried and failed to place the manuscript with a magazine.

When no buyers were found, Fanny, bereft of tact, offered to take over the tale and try her hand with it. Wearily—she was visiting Skerryvore

at the time—Mrs. de Mattos agreed, but in such a way that everyone save
Fanny concluded she would rather not release her work. She handed over
the manuscript, and even Louis told Fanny she should take the matter no
further. But when her unassuaged appetite for recognition was involved,
Fanny heard nothing. She rewrote the story, retaining much of Katharine's
original. Early in March of 1888 it appeared—the Stevenson name having
had its usual magical effect on her husband's publishers—in *Scribner's*. It
was credited to Fanny Van de Grift Stevenson alone. Louis had an article,
"Beggars," in the same issue.

Henley had read the magazine, and his letter was marked "Private and
Confidential." It began conventionally enough, upbraiding Louis for staying in America. "Dear Boy," he began, "If you will wash dishes and haunt
backkitchens in the lovely climate of the Eastern States, you must put up
with the consequences . . ." There followed the usual gossip, some good-
natured jokes. Then, with that alarming, almost devious, change of mood
which was one of Henley's characteristics after years of whisky and physical pain, there came a six-line paragraph.

> I read *The Nixie* with considerable amazement. It's Katherine's; surely it's
> Katherine's? The situation, the environment, the principal figure—*voyons!*
> There are even reminiscences of phrases and imagery, parallel incidents—
> *Que sais-je?* It is all better focused, no doubt, but I think it has lost as much
> (at least) as it has gained; and why there wasn't a double signature is what
> I've not been able to understand.

Henley knew what he was about. He could not have imagined that
Louis would take from the paragraph any less than was intended. Yet still,
eaten with a jealousy vicious as a tapeworm, having taken Louis's money
and resented having to take it, despising "semi-educated" Fanny, and having disparaged Louis's success behind his back to Savile Club cronies, he
revealed uncomfortable knowledge of his own malice.

> Don't show this to *anybody*, & when you write, don't do more than note
> it in a general way—By the time you *do* write, you will have forgotten all
> about it, no doubt. But if you haven't, deal vaguely with my malady. Why
> the devil do you go and bury yourself in that bloody country of dollars and
> spew? . . . However, I suppose you must be forgiven, for you have loved

me much. Let us go on so to the end . . . Forgive this babble, and take care
of yourself & burn this letter.

Your friend

W.E.H.

Plainly, he understood what he had done, and how much damage he
might cause ("burn this letter") but could not bring himself to draw the
barb. Perhaps he was drunk; perhaps he truly believed that the "Dear
Boy" would enter such a conspiracy of silence against his own wife after
having taken the shaft meant for her, or even, most insulting of all, accept
what amounted to an order to enter such a conspiracy. Outrage was not
the word for Stevenson's reaction; pain and disbelief were mingled with
horror. His faith in friendship, so fundamental to his character, was
shaken. The only mercy was that Fanny, mildly paranoid at the best of
times about the set Henley represented, was not present. She would have
taken it, hysterically no doubt, as confirmation of her beliefs—with some
justice.

McClure, who visited London at around this time, recalled that "most
of Stevenson's set was very much annoyed by the attention he was receiving in America, a most extraordinary spirit of hostility and jealousy. They
were resentful of the fact that Stevenson was recognised more fully, more
immediately, and more understandingly in America than in England at
that time. Some of Stevenson's London friends agreed that he was a much
overrated man."

Only Henry James, the expatriate American and the sole man of stature among them, was exempt. McClure put his finger on part of the
problem. It was jealousy, he said, "of the American appreciation of
Stevenson . . ." He nominated Henley as suffering most from "this strange
jealousy." R.L.S., who had long since grown tired of those friends who
felt no compunction in telling him his work was "bosh," came to agree.

For the moment he agonised. It took him days to compose a reply.
How to answer such charges from one of his oldest friends? How to deal
with a lie? How to defend his wife? How to trust anyone again as he had
once trusted Henley? Louis's emotions ran close to the surface at the best
of times. His temper could be awesome—he had once smashed a bottle

of wine against a Paris restaurant wall because it was corked. He wept easily, loved fiercely. A kind word could transport him skywards; an argument could demoralise him for days. When Fanny persisted in her fury long after he had recovered a kind of equanimity, he showed how little appetite he had for the casual passions that others thought normal. "I envy you flimsy people," he wrote, "who rage up so easily with hate . . ."

Stevenson had quarrelled with Henley before, but never in such circumstances. He had been irritated by Henley's patronising attitude when he had refused to accept his full fee for "The Body-Snatcher" because he thought the piece unworthy. He had been furious when Henley's brother Teddy, touring the States in the winter of 1887 with *Deacon Brodie* (and doing the poor play few favours), had become involved in a drunken brawl in Philadelphia, escaping with a fine before decamping to New York to live in a better hotel than Louis could afford, and *then* trying to sponge money from him. Louis's reaction to that episode was revealing of the difference between his character and that of the thoughtless W. E. Henley. He confided, if that is the word, to Baxter:

> The drunken whoreson bugger and bully living himself in the best hotels, and smashing inoffensive strangers in the bar! It is too sickening . . . The violence of this letter comes from my helplessness: all I try to do for W.E. (in the best way) by writing these plays is burked by this inopportune lad. Can nothing be done? In the meanwhile I add another £20 to W.E.'s credit.

It has been said in Henley's defence that over the years he had done more for Louis, acting as his unpaid agent, than R.L.S. had ever repaid with his "loans." But that, in a way, merely explains the depths of Henley's rancour. He continued to expect gratitude, not to mention deference, long after it was clear that handling Louis's manuscripts was doing the name of William Ernest Henley as much good as it did that of Robert Louis Stevenson. Money aside, he forgot how Louis had kept his pitiful magazines afloat with unpaid labours, and continued to dispense advice— even telling Louis where and how he should live—long after it was clear to all who the real artist was. Gentle Sidney Colvin summed Henley up in a letter to Graham Balfour towards the end of the First World War, long after the combatants in the "great literary quarrel" were cold in their graves. W.E.'s disloyalty, he said, was "chronic," the result of bad blood, it-self the result of scrofula, whisky, jealousy of Louis, resentment of Fanny, "and the blind flattery of his own bodyguard, including some foolish women . . ." He may well have meant the equally disloyal Katharine de Mattos by that last remark.

Henley could be a blustering, drunken, tactless oaf. Stevenson knew it perfectly well (for Fanny told him), but he had accepted everything in the name of friendship. Not this. He drafted his reply half a dozen times. In the final version he came straight to the point:

> My dear Henley,
>   I write with indescribable difficulty; and if not with perfect temper, you are to remember how very rarely a husband is expected to receive such accusations against his wife. I can only direct you to apply to Katharine and ask her to remind you of that part of the business which took place in your presence and which you seem to have forgotten . . .

Louis went on to draw attention to Henley's strange insistence on "Pri-vate and Confidential," which, he said, had tied his hands. But he was de-termined not to let the slander survive.

> I wish I could stop here. I cannot. When you have refreshed your mind as to the facts, you will, I know withdraw what you said to me; but I must go farther and remind you, if you have spoken of this to others, a proper explanation and retraction of what you shall have said or implied to any person so addressed, will be necessary.

His advocate's training had not gone entirely to waste. But Stevenson also prided himself on being a gentleman. He believed from the bottom of his soul that what Henley had written had "been merely reckless words." Nevertheless:

> . . . it is hard to think that anyone—and least of all my friend—should have been so careless of dealing agony . . . You will pardon me if I can find no form of signature; I pray God such a blank will not be of long endurance.
>   Robert Louis Stevenson

He wasted his time. No real apology was forthcoming, only a disingenuous whining that Louis could think so of his old friend, and how upset
Henley was at having hurt Stevenson's feelings without meaning to. "I
thought the matter of little consequence," Henley wrote back. There was
no mention of Fanny's honour. R.L.S. was not deceived and did not
hesitate—despite Henley's demand for privacy—to tax Katharine de Mattos on the matter. She affected a sudden vagueness and distaste for the
whole business (it made her "ill"). Henley, she said, "had a perfect right
to be astonished but his having said so has nothing to do with me." Finally she refused to continue with the debate, protesting that there was
"devilry in the air."

"I fear that I have come to the end with Henley; the lord knows if I
have not tried to be a friend to him . . . There is not one of that crew
that I have not helped in every kind of strait . . ." Louis said in a long letter to Baxter in which he struggled to identify the fault in *himself* that had
caused such an outrage. Baxter, fair as ever (and knowing Fanny), did not
accept that Henley had "wilfully" intended to injure.

Through it all Fanny was ill. She had been unwell, and often in bed,
throughout the winter, and a growth in her throat had been troubling her
for some time. In the midst of the tumult the doctors operated but found,
to the relief of all, that there was no cancer. Typically, she was more concerned with the upset the row was causing Louis than with herself.

Louis's mood turned from anger to despair. "If this be friendship," he
told Charles Baxter, "I am not robust enough to bear it. If it be want of
tact, it is strangely like want of heart . . ." Young Lloyd was appalled that
his two heroes should quarrel so, but there was little he could say or do.
Fanny thought the injury could never be condoned and swore, in the language of high tragedy, that only the thought of Louis kept her from suicide, that she never wanted to see England again. The gossip columns
were, meanwhile, making the most of it.

Oddly, R.L.S. did eventually condone the slight. He and Henley resumed a kind of friendship—or at least a correspondence—until the day
in 1890 when W.E., in Edinburgh to work on the *Scots Magazine*, did not
take the trouble to call on Maggie Stevenson on her temporary return
from the Pacific. That, for Louis, was unacceptable, the last straw. Such

behaviour could only be understood as a calculated insult. For a bohemian Stevenson could be very particular.

Soon after the row he sent Baxter a codicil to his will. His father had
enjoined him to look after his cousin Katharine. Louis instructed that an
annuity be provided for her daughter. He also asked Baxter to arrange
that a small allowance be provided for Henley, taxing the ingenuity of the
lawyer yet again by asking him to ensure that it would seem to come from
"anybody but me." Had she had her way, Fanny, likely to be executrix,
would have seen to it that neither party received a penny piece. She was
not best pleased when told of her husband's decision.

The true measure of Henley's strange, unpleasant mind was not to be
had until long after Louis was safely dead. In 1901 the *Pall Mall Magazine*
sent him Balfour's biography for review. He affected reluctance but, having said his piece, refused to moderate his remarks for the December issue. They were, his own biographer wrote, "mercilessly cruel,"
particularly where Fanny was concerned. He belaboured Balfour, with
some justice, for creating a "barley sugar effigy of a real man." But as
J. C. Furnas points out, it is the patronizing tone of the piece that is so
breathtaking. Stevenson's style, Henley argued with wonderful complacency, "is so perfectly achieved that the achievement gets obvious . . ."
Even today, you itch to ask the aged blustering viceroy of English letters
what, precisely, he had himself achieved, obvious or otherwise, that entitled him to judge?

He had perhaps been insulted by a well-concealed reference—no one
else could have made the link—to Lewis's (he persisted in pretending that
he had known R.L.S. before the spelling was changed) "loans" to himself.
Furnas deduced that Henley spotted a reference in Balfour's *Life* to a letter
written by Louis to Baxter not long before he died. In it he had given instructions for Henley to be allowed, *in extremis*, five pounds a month—but
no more: ". . . if I gave him more it would only lead to his starting a gig
and a Pomeranian dog." Balfour named no names, intending only to illustrate Stevenson's generosity, but Henley recognised himself and hit back,
doubtless confusing most of his readers with the passions that could be
aroused by Pomeranians.

It makes sense, but does not explain all. It does not explain the pathetic
malice and the jealousy: the fuse was not the dynamite. Henley had

nursed his wrath for years and it had blistered his heart. He had come a long way from the brave, talented youth lying in the infirmary in Edinburgh, and had lost whatever quality Stevenson first saw in him. Fanny, no amateur at enmity herself, believed he was drunk when he wrote it. Perhaps, but a writer, of all people, should be taken at his word. What did Henley think of R.L.S. as he faced the monument Balfour had constructed?

> For me there were two Stevensons: the Stevenson who went to America in '87; and the Stevenson who never came back. The first I knew, and loved; the other I lost touch with, and, though I admired him, did not greatly esteem. My relation to him was that of a man with a grievance; and for that reason, perhaps—that reason and others—I am by no means disposed to take all Mr Balfour says for gospel . . .

The Stevenson Balfour knew was not the Stevenson Henley, alone of all, could claim to have known. Yet his cherished memories did not restrain his spite. He was determined, as no later "debunker" was ever to be so determined, to reduce R.L.S. to imperfect, even petty, humanity.

> At bottom Stevenson was an excellent fellow. But he was of his essence what the French call *personnel*. He was, that is, incessantly and passionately interested in Stevenson. He could not be in the same room with a mirror but he must invite its confidences every time he passed it; to him there was nothing obvious in time and eternity, and the smallest of his discoveries, his trivial apprehensions, were all by way of being revelations, and as revelations must be thrust upon the world; he was never so much in earnest, never so well pleased (this were he happy or wretched), never so irresistible, as when he wrote about himself.

At this distance it is hard to understand why a man with the piercing vision of William Ernest Henley put up with the vain, small-minded, self-obsessed "Shorter Catechist" for so long. "Lewis" was no wit, a rotten musician. A writer? "To tell the truth his books are none of mine: I mean, that if I want reading, I do not go for it to the 'Edinburgh Edition' . . ." Drunk or sober, Henley, as in the Nixie letter, did not mean to be mistaken: "I remember, rather, the unmarried and irresponsible Lewis: the friend, the comrade, the *charmeur*." *Unmarried* is the stab: Fanny's theft of the "dear boy" was not forgiven. Henley, often desperately ill himself, would not even allow that R.L.S. had attained any heroism in illness.

> Let this be said of him, once for all: 'He was a good man, good at many things, and now this also he has attained to, to be at rest.' That covers Sophocles and Shakespeare, Marlborough and Bonaparte. Let it serve for Stevenson; and for ourselves, let us live and die uninsulted, as we lived and died before his books began to sell and his personality was a marketable thing.

Louis had sinned by being successful and loved. Henley speaking for the uninsulted was a blind man speaking of sight. His snobbery was rank, yet his attitude was not so different from the streak of contempt for Stevenson the person that was to run through much criticism after the Great War, and which persists. Louis had dared exile and romance, yet he was applauded for it, praised for it, *paid* for it. It would not do. Henry James, the Master, sketched Henley's character in a letter to Graham Balfour written in November 1901 and now held in the National Library of Scotland. Of the *Pall Mall* article, he said:

> The interest the thing *does* present is of a documentary sort in respect to H himself—and in that particular is curious: the long-accumulated jealousy, rancour—I suppose of invidious vanity, so getting the better of a man of his age and experience that, your book at last making the cup overflow, he tumbles it all about before a mocking world. Only indeed that world isn't mocking, but stupid, passive, easily muddled—which ensures him a certain impunity.

And was Fanny a plagiarist? Yes, by common standards. That is the irony of it all. Henley's central charges were accurate: she had used Katharine's material and failed to give credit. Louis certainly wished she had left the worthless little story alone. But for him, that had never been the point any more than it had been the point of his old friend's vicious little assault. Fanny was his wife; the bond surpassed all, whether Henley liked it or not. And if she was a wilful, difficult, neurotic, steadfast, and heroic wife—sometimes simultaneously—that was Louis's problem, and his joy.

~

Before long Louis, Lloyd, Maggie, and Valentine were in New York again. He was sick of Saranac, especially with Fanny away in California. The winter had improved his health—the haemorrhages had stopped entirely—but the claustrophobia of the place oppressed him. In the city he spent an afternoon in Washington Square talking literature with Mark Twain, who afterwards recalled, as everyone recalled, the remarkable eyes of the Scotsman. These two most practical of craftsmen discussed their mutual trade, and remained in touch, on and off, in the years to come.

When New York palled—"Low, get me out of this," he told his friend—the group left the Hotel St. Stephen and moved to an inn at Manasquan, in New Jersey, where Stevenson, his stepson, and Will Low developed a craze for sailing in broad, round-bottomed catboats. He took long walks; Saint-Gaudens came to visit; *The Master of Ballantrae* was "laid aside" while he tinkered with *The Wrong Box*. For six weeks nothing was heard from Fanny. Their eighth wedding anniversary saw them on opposite sides of the continent.

In his memoirs Low recalled that during one lunch at the inn a telegram arrived. Louis glanced at it then asked his mother to read it aloud. "Can secure splendid sea-going schooner yacht 'Casco' for seven hundred and fifty a month with most comfortable accommodation for six aft and six forward," it said. "Can be ready for sea in ten days. Relpy immediately."

Louis did not hesitate. In the aftermath of Henley's assault it was all he could have hoped for. Capable Fanny, no great lover of sailing or the sea, had done her bit as an adventurer's companion. He composed a reply and handed it to the waiting telegram messenger. "Blessed girl," he wired back, "take the yacht and expect us in ten days."

The party returned to New York, moved on to Chicago, and headed west in a cramped train. Fanny met them at Sacramento on 7 June. Louis, tired by the long journey, took to his bed on doctor's orders while his wife pressed ahead with arrangements for the voyage.

A new world of wide skies and blue oceans was opening up to the traveller. He wanted this otherness even before he knew what it was. The "great affair" had been resumed. The Pacific beckoned and he did not even think to resist.

Europe was behind him now, and America, too, was to fall away. The world in which W. E. Henley stumped around making a small name from his small talent, where lives were consumed by pettiness and art was no more than the chatter of salons, where everyone who could not write felt entitled to instruct the writer, must manage without him for a while. In such circumstances the *only* affair was to move. As things turned, his friends, true or false, would have to manage without him ever after. Stevenson did not return.

14 *1888–1889*

. . . I have often marvelled at the impudence of gentlemen who describe and pass judgement on the life of man, in almost perfect ignorance of all its necessary elements and natural careers. Those who dwell in clubs and studios may paint excellent pictures or write enchanting novels. There is one thing they should not do: they should pass no judgement on man's destiny, for it is a thing with which they are unacquainted . . .

THE WRECKER

*T*he owner of the *Casco* adored his yacht and had no high opinion of writers or of their ability to look after his vessel. "You may think your husband loves you," he told Fanny, "but I can assure you that I love my yacht a great deal better." Given all he had read in the press, this Scotch writer sounded less trustworthy than most. The *Casco*—"74 tons register," 95 foot, fore-and-aft topsail schooner—sat, Graham Balfour said, "like a bird upon the water," and a photograph of it confirms as much. She had been built to sail in coastal waters but had once been taken as far as Tahiti. Before Dr. Samuel Merritt would let her out of his sight, he intended to interview the plainly rich but obviously eccentric bohemian. "I'd read things in the papers about Stevenson, and thought he was a kind of crank," Balfour recorded the millionaire doctor as recollecting, "but he's a plain, sensible man that knows what he's talking about just as well as I do."

The interview went well. Merritt's only stipulation—wise, considering that he had fitted the boat out to luxury standards—was that his own skipper, Captain A. H. Otis, be engaged. Privately, after having exam-

ined the specimen of a Scotsman, he told the captain to be prepared to
bury the "crank" at sea. The voyage, intended to last seven months, was
costing Louis at least two thousand of the three thousand pounds he had
inherited from his father. Under the agreement he was to pay Merritt
five hundred dollars a month and was to bear all the other costs of the
voyage. Stevenson told Baxter: "If I cannot get my health back (more or
less) 'tis madness; but, of course, there is hope. . . . If this business fails
to set me up, well, £2,000 is gone, and I know I can't get better. We
sail from San Francisco, June 15th, for the South Seas in the yacht
Casco."

In reality, Louis's deal with McClure meant that penury would be
avoided without much difficulty if his pen did not fail him. The New
York *Sun* had agreed to pay ten thousand dollars for fifty letters despatched en route, and McClure had also come up with five thousand dollars for the British rights. There was little for R.L.S. to worry about.
Writing a farewell letter to Henry James—who hoped, plaintively, to
"spoil your fun" by making Louis homesick—he was more positive:

> This, dear James, is valedictory. On June 15th the schooner yacht *Casco*
> will (weather and a jealous providence permitting) steam through the
> Golden Gates for Honolulu, Tahiti, the Galapagos, Guyaquil, and—I hope
> *not* the bottom of the Pacific. It will contain your obedient 'umble servant
> and party. It seems too good to be true, and is a very good way of getting
> through the green-sickness of maturity, which, with all its accompanying
> ills, is now declaring itself in my mind and life.

While in San Francisco, Fanny met the woman Sam Osbourne had
married after their divorce. It was a sad and satisfying encounter. Sam,
characteristically, had disappeared several years before. His wife, Paulie,
had prepared his supper yet he had never arrived to eat it. No one knew
what had become of him (much later it was claimed he had been sighted
in South Africa, though the claim was never confirmed). According to
Nellie Sanchez, Fanny's sister, Paulie had once been pretty but was now
deaf, lonely, very poor, and "notorious." The story went that she had
fallen to her knees before Fanny and wept, saying, "You were right about
that man and I was wrong!" Fanny gave her some money and wrote to

Louis: "Imagine how humble I felt in my good fortune when I sat side by side with that poor woman whose case might have been mine—but for you . . ."

Stores were laid in on the *Casco* and gifts for the natives procured while Louis read Melville's accounts of the Pacific. Fanny, Maggie, and Valentine were kitted out with tropical gear, notably the long, flowing "Mother Hubbard" gowns and underskirts—*muumuu* and *holuka*—with which missionaries had attempted to make island girls modest. Fanny worried about Belle, whose marriage to Joe Strong was disintegrating because of his incessant drinking. There was no time to stop or think. On 26 June—not 15—they boarded the *Casco*. On the twenty-eighth, after farewells had been made and parting gifts received, the vessel was towed through the Golden Gates by the tug *Pelican*. Belle sent one last, heartbroken note to her mother with the tug. Fanny, touched, despatched a reply for the little boat to carry ashore. Maggie Stevenson, writing to her sister Jane by the same means, admitted that the voyage fulfilled some of her own "childish longings." There would be no more letters for weeks.

As they moved towards the open sea, the ferryboats in the bay whistled in salute. Then Captain Otis snapped out the order, and Louis, standing on deck excited as any child, saw the white sails unfurl and billow as the Pacific winds caught them and the yacht glided into open water. For other children he had once made a verse:

> *If I could find a higher tree,*
> *Farther and farther I should see,*
> *To where the grown-up river slips*
> *Into the sea among the ships . . .*

It was the final phase, though he did not yet know it. He still planned to return to Europe someday after this latest and best adventure was over. But only six years remained.

The first days were rough at sea. Fanny, Lloyd, and Valentine stayed in their bunks for three of them, unable to rise above their nausea. Only Maggie and Louis, seafaring Stevensons, found their legs quickly. The *Casco* was a fast ship, a racing ship, and soon turned south-southwest to-

wards the Marquesas as the weather grew warmer, with pilot birds for
escort and the Southern Cross above at night. They sailed for a month,
three thousand miles, with Louis spending each morning writing and
Fanny interfering with the running of the vessel. Captain Otis—the
original of Nares in *The Wrecker*—grumbled at first. When she persisted
in chattering to the man at the wheel, the captain ventured: "Please
don't talk to him today, Mrs Stevenson. Today I want him to steer." But
soon Otis was obliged to concede that this eccentric little woman had,
by dint of badgering the cook, improved the food. He had sailed short-
handed, and Fanny's efforts sometimes produced better results than his
furious haranguing of the inept crew. If nothing else, it distracted her
from her habitual seasickness. Meanwhile, the captain developed an admiration for Maggie Stevenson's ability at whist, honed to sharpness in
the drawing rooms of Edinburgh, while concluding that the Scotch
writer—whose *Treasure Island* he had thought little of—was not such a
bad sort.

Four weeks out of San Francisco, Louis, playing his part to the hilt,
called out "Land!" and they arrived at Nukahiva, part of the French
Marquesas and the scene of Melville's *Typee*. The first chapter of *In the
South Seas* describes the moment Stevenson had long sought and dreamt
of, the first encounter from the sea with a strange, glorious new world.
He regretted that it could only happen once:

> The first experience can never be repeated. The first love, the first sunrise,
> the first South Sea island, are memories apart and touched a virginity of
> sense. On the 28th day of July 1888 the moon was an hour down by four
> in the morning. In the east a radiating centre of brightness told of the day;
> and beneath, on the skyline, the morning bank was already building, black
> as ink . . . Although the dawn was preparing by four, the sun was not up
> till six; and it was half-past five before we could distinguish our expect is-
> lands from the cloud on the horizon. Eight degrees south, and the day two
> hours a-coming. The interval was passed on deck in the silence of expec-
> tation . . . Slowly they took shape in the attenuating darkness. Ua-huna,
> piling up to a truncated summit, appeared the first upon the starboard bow;
> almost abeam arose our destination, Nuka-hiva, whelmed in cloud; and
> betwixt and to the southward, the first rays of the sun displayed the needles
> of the Ua-pu. These pricked about the line of the horizon; like the
> pinnacles of some ornate and monstrous church, they stood there, in

the sparkling brightness of the morning, the fit signboard of a world of wonders.

They dropped anchor at Anaho, a collection of grass huts and a few stores beside the bay, while the passengers of the *Casco* "craned and stared, focused glasses, and wrangled over charts . . ." The only white man in the place was a German merchant named Regler. Accompanied by the chief, Taipikikino—who was tattooed across the face with bands of blue yet wore immaculate white linen trousers and coat—the German came out in a canoe to greet the visitors. A large boat bearing fruit and baskets for sale followed. The people, remembered Maggie Stevenson, "were in every state of undress. The display of legs was something we were not accustomed to; but as they were all tattooed in most wonderful patterns, it really looked quite as if they were wearing open-work silk tights." These people had been cannibals not so very long before, a fact which made social intercourse a delicate business. Other canoes followed the merchant to the *Casco*, as Louis recalled.

> . . . till the ship swarmed with stalwart, six foot men in every stage of undress; some in a shirt, some in a loin-cloth, one in a handkerchief imperfectly adjusted; some, and these the more considerable, tattooed from head to foot in awful patterns; some barbarous and knived; one, who sticks in my memory as something bestial, squatting on his hams in a canoe, sucking an orange and spitting it out again to alternate asides with ape-like vivacity.

The natives tried to trade and became irritated and insulting when "island curios at prices palpably absurd" were refused. It became a little frightening as they jostled and gesticulated. "The ship," said Louis, "was manifestly in their power; we had women on board; I knew nothing of my guests beyond the fact that they were cannibals . . ." Were they to be "butchered for the table"? Nothing came of it, though R.L.S. was soon pondering this first clash between cultures. That night he felt "a kind of rage" that he could not communicate with people who might as well have been "the dwellers of some alien planet." It was the last time he received such a reception in the islands.

His description of the people accords with those of Captain Cook, who said they were "scarcely ever less than six feet," and of Melville, who wrote: "In beauty of form they surpassed anything I had ever seen." Jack London, following in conscious imitation of Louis in his boat *Snark** in 1907, blamed white man's diseases for the islanders' subsequent decline. Certainly they had been hit hard: smallpox, TB, venereal diseases, "South Sea elephantiasis." Melville had seen "not a single instance of natural deformity"; London found the valley of Typee to be "the abode of death."

Stevenson did not pass in ignorance of any of this. He saw, as London would, how the idols and dwellings of older generations were being swallowed by vegetation as the population, often apathetic, dwindled. He questioned why some islands had suffered while others had not, and put forward his own explanation in the fifth chapter of *In the South Seas*. It is a modern-sounding one, and sensible, but odd coming from the future colonist and laird of Vailima.

> Upon the whole, the problem seems to me to stand thus: Where there have been fewest changes, important or unimportant, salutary or hurtful, there the race survives. Where there have been most, important or unimportant, salutary or hurtful, there it perishes. Each change, however small, augments the sum of new conditions to which the race has to become inured . . . It is easy to blame the missionary. But it is his business to make changes. It is surely his business, for example, to prevent war . . . I take the average missionary; I am sure I do him no more than justice when I suppose that he would hesitate to bombard a village, even in order to convert an archipelago. Experience begins to show us (at least in Polynesian islands) that change of habit is bloodier than a bombardment.

Such thinking was to shape his behaviour later on Samoa. In the meantime, R.L.S. (soon to be known as *Ona*—"owner," the first of his South Seas honorifics), Otis, and Lloyd went ashore first, leaving Fanny, Maggie, and Valentine to cope with the natives who swarmed over the *Casco*'s deck. Maggie Stevenson, ramrod straight in her white widow's cap, refusing to go barefoot as the others had done, coped without batting an eyelid: years of dealing with Edinburgh tradesmen had stood her in good stead. Later, the chief and his wife and party were invited back on board,

*See, generally, London, J.: *The Cruise of the Snark* (New York, 1911).

and the native women goggled at the luxuries of the ship while one lady decided to "strip up her dress, and, with cries of wonder and delight, rub herself bare-breeched upon the velvet cushions." Meanwhile, Otis took on a mate, making life on board and his own mind easier. He also replaced the drunken cook. Ah Fu had been brought to the Marquesas from China as a bond boy and joined the party gladly. He was to stay with the Stevensons for two years and become devoted to Fanny, who coached him in the culinary arts.

They remained on Nukahiva for six weeks. Louis, soon exploring the hinterland, picked up his first few Polynesian words, learning from a French missionary something of the island's cannibal history. R.L.S. was alert and eager, already sensitive to the changes wrought by colonisation. Yet again he was comparing a new place to his homeland:

> Not much beyond a century has passed since [the Scottish Highlanders and Islanders] were in the same convulsive and transitory states as the Marquesans of today. In both cases an alien authority enforced, the clans disarmed, the chiefs deposed, new customs introduced, and chiefly that fashion of regarding money as the means and object of existence ... In one the cherished practice of tattooing, on the other a cherished costume, proscribed ... The grumbling, the secret ferment, the fears and resentment, the alarms and sudden councils of Marquesan chiefs, reminded me continually of the days of Lovat and Struan. Hospitality, tact, natural fine manners, and a touchy punctillio are common to both races: common to both tongues the trick of dropping medial consonants.

"I did not dream there were such places or such races," R.L.S. wrote to Colvin. His health, already bolstered by the voyage, seemed almost normal now; certainly he was more vigorous than he had been for years. Deeply tanned, he walked and rode for hours, fascinated by everything he saw and heard. All of the party responded to the atmosphere. Fanny, writing to Henry James, evoked the picture of Presbyterian Maggie Stevenson "taking a moonlight promenade on the beach in the company of a gentleman dressed in a single handkerchief." Once a chief drunk on rum responded to a request to display his tattoos by stripping "to the buff." Neither woman admitted to embarrassment. Meanwhile, the people showered gifts on the visitors, including many of the objects they had tried to barter during that first disagreeable encounter. Maggie Stevenson, of all people, even began to doubt if missionary work had any point when the people were obviously so happy and content. One can only wonder what she would have made of the Mormons on Samoa today.

They set out for the Paumotus, en route to Tahiti. There was some doubt that their racing yacht was suitable for such a voyage—though Otis later rebutted Graham Balfour's suggestion that it was not—but they decided to risk the trip. They became lost for a day and a night on the way, and once almost ran aground on an atoll thirty miles from where it was supposed to have been. During the tricky voyage Louis had a curious vision of Drummond Street, the dark, narrow Edinburgh street which housed Rutherford's bar, "The Pump" of his student days. He wrote of the experience to Colvin:

> It came on me like a flashing of lightning. I simply returned thither, and into the past. And when I remember all I hoped and feared as I pickled about Rutherford's in the rain and the east wind; how I feared I should make a mere shipwreck, and yet timidly hoped not; how I feared I should never have a friend, far less a wife, and yet passionately hoped I might; how I hoped (if I did not take to drink) I should possibly write one little book. And then now—what a change! I feel somehow as if I should like the incident set upon a brass plate at the corner of that dreary thoroughfare for all students to read, poor devils, when their hearts are down.

It remains one of the most moving passages he wrote. Stevenson's feeling for the movement of time, the way in which the texture of memory could catch in his throat, was a remarkable thing. It was more than just nostalgia (though that was in it); it was more than craftsman's tricks (though they are in it: lightning, rain, shipwreck, in a chain of images); it was more even than honest autobiography (though the recollections of his pathetic youthful self ring true). It was a knowledge of the trail he had left, the route he had taken, and an awareness of how time and memory act on character. *What a change!* and yet, as he implies, nothing essential had changed, a thought from which the poor devils could take heart and every reader of Stevenson should remember. The past was always with him.

After five days they arrived at the lagoon of Fakarava, the main coral atoll, and anchored opposite the French residency. It became oppressively hot on the *Casco*. A cottage was rented on the horseshoe-shaped island, and they spent their days bathing in the lagoon, collecting shells, and their evenings listening to the stories of the half-Tahitian, half-French vice president of the island. "Night after night we sat entranced at his feet," Fanny recalled. Louis remembered some of those tales when he was composing the remarkable *Island Nights' Entertainments*, particularly the "Isles of Voices." "I know I never read it," Fanny wrote, "without a mental picture rising before me of the lagoon, and the cocoa palms, and the wonderful moonlight of Fakarava."

The atoll had another side to its character. Louis was conscious, here as elsewhere in the Pacific, of what could lie beneath the thin veneer of magnificence, of the cycle of fantastic growth and gross decay beneath the charming surface. Life could be precarious on these isles; there was, to a European, a kind of biological decadence at work. Some of the fish in the lagoon, so breathtaking in their shimmering beauty, were poisonous. Stevenson recalled how on other coral islands he had broken off "great lumps of ancient weathered rock" and found them "full of pendent worms as long as my hand, as thick as a child's finger, of a slightly pinkish white, and set as close as three or four to the square inch." There was another side to paradise in such places, where the land itself was "not of honest rock, but organic, part alive, part putrescent . . ."

Suddenly, as though the past was reaching out to reclaim him, Stevenson, recently so invigorated, fell ill. It began with a cold but a haemorrhage followed. Fanny, demanding a doctor, instructed Otis to get the *Casco* under way for Tahiti. The captain, uncertain of the overcast skies, would do no such thing. Fanny raged, but the seaman would not budge, refusing, rightly, to risk several lives for one, until the clear dawn broke.

They anchored off Papeete, the main town of Tahiti. Louis was very sick, and the French doctor they had found forecast that the next spurt of blood from his lungs would kill him. R.L.S., smoking a cigarette all the while, sent for Otis and gave him exact, sober instructions of what should and should not be done if the doctor was right. The captain's last reservations about this odd, skinny, excitable Scotsman turned to solid respect and affection.

Death was patient. Louis began to recover, and they moved to a small rented house close to where Melville and the mutineers had once been imprisoned by the French. But Papeete was not Stevenson's idea of the South Seas. The human flotsam of the eastern Pacific seemed to wash up there (an observation utilised in *The Ebb Tide*); the Polynesians seemed degraded. It was a depressing place; a "sort of halfway house between savage life and civilisation," Maggie called it. When locals informed them that the other side of the island was certainly beautiful but, sadly, inhabited by a people "almost as wild as the people of Anaho," Louis decided that it was just the spot for him.

They sailed first to Taravao but were disappointed by its dullness, its climate, and its maddening insect life. Two horses and a wagon were obtained from a recalcitrant old Chinese and a search made for a more congenial spot. Fanny demanded to be taken to "the largest native village and the most wild." Thus they fetched up at Tautira, where there commenced a strange episode in Stevenson's medical history.

He had not fully recovered from the illness that had taken him to Papeete, and the sixteen-mile drive to the village, involving numerous river crossings, had weakened him further. He fell into a fever, his lungs congested, and Fanny began to wonder what she had done by taking him so far from the reach of doctors. There was a knock on the door and a beautiful native woman, speaking English, identified herself as Möe. She had heard there was sick foreigner in the house and had therefore prepared a special dish for him. Somehow mullet soaked in brine with a sauce of coconut milk, lime juice, and pepper was fed to Louis several times a day. Within a week he was walking again. It is interesting to imagine what uncle George Balfour would have had to say about the unconventional therapy with which the "princess" Möe saved the life of his nephew. Fanny certainly believed that was what happened, and Stevenson later wrote a poem in honour of his saviour.

Meanwhile, dry rot had been discovered in the spars of the *Casco*: given the seas the yacht had come through, they had had a lucky escape. The Stevenson party settled down to wait while urgent repairs were carried out at Papeete. Louis returned to *The Master of Ballantrae*, that maddening book, and began to learn Tahitian, even attempting a couple of interminable ballads in what he assumed to be traditional style. Lloyd took photographs; they bathed in the sea; intrepid Valentine tried to learn to cook in the native style, out-of-doors; Maggie Stevenson was much taken with the Protestant villagers and their prayer meetings. She gave a feast for them involving six hens and a hundred coconuts. Each day they waited with impatience for the return of the *Casco*.

After a month they began to believe they were stranded. Their money and supplies were running low. When word came that their vessel required yet more work, the kindness of the natives, who offered to share their food, reduced both Louis and Fanny to tears. It was Christmas Day, 1888, two months after they had arrived in Tautira, before they could sail. Everyone wept again.

Those eight weeks transformed Louis from a tourist, however perceptive, to a man truly at home in the South Seas. Dressing and eating as a native, learning their language, their songs, and their customs, he shed another layer of his old self. He even became a "brother" to the tall, magnificent subchief Ori by "exchanging names" with him in the native way (Fanny exchanged hers with Möe). It was Ori, most of all, who had kept them from starvation, and this first real friendship with a man of the South Seas was never forgotten. Stevenson's character was becoming a composite of his present existence and his memories of Scotland. Much that had lain in between was forgotten, discarded. The past had a reality only in memory; for the present Louis was again a vagabond, a deliberate exile, a man of no country but that of his own imagination. It was his way of reaching maturity.

It took the *Casco* a month to reach Hawaii through alternating calms and storms. At one point they were faced with the choice of riding out a hurricane or running with it. Otis put the question to Louis and was mightily impressed with the Scotsman's unhesitating answer: "Run for it." The seamen were lashed to their posts; the passengers confined to their cabins; the storm struck them hard. It must have been terrifying, in a yacht so lately repaired, but Louis was exhilarated.

Fanny was seasick almost continuously as they battled on, and their supplies (even the precious tobacco) were all but exhausted when at last they reached Honolulu. Belle, waiting for the voyagers there with Joe Strong and their eight-year-old son, Austin, began to believe that the party had been lost to the Pacific. When at last they arrived, having been becalmed for a week just short of port, she sailed out to meet them and was relieved to find the family more than well, if a little obsessed with food. That night, at the Royal Hawaiian Hotel, they fell on their meal as though it was the first they had eaten in a year.

They rented a house—with a grand piano—near the beach at Waikiki and remained there for four months. Fanny had developed an aversion to the ocean and an ambivalence towards the whole adventure. Freedom for R.L.S. could often seem like nothing more than another upheaval for her, she whose life had been a series of dislocations. They talked of returning to Europe, of wintering on Madeira. Much of it, one suspects, was for Fanny's benefit: R.L.S. was already besotted with the Pacific. His wife wrote to Frances Sitwell:

> As for myself, I have had more cares than I was really fit for. To keep house on a yacht is no easy thing. When Louis and I broke loose from the ship and lived alone among the natives I got on very well. It was when I was deathly seasick, and the question was put to me by the cook, 'What shall we have for the cabin dinner, what for tomorrow's breakfast, what for lunch? and what about the sailors' food. Please come and look at the biscuits, for the weevils have got into them . . .' In the midst of heavy dangerous weather, when I was lying on the floor clutching a basin, down comes the mate with a cracked head, and I must needs cut off the hair matted with blood, wash and dress the wound . . . I do not like being 'the lady of the yacht,' but ashore—O, then I feel I am repaid for all! . . .

Even Louis conceded that the voyage had been a "foolhardy venture" which might easily have cost him even more money than he actually expended. Suspicions about the fitness of the *Casco* for such a trip seemed confirmed, whatever Captain Otis claimed. The captain was paid off and the maid Valentine, who had become involved with a seaman, dispensed with. She adored Louis but, having followed him halfway round the world, did not regret the parting from Fanny.

On Hawaii, R.L.S. accepted that a break from travel was necessary, if only to allow him to get on with his work. He finished *The Master* at last, glad to see the back of it and get his obligation to *Scribner;s*, which was already running the novel as a serial, off his neck. The technical problems he had set himself had almost defeated him. "*The Master* is finished," he wrote of the "hardest job I ever had to do," "and I am quite a wreck and do not care for literature." When the book was published in the autumn of 1889, the public thought better of it than its author, who never felt he had really resolved the problem of the ending, such a contrast was it to the rest of the story in style and structure.

Louis went back to writing his articles for McClure and turned his attention again to reworking *The Wrong Box*, "toiling like a galley slave." Fanny was still suffering from the aftereffects of the voyage and Stevenson from the hospitality of Kalakaua, the last king of Hawaii and a famous host, with whom Belle, resident on the island for several years, had become acquainted through the "royal set."

The imposing king thought himself a gentleman and a modern monarch. His taste for European luxuries ran to champagne by the case, a habit which doubtless fuelled several of his eccentric schemes to restore Polynesian pride in the face of foreign pressure. He was a political and cultural nationalist, struggling to preserve Hawaii from the predations of America. It was a hopeless effort: the dynasty ended with Kalakaua's death and the establishment of U.S. control (with the aid of the missionaries) over his former kingdom.

Nevertheless, contact with this extraordinary monarch, even through the haze of his formidable hospitality, gave R.L.S. his first inkling of the complexities of Pacific politics. He soon identified Germany as the chief villain of the piece, and wrote to *The Times* to say so. The letter was simplistic and misinformed, but the substance of it was sound. In the process Louis also learned that Samoa was at the eye of the political storm.

Kalakaua had read *Treasure Island* and *Dr. Jekyll*. He enjoyed talking to Stevenson about the islands and their history. He arranged for Louis to have language lessons and worked, in his tipsy way, to win the famous writer to his cause. Fanny, meanwhile, was worried that the book Louis planned to write about their experiences was not at all the sort of thing she thought worthwhile. Forgetting the plays, she argued that he was wasting his time and his talents. She wrote to Colvin to win his support, a shrewd-enough move given that S.C. was becoming increasingly sceptical about the whole Pacific adventure:

> Louis has the most enchanting material that any one ever had in the whole world for his book, and I am afraid he is going to spoil it all. He has taken into his Scotch-Stevenson head that a stern duty lies before him, and that his book must be a sort of scientific and historical, impersonal thing, comparing the different languages (of which he knows nothing really) and the different peoples . . . I am going to ask you to throw the weight of your influence as heavily as possible in the scales with me . . .

Fanny underestimated how involved Louis had already become with the South Seas. Nevertheless, her persistence in believing that she knew what was best for him was awesome. Even while Stevenson was trying to tell the world certain truths about life in the Pacific, and about what "civilisation" was doing to the islanders, she persisted in trying to guide his genius. "It is," she said with more exasperation than usual, "like managing an overbred horse! Why, with my own feeble hand I could write a book that the whole world would jump at . . ."

Louis, for his part, itched to be off again. Honolulu, with its electric lights and telephones, was a deal too civilised for his tastes. There was no more talk of Europe; instead his thoughts turned to Butaritari in the Kingsmills (Gilberts) and Ponape. From there, perhaps, to the Philippines or China. Ah Fu would be able to go home at last. Some Boston missionaries were about to set off for the Kingsmills aboard the *Morning Star*, but negotiations to secure passage with them proved difficult. Then Louis heard that the *Equator*, a trading schooner, would soon be arriving at Hawaii on its way south. The vessel's owner, a Mr. Wightman of San Francisco, was more than happy to agree to a charter, but on his terms: the Stevensons could stop at any port but must allow the master, a young Scot named Denny Reid, to pursue the copra trade. Fanny recalled the arrangement in a note published with *The Wrecker*.

> By the 'charter party' of the *Equator* we agreed to pay a fixed sum down for the trip from Honolulu to Butaritari and through the Kingsmill group, with the proviso that whenever the ship's anchor went down, if for no more than five minutes, my husband should have the right to hold the ship

there for three days without extra charge. At the same time we always tried
to consider the owner's interests, not allowing ours to clash with his.

Maggie Stevenson did not join them, choosing instead to return to Edinburgh, where Aunt Jane was ill. The plan was for the rest of the party
to take ship from China and join her, sooner or later, in Britain. Valentine
Roch, meanwhile, travelled to San Francisco without a backward glance,
making her home there for the rest of her long life.

Louis, Fanny, Lloyd, and Ah Fu were all that remained of the *Casco*
party. While Fanny braced herself for another contest with the ocean—
this time in a "tiny boat" of sixty-four tons—her husband drew up a new
will. Joe Strong, who had participated in a drunken embassy on behalf
of Kalakaua, had already briefed Louis about Samoa: a seed had been
planted.

When they did at last depart, the *Honolulu Advertiser* bade Stevenson a
wry, if less than accurate, farewell: "It is to be hoped that Mr Stevenson
will not fall victim to native spears; but in his present state of bodily
health, perhaps the temptation to kill him will not be very strong."

The *Equator*, off in San Francisco, was unable to receive its charter
party until June, however. In the meantime, Louis continued to gather
copy for McClure. He had a journalist's instincts—if not the objectivity
supposed necessary by some—and knew a good story when he heard one.
Leprosy, common in the South Seas, had already created controversy in
Hawaii, partly because of its policy of forcibly isolating victims and partly
because of the sectarian tensions it had created between Catholics and the
Protestant majority. Louis decided to visit the lepers' prison on Molokai.

In her preface to *Lay Morals*, Fanny remembered an incident during
their time at Anaho:

I remember one afternoon . . . when my husband and I, tired after a long
quest for shells, sat down on the sand to rest awhile, a native man stepped
out from under some cocoanut tree, regarding us hesitatingly as though
fearful of intruding. My husband waved an invitation to the stranger to join
us, offering his cigarette to the man in the island fashion. The cigarette was
accepted and, after a puff or two, courteously passed back again according
to native etiquette.The hand that held it was the maimed hand of a leper.
To my consternation my husband took the cigarette and smoked it out.

After another incident with a leprous girl, Louis became determined to visit the settlement on Hawaii. "The more he saw of leprosy, and he saw much in the islands," Fanny remembered, "the higher rose his admiration for the simple priest of Molokai. "I must see Molokai," he said many times . . ." The priest's name was Damien.

Jack London was to make the same trip years later and watch the lepers enjoying horse and donkey races. He mingled freely with the sufferers and was at pains to stress how isolation had helped to combat the disease. It was, London said, a "happy colony." He found "horrors" on the remote peninsula, but that was in the nature of the disease. "One thing is certain," he wrote in *The Cruise of the Snark*. "The leper in the Settlement is far better off than the leper who lies in hiding outside."

In Stevenson's day things were less civilised. Once out of sight, the lepers were out of Hawaii's mind. The settlement had been neglected, at least until a Belgian priest, Father Damien, volunteered to spend the rest of his days there. Eventually he too fell victim to the disease and died of it.

Catholics thought Damien a hero, and wanted to erect a monument to him. His Protestant rivals, who had been fighting a missionary war with the Church of Rome for decades, preferred to spread unpleasant tales, mainly to the effect that the priest took leprous women to bed with him. Many such un-Christian stories were current when R.L.S.—"after the waste of much time and red tape"—took the steamer to Kalawao-Kalaupepa with a group of nuns and several lepers. He tried to be resolute but was, at first, afraid, as he told Fanny:

> My horror of the horrible is about my weakest point; but the moral love-liness at my elbow blotted all else out; and when I found that one of them was crying, poor soul, quietly under her veil, I cried a little myself; then I felt as right as a trivet, only a little crushed to be there so uselessly. I thought it was a sin and a shame she should feel unhappy; I turned round to her and said something like this: 'Ladies, God himself is here to give you welcome. I'm sure it is good for me to be beside you; I hope it will be blessed to me; I thank you for myself and for the good you do me.'

He stayed for eight days, tolerating the Catholicism much as he had years before at Our Lady of the Snows in the Cévennes, talking to the lepers and trying to live as they lived. He learned what he could of Damien, long dead, and described him to Colvin:

> He was a European peasant, dirty, bigoted, untruthful, unwise, tricky, but superb with generosity, residual candour and fundamental good humour; convince him that he had done wrong (it might take hours of insult) and he would undo what he had done and like his corrector better. A man, with all the grime and paltriness of mankind, but a saint and hero all the more for that.

Damien's heroism was, for Louis, authentic. Yet towards the end of the year, when he was on Samoa, he learned that the priest had been denounced and that the monument might not be erected. Later still, while in Australia, he read the letter written by the Reverend C. M. Hyde of Honolulu which accused Damien of vice and incompetence. It suggested in a mealymouthed way, that the priest had contracted leprosy through sex. The text demonstrated to R.L.S., the old enemy of cant and pious liars, that there was no hypocrite like a god-fearing hypocrite. "I'll not believe it," Fanny recorded him as saying before he saw the letter in print, "unless I see it with my own eyes; for it is too damnable for belief!" On 2 August 1889, Hyde had indeed written to the Reverend H. B. Gage, describing Damien:

> The simple truth is, he was a coarse, dirty man, headstrong and bigoted. He was not sent to Molokai, but went there without orders; did not stay at the leper settlement (before he became one himself) . . . He had no hand in the reforms and improvements inaugurated . . . He was not a pure man in his relations with women, and the leprosy of which he died should be attributed to his vices and carelessness.

Stevenson's "Open Letter to the Reverend Dr. Hyde of Honolulu," dated 25 February 1890, was superbly passionate if ill conceived. He did not seem to doubt that Hyde's allegations were accurate—though others have questioned them—but chose instead to explore his old idea that bad men can do good things, and vice versa. The diatribe is not perhaps all that Damien himself would have wanted for a defence, but it proves that the Scottish bar lost a formidable advocate when it lost Louis.

The plight of the lepers had moved R.L.S. deeply: that was the heart of it. It was a foolish or an unlucky man who assailed the object of his affections at any time. On this occasion it was Hyde's misfortune to become the victim of one of the most sustained, comprehensive, delicate, penetrating and vicious pieces of invective in the language. Years of contempt for bad faith and sanctimonious frauds poured on the reverend doctor's head. He deserved it. Stevenson had met him once, but was not restrained by any affection.

Damien was poor, he wrote; the Protestant missionaries (Hyde included) had grown rich:

> Your Church and Damien's were in Hawaii upon a rivalry to do well: to help, to edify, to set divine examples. You having (in one huge instance) failed, and Damien succeeded, I marvel it should not have occurred to you that you were doomed to silence; that when you had been outstripped in that high rivalry, and sat inglorious in the midst of your well-being, in your pleasant room—and Damien, crowned with glories and horrors, toiled and rotted in that pigsty of his under the cliffs at Kalawao—you, the elect who would not, were the last man on earth to collect and propagate gossip on the volunteer who would and did.

Louis, writing in the sure knowledge that he could face ruinous legal action, was determined that Hyde should not misunderstand him. He understood the core of the Christian faith better than Damien's spiteful enemy:

> . . . to bring it home to you, I will suppose your story to be true. I will suppose—and God forgive me for supposing it—that Damien faltered and stumbled in his narrow path of duty; I will suppose that, in the horror of his isolation, perhaps in the fever of incipient disease, he, who was doing so much more than he had sworn, failed in the letter of his priestly oath—he, who was so much a better man than either you or me, who did what we have never dreamed of daring—he too tasted of our common frailty. 'Oh, Iago, the pity of it!' The least tender should be moved to tears; the most incredulous to prayer. And all that you could do was to pen your letter to the Reverend H. B. Gage!

Louis did not hesitate to publish but took the trouble to discuss the matter with his family. If he was to be bankrupted by Hyde they should at least have the chance to offer an opinion. Belle recorded that Fanny rose to the challenge and gave him her full support:

> Throwing the manuscript on the table, he turned to his wife. She, who never failed him, rose to her feet and, holding out both hands to him in a gesture of enthusiasm, cried: 'Print it! Publish it!'

A lawyer named, appropriately enough, Mr. Moses, advised that Stevenson's diatribe was unpublishable in the legal sense. He was right, and Louis had the "Open Letter" printed privately. It did not stay private for long. In Honolulu it appeared in translation in a native newspaper and was afterwards circulated widely, in the Pacific and elsewhere. Ever after—drawing the line "at cannibalism"—he refused any payment for it. When the piece was published as a pamphlet, the proceeds went to the lepers. Fanny, meanwhile, used Louis's visit to Molokai as background to a short story of her own, an overwrought piece entitled "The Half-White," which a dutiful *Scribner's Magazine* published.

Stevenson's adversary with the fateful surname chose not to sue, however, doubtless reasoning that a court case would attract still more unwelcome publicity. Theological debate might be no business of a ruffian like Louis, but Hyde knew from the "Open Letter" that he had stirred a hornet. He contended that his own letter had not been meant for publication: it was Iago's excuse and excused nothing. Afterwards, R.L.S. thought he had been too harsh on Hyde in his eagerness to defend Damien, but he hit the right target. The reverend doctor was typical of the *haoles* (whites) corrupting the South Seas with Christ and commerce. If nothing else the episode gave Stevenson some sense of his own powers as a celebrity, a political animal, and a polemicist. He knew where he stood.

The "Open Letter" also demonstrated an essential decency that others would later try to devalue. Louis in full cry, righting wrongs with the point of his pen, was a magnificent spectacle. He had meant every word that he wrote, and his sincerity had animated his prose. He had taken responsibility for a stranger's good name, and the gesture, so typical, did as much to make his own as any fiction. Fanny, no writer, got it succinctly right in her preface to *Lay Morals*:

> Father Damien was vindicated by a stranger, a man of another country and another religion from his own.

It was a foretaste of battles to come.

15 *1889*

There is no duty we so much underrate as the duty of being happy. By being happy, we sow anonymous benefits upon the world, which remain unknown even to ourselves, or when they are disclosed, surprise nobody so much as the benefactor.

"An Apology for Idlers"

A fter ten heavenly days my husband determined to make his home for ever in the islands," Fanny wrote, years later, of the voyage of the *Equator*. He may have said some such thing, but it was not until they were entrenched at Vailima on Samoa that he accepted, finally, that he would never return to Europe to live. Even then, Scotland and France tugged at him, old friendships still stirred him, the past still shadowed him. Until Vailima, the only decision he made was that he would not be settled, not tied.

Even aboard the *Equator* he had no thought of putting down roots: instead he planned to live as an island trader (how he was to write was unclear) on a schooner he would buy with the proceeds of *The Wrecker*, another collaboration with Lloyd. He already had a name in mind for the vessel—the *Northern Light*. Trading would make his fortune while the South Seas preserved his health; Denny Reid would be his captain. "All details were arranged," Fanny remembered of the ninety-ton vessel they planned, "even to the rifle racks, the patent davits, the steam launch, the library, and the price—fifteen thousand dollars." They would head for Samoa, which Louis had heard was well served by the mail steamers necessary to make serial publication possible, and stay there until the money for the fantasy was earned.

Nothing came of it, fortunately. It was another scheme in a long line of Stevenson's schemes, quickly forgotten, though he earned the fifteen thousand dollars soon enough. Fanny put the change of heart down to the discovery that South Sea trading often involved near-criminal behaviour—and was shocked to note, in her reminiscences, that Denny Reid, with his "Scotch bonnet" and his winning ways, had ended up a convict in Fiji, charged with the fraudulent sale of a vessel. Nevertheless, the episode showed how Louis's mind was running.

Literature never lost R.L.S., but at times he grew distant from it. Knocking out books with Lloyd and scribbling articles for McClure, always for easy money, he seemed for a while to evade his talent. It is usual to say that he drove himself to keep his family; it is more true to say that he drove himself to keep himself *and* his family in the style to which they strove to become accustomed. Had he lived in Europe, Louis would have been both rich and famous. In the Pacific money went through his hands like a receding tide.

To be fair, other matters engaged him. His projected volume on the Pacific was intended as serious scientific and social journalism; today we would call it anthropology. In the meantime his taste for the real challenges of his art seemed to desert him, perhaps because his struggle with *The Master of Ballantrae* had made him doubt himself, or simply because he was having too much fun. And though letters kept him in touch with his profession, fame seemed a remote thing. The literary life embodied by Henley was, in any case, no longer to his taste. The *Equator* dropped the party at Butaritari and they stayed for six weeks, during which time Louis barely wrote a word. He was becalmed between novels and seemed happy to be so.

The Wrecker has many good things in it, but like all of Stevenson's collaborations with Osbourne, it also has the air of art prefabricated, as though written to a formula. It seems compromised, and was: Stevenson was ever ready to sacrifice his art for his family and did not always try to curb the instinct.

At Honolulu he had become fascinated with the plight of some sailors whose vessel had been wrecked and whose story sounded like fiction. He had tried and failed, according to Fanny, to penetrate the mystery. She later recalled the bare bones of the narrative R.L.S. heard:

> While we were submerged in preparations for the voyage, Honolulu was thrilled by the landing of a number of castaways picked up on Midway Island by a passing vessel. This, in itself, was not so extraordinary, but the circumstances were unusual and mysterious. The story, which was far from convincing, as told by the captain of the wrecked ship, a barque called the *Wandering Minstrel*, was that he had fitted out his vessel in Hong Kong for the purpose of catching sharks. He meant, he said, to make spurious cod-liver oil from the livers of the sharks, and sell the dried fins to the Chinese . . . it was plain that fishing for sharks was not the sole object . . . The wages of the sailors, for one thing, were to be far beyond the usual rate of payment.
>
> Almost nothing was saved from the stores of the *Wandering Minstrel*; the castaways were soon in desperate circumstances, and in no condition to make terms with a ship that answered their signals of distress. The captain of the rescuing vessel first ascertained exactly what amount of money had been saved from the wreck; it was just this sum, several thousand dollars . . . that the stranger demanded as his price for carrying the miserable creatures to the nearest civilised port, where they were dumped, penniless, on the wharf.

During the voyage out on the *Equator*, he and Lloyd talked the business over, but no matter how intriguing their conversations, they did not translate their excitement into prose. Readers of *The Wrecker* are obliged to be patient if they want the meat of the tale. First come several chapters full of material on the lives of artists in Paris and Barbizon—interesting enough in themselves—and spurious recollections of Edinburgh, followed by some nonsense business concerning an invented American state ("Muskegon"), then more memories, this time of San Francisco. For once, Louis allowed his autobiographical streak to overwhelm his artistic instincts.

Later in the book there are fine passages: the storm, the wreck on Midway Island, the massacre. After R.L.S. was dead, Lloyd claimed authorship of the book's better parts (he could hardly claim Edinburgh or Barbizon), though few people have been inclined to believe him. There are times when an admirer of Stevenson wishes the pushy young protégé had fallen overboard in the South Seas.

Louis, obviously aware of the book's defects, added an "epilogue" dedicated to Will Low in which he attempted to justify its construction in the name of "theory."

> It was plainly desirable . . . that our hero and narrator should partly stand aside from those with whom he mingles, and be but a pressed man in the dollar hunt. Thus it was that Loudon Dodd became a student of the plastic arts, and that our globe-trotting story came to visit Paris and look in on Barbizon.

Stevenson was rarely so defensive or transparent in print. Nevertheless, *Scribner's* gave him his fifteen thousand dollars for the novel, and serialisation began in August 1891. In a letter to Colvin from Vailima towards the end of that year, Louis was more honest about the defects of *The Wrecker*, yet still insisting that he had never had any great literary ambitions for the book:

> The part that is genuinely good is Nares, the American sailor; that is a genuine figure; had there been more Nares it would have been a better book; but of course it didn't set up to be a book, only a long tough yarn with some pictures of the manners of to-day in the greater world . . .

Nares was modelled on Captain Otis, and its "genuinely good" parts meant that *The Wrecker* was soon outselling *The Master of Ballantrae*. Had he put aside his desire to help Lloyd—or quelled his own laziness—it would have been a better novel than it is. One contemporary critic, at least, wondered if Louis was chancing his hand and testing the public by palming inferior material off on them.

The voyage produced another literary oddity, a little story, lost for decades, called "The Enchantress." Louis composed it sometime during the voyage, but the twenty-seven-page manuscript was only discovered in 1990, when Professor David Mann of Miami University in Ohio found it among uncatalogued papers at Yale. Set in France and first entitled "A Singular Marriage," it tells of a gambler, Hatfield, who sets out to snare a wealthy orphan, Miss Croft, and is himself ensnared.

The tale, of no great merit, seems to have been suppressed by Lloyd, who may have thought the female character bore too close a resemblance to Fanny. Certainly the manuscript was sold in 1914, the year she died, and disappeared after 1923. As the inimitable Associated Press informed the world's newspapers when the piece was rediscovered: "In cumbersome Victorian English, Hatfield puts the bite on Miss Croft, who identifies him as a gentleman. She gives him 1000 francs—a bundle in those days—turns up the charm and makes a proposition."

The proposition is marriage, on certain terms: if Hatfield refuses, she will set him up in business and never see him again; if they marry, he will have three hundred pounds a year (less than he would if he refuses) and must accept all her orders. They marry and Hatfield, now in love, attempts to end the bargain over the three-hundred-pound stipend. After the wedding the Enchantress orders him to return to his hotel. Two days later a lawyer's letter arrives, saying she has left the country. The twist, it transpires, is that Miss Croft had just turned twenty-one but could not gain control of her inheritance from her guardian until she married. Doubting her guardian's ability to preserve her fortune, she had done just that. Hatfield, the con artist, has been conned.

Joe Strong had joined the party on the *Equator*, but his wife had chosen to remain in Hawaii. His drinking, opium taking, and spendthrift habits had poisoned a marriage that had ceased to exist in anything but name. The husband's health, mental and physical, was poor after years of self-abuse. Soon he was trying everyone's patience. In Hawaii, Fanny and Louis had tried to discipline him, extracting promises and abject apologies. Joe had even signed a legal document putting "his affairs absolutely in Louis's hands." Nevertheless, Belle Strong had seen him depart on the cruise with "positive relief . . . I felt that I didn't have to worry about him any more."

She had also quarrelled with Louis over his decision to send her and Austin to Sydney while the *Equator* journeyed around the islands. Her accommodation was already chosen and financial arrangements made when Stevenson broke the news. Asked what she was to do when she got to Australia, the stern stepfather replied: "Wait till called for." Fanny and Louis had decided, evidently, that Joe was not the only one capable of misbehaving. Prodded by his wife, R.L.S. played the patriarch. As the one who was paying the bills, he was entitled to the role, but the shade of

Thomas Stevenson must have found it all amusing. Joe was to become more than a nuisance as the voyage went on.

The first days were idyllic, the weather fine, the seas kind. Near the equator, they made landfall at the Kingsmills, a group inhabited by Micronesian people very different from the Polynesians. Here they were truly remote. Writing for *In the South Seas*, Louis said: "No posts run in these islands; communication is by accident; where you may have designed to go is one thing, where you shall be able to arrive another." On 14 July, while the *Equator* set off to trade for copra, R.L.S. and his party waded ashore (the tide was out) at Butaritari, on the island of Great Makin. American influence was strong there, and Wightman, owner of the *Equator*, had a trading post. Unfortunately, the Stevensons chose to arrive in the aftermath of the Fourth of July celebrations.

The entire population seemed to be drunk. King Tebureimoa had lifted the *tabu* on alcohol to mark America's national day and turned Butaritari into a madhouse. "For ten days," by Louis's account, "the town had been passing the bottle or lying . . . in hoggish sleep; and the king . . . continued to maintain the liberty, to squander his savings on liquor, and to join in and lead the debauch." The monarch was, Fanny said in her note to *The Wrecker*, "a besotted, dull, obese man."

> Those of the natives who had money thronged the bars of the two saloons, the 'Sans Souci' and 'The Land We Live In'; while the rest contented themselves with the fiery spirit made from the sap of the cocoanut blossom. This beverage, called sour toddy by the traders, causes the person intoxicated with it to 'see "red".' Scenes of atrocious barbarity were common, and our own safety seemed doubtful.

The cottage they had rented from a missionary was next door to the Sans Souci. The trader there finally closed its doors, but this only made matters worse: ". . . a crowd gathered round the place, fighting and clamouring for drink . . . Little work was done during our six weeks stay in Butaritari." Louis recalled:

> The whites were the authors of this crisis; it was upon their own proposal that the freedom had been granted at first; and for a while, in the interests of trade, they were doubtless pleased it should continue. That pleasure had

now sometime ceased; the bout had been prolonged (it was conceded) unduly; and it now began to be a question how it might conclude.

The king was a thug and his men, fighting drunk, were armed with rifles. It was Stevenson's belief that "too surly a refusal" to sell them booze "might prove the signal for a massacre." Louis, Fanny, and the rest felt themselves under threat, and made a point of pistol practice on the beach—"to the admiration of the natives"—with the many empty bottles that were strewn around. At night, shots were fired and the visitors seemed in real danger. Eventually, after stones had been hurled at him on two occasions ("the mark of some intimidation") while he was on the verandah, R.L.S. took a hand. A birthday celebration was being prepared for a "little princess"; state visits were expected from tributary chiefs: ". . . if the debauch continued after the bulk of them had come, a collision, perhaps a revolution, was to be expected." With no little difficulty he managed to have the *tabu* on alcohol restored.

Sunday, July 28.—This day we had the afterpiece of the debauch. The king and queen, in European clothes, and followed by armed guards, attended church for the first time, and sat perched aloft in a precarious dignity under the barrel-hoops. Before sermon his majesty clambered from the dais, stood lopsidedly upon the gravel floor, and in a few words abjured drinking. The queen followed suit . . . All the men in church were next addressed in turn; each held up his right hand, and the affair was over—throne and church were reconciled.

The *Equator* was late in returning. When she at last appeared, the Stevenson party set off to investigate one of the legends of the Pacific, King Tembinoka, the absolute ruler of Apemama, Kurai, and Araukai, whose territorial ambitions were kept in check, though only just, by the Royal Navy. Louis hoped to see life in Tembinoka's kindgom at first hand, a foolhardy idea given that the ruler's viciousness was no myth. There was, R.L.S. discovered, ". . . only one white on Apemama, and he on sufferance, living far from court, and hearkening and watching his conduct like a mouse in a cat's ear." The visitor would need his wits about him.

Tembinoka protected his copra monopoly by paying a personal visit to every trading vessel. He also had a taste for western goods, fake western "brandy" and western clothes, mixing male and female attire as the fancy took him. He earned himself a chapter in *In the South Seas*:

> His corpulence is now portable; you would call him lusty rather than fat; but his gait is still dull, stumbling, and elephantine. He neither stops nor hastens, but goes about his business with an implacable deliberation. We could never see him and not be struck with his extraordinary natural means for the theatre: a beaked profile like Dante's in the mask, a mane of long black hair, the eye brilliant, imperious and inquiring: for certain parts, and to one who could have used it, the face was a fortune. His voice matched it well, being shrill, powerful, and uncanny . . . Where there are no fashions, none to set them, few to follow them if they were set, and none to criticise, he dresses . . . 'to his own heart.' Now he wears a woman's frock, now a naval uniform; now . . . figures in a masquerade costume of his own design: trousers and a singular jacket with shirt tails, the cut and fit wonderful for island workmanship, the material always handsome . . . In the woman's frock he looks ominous and weird beyond belief.

The king came aboard the *Equator* and began immediately to assess its contents. A battered dressing case of Fanny's caught his eye. He informed the whites that he would buy it and counted out some twenty pounds in gold sovereigns and half sovereigns. At first the Stevensons refused, but then, having learned something of local tradition, said he might have it as a gift. His face fell: he could not refuse, and now he was in the debt of these whites. "I shamed," he said. In exchange for Fanny's case Tembinoka was obliged to allow the party ashore, and to treat them well. Fanny remembered his hospitality after the schooner had gone trading once more. The king

> . . . had four houses moved from another part of the island to be set up for our use near some brackish water that filtered through the coral of the beach into a turbid pool rising and falling with the tides. Every evening an old man we called Uncle Barker, because his speech was like the barking of a dog, brought us green cocoanuts fresh from the trees for our drinking, so we need use the pool only for washing and bathing. Besides Uncle Barker, several slaves were given to us, including three buxom young damsels who spent most of their time frolicking in the pool. Our premises were

enclosed within a taboo line which it was death for any native commoner, not connected with our family, to cross.

Here we lived in peace of mind for more than three weeks. At last a real beginning of *The Wrecker* was made, and several poems and many letters were written besides.

Their houses in "Equator Town," as they called their hamlet, were "something like bird cages, standing on stilts about four feet above the ground," according to Fanny. Lloyd thought his like "a sort of giant clothes basket." The time passed easily, there and at the "palace" stuffed with rusting knickknacks and gadgets the king had bought from traders. Defeated by etiquette, Tembinoka made friends with Stevenson. Living in a kind of harem himself—as a "popular master in a girls' school might," Louis thought—he also developed an admiration for Fanny, who was plainly a woman of status. The king played cards with his guests, in a game of his own devising (which R.L.S. alone of whites was able to master), composed poetry, or quizzed Louis in simple but direct English on the mysteries of western ways. Tembinoka was no fool and hoped to learn much from Stevenson:

> After etiquette, government, law, the police, money, and medicine were his chief interests—things vitally important to himself as a king and the father of his people. It was my part not only to supply new information but to correct the old. 'My patha he tell,' or 'White men he tell me,' would be his constant beginning; 'You think he lie?' Sometimes I thought he did.

The *Equator* was gone so long they thought it lost and almost took passage on the *Tiernan* bound for Samoa. Lloyd remembered that the price had been too high; Fanny said she had had an intuition. The vessel sank, in any case, and all but three of its hands died.

Early in November, Reid returned and the Stevensons made their farewells to the tearful king. He had developed a real fondness for Louis:

> Miss Stlevens he good man, woman he good man, boy he good man; all good man . . . I think Miss Stlevens he big chiep all the same cap'n man-o'-wa'. I think Miss Stlevens he rich man all the same me. All go schoona . . . You no see king cry before. King all the same man: feel bad, he cry. I very sorry.

The plan was to sail to Samoa and pick up the mail steamer bound for Sydney. From there they would return by stages to Britain for a visit. The delay waiting for the *Equator's* return had meant that the party was on a reduced diet for several weeks, and none felt especially fit. Equally, the voyage to Samoa proved difficult: once they ran aground; once they narrowly avoided a reef; once, in a sudden squall, the foretopmast snapped and the rigging became entangled. Reid was otherwise engaged, and only Ah Fu had the good sense to cut the right line. Louis, of all people, admitted to Colvin in a letter that "the sea is a terrible place," with its confinements, ceaseless motion, and poor food.

Still, he had the makings of a book, even if it was a book which Fanny opposed and to which Colvin objected. Sailing to Samoa, after setting down the bulk of his material during the eight weeks on Apemama, Louis wrote to S.C., explaining what he had in mind:

> My book is now practically modelled; if I can execute what is designed, there are few better books now extant on this globe, bar the epics, and the big tragedies, and histories, and the choice lyric poets and a novel or so—none. But it is not executed yet; and let not him that putteth on his armour, vaunt himself. At least, nobody has had such stuff; such wild stories, such beautiful scenes, such singular intimacies, such manners and traditions, so incredible a mixture of the beautiful and horrible, the savage and civilised.

This was high ambition for a work that was to remain unpublished in anything like the form he intended until after his death. The history of *In The South Seas* is tangled; it never became the large, definitive study he intended; but the main reason for the abortion was a simple one: Fanny was opposed, "and I prefer her peace of mind to my ideas."

The use of the phrase "peace of mind" was to acquire significance. It is, even in this context, an odd way to describe what was, essentially, an intellectual argument, but then Fanny suffered and celebrated with all parts of her being simultaneously. Her objections to his writing of "his own theories on the vexed questions of race and language"—so she described them to her ally Colvin—were passionate.

R.L.S. was equally passionate. In 1893 he told a Honolulu editor that he intended a "prose-epic," one that would deal with the "unjust (yet I can see the inevitable) extinction of the Polynesian Islanders by our shabby civilisation . . ." He had no interest in exploiting these truths for the autobiographical romances that Fanny insisted were his metier. Neither won the battle. The real point is that Louis was prepared to give up a book over which he lavished so much work for Fanny. Whether he did it for love or for peace of mind, the decision must still be accounted a mark of weakness. His wife, meanwhile, wrote one of the conspiratorial letters she reserved for Mrs. Sitwell:

> He says I do not take the broad view of the artist, but hold the cheap opinions of the general public that a book must be interesting. How I do long for a little wholesome monumental correction to be applied to the Scotch side of Louis's artistic temperament.

As well ask the wind to stop blowing. Sadly, McClure and the New York *Sun* were also disappointed with what Stevenson eventually sent them, no doubt to Fanny's satisfaction. McClure chopped the copy hard, and wrote to R.L.S. early in 1891 that "the letters did not come as letters are supposed to come. They were not a correspondence from the South Seas . . ." In other words, they did not meet the terms of the *Sun* contract. Yet Louis had warned McClure repeatedly that this would be the case, maintaining all along that he would send chapters, not letters. Nevertheless, the newspaper ran only thirty-seven instalments rather than fifty; Louis earned, from British, American, and Australian serialisations, only a thousand pounds or so.

Fanny's commercial instincts may have been right, but her artistic instinct was flawed, even if, ironically, it was she who demanded that her husband stick to "art." Lloyd, puffed up with "collaboration," agreed with her and matched her mistake. Even now, in editions (such as the Swanston) in which Stevenson's other Pacific nonfiction has been added to the early material, the book is not as he intended. Yet it has many passages which are magnificent; it has a spirit unprejudiced, eager to learn and inform; and it has an instinctive sympathy the modern tourist cannot comprehend.

Colvin's reaction was somehow emblematic of the western ignorance that R.L.S. was attempting to combat. "I see that romantic surroundings are the worst surroundings possible for a romantic writer," whinnied Oscar Wilde a few years later. "In Gower Street Stevenson could have written a new *Trois Mousquetaires*. In Samoa he wrote letters to *The Times* about Germans." Such sentiments explained why Louis was in the South Seas and the likes of Oscar and S.C. were not: even if he had remained in Europe, Stevenson would not have been languid in Gower Street applying a coat of varnish to Dumas.

Those who had waited years for Louis to mature now found, to their alarm, that his maturity was leading him where they could not follow. He had become a serious artist and such do not take tuition from the likes of Colvin or Henley. He knew that what was happening in the Pacific was of importance for all of humanity and struggled to understand it. His "realism" was as truthful as anything in Zola, but it did not transgress his own laws of narrative.

Glib words like "vagabond" and "civilisation" still set up false oppositions. To see entire cultures destroyed had, for a Scot, historical significance. The large ate the small and art was no defence: were not the Polynesians as cultured as the Gaels?

Yet there was more to it than that. How was civilisation to proceed if all it could do was to destroy the weak? How was the effort of understanding between cultures to be made? Stevenson was never optimistic about the future of Polynesia. It was both a practical and a moral issue, shorn of romance. How to understand humanity? How to make justice? His art, when he returned to it, would never be the same again.

So much was possible. On the morning of 7 December 1889, after twenty-six days at sea and a birthday party with shark and champagne, the mass of Upolu rose before the *Equator*. "Come up and see Samoa!" Fanny shouted, and he did: a sheet of jungle streaked with lava flows, worn volcanic shapes rising from the ocean floor, plantations of coco palms, some houses and churches scattered on the slopes, the surf thunderous on the barrier reef. Then, the narrow coral neck of Apia harbour littered with the wrecks of foreign warships dealt a lesson in a storm eight months before. Canoes came out to greet them, followed by a boat with an American trader named Harry Moors, a friend of Joe Strong. He offered to take the party ashore.

Soon enough there was to be "a hard and interesting and beautiful life" on this island only forty-five miles long. That was not yet part of the plan—Louis meant only to do a little work on his South Seas book before moving on—but the plan was made to be flawed. The end had begun. Years before, in 1878, in a piece that became, ironically enough, a favourite of Henley's, he had written of El Dorado and the search that cannot end:

> Happily we all shoot at the moon with ineffectual arrows; our hopes are set on inaccessible El Dorado; we come to an end of nothing here below. Interests are only plucked up to sow themselves again, like mustard . . . We may study for ever, and we are never as learned as we would. We have never made a statue worthy of our dreams. And when we have discovered a continent, or crossed a chain of mountains, it is only to find another ocean or another plain upon the further side.

16 1890–1892

The Reverend W. E. Clarke of the London Missionary Society, who was to come to know Louis well and preside at his funeral, remembered the strange group of vagabonds who arrived off the *Equator* that day. His memoir is worth quoting at length:

A cloudless tropical morning, the sun relentless; the trade wind sweeping across the bay, driving the huge Pacific rollers against the barrier reef in great masses of foam. The two giant palms which mark the approach of the mission compound were arching and creaking in the gale . . . Making my way along the 'Beach'—the sandy track with its long, straggling line of 'stores' and drink saloons—I met a little group of three European strangers,—two men and a woman. The latter wore a print gown, large gold crescent earrings, a Gilbert-island hat of plaited straw, encircled with a wreath of small shells, a scarlet silk scarf round her neck, and a brilliant plaid shawl across her shoulders: her bare feet were encased in white canvas shoes, and across her back was slung a guitar.

The younger of her two companions was dressed in a striped pyjama suit . . . a slouch straw hat of native make, dark blue sun-spectacles, and over his shoulders a banjo. The other man was dressed in a shabby suit of white flannels that had seen many better days, a white drill yachting cap with a prominent peak, a cigarette in his mouth, and a photographic camera in his hand. Both the men were barefooted. They had evidently just landed from the little schooner now lying placidly at anchor, and my first thought was that, probably, they were wandering players *en route* to New Zealand, compelled by their poverty to take the cheap conveyance of a trading vessel.

So were they reduced, deprived of civilisation's restraints, to banjos and bare feet. Harry Moors, a businessman of some standing in Samoa and a force in local politics, had thought R.L.S. looked "weak" on his arrival. Soon the visitor "could not stand still" in his eagerness to investigate his surroundings. Moors and his Samoan wife insisted on putting the writer and his party up until they could find a place to stay.

Apia, the only town of significance, had once serviced whalers in the days when the fourteen islands of the group were known as the Navigators. By Stevenson's day it had become a society of bums, beachcombers, runaways, and castaways, the flotsam of the South Seas, some three hundred of whom were white or of mixed race. Most lived in the shadow of the Great Powers; they, in turn, were squaring up like prizefighters, in the Pacific as in Africa, with strategic advantage and imperial gain the purse. The people of the Beach worked hard, if they worked at all, and played hard. The Reverend Clarke's disdainful description of " 'stores' and drink saloons" gives some idea of what decent folk thought of it all. Like many Pacific ports Apia had acquired a justified reputation for decadence, but that did not trouble R.L.S. Germany had its plantations; Britain its missions; America its traders. It was a volatile community, not least among the native Samoans, whose feelings and rights were abused routinely.

A cottage was soon rented, and Louis set to work gathering Samoan material for his McClure letters while passage to Australia was arranged. He was not, at first, much impressed by the site of his latest landfall. The scenery was less dramatic than he had seen elsewhere in the islands; the natives seemed less attractive than the Tahitians. Within six weeks, however, he had decided to buy land on Upolu.

Moors may have had something to do with it. He was persuasive, a born salesman, and one who recognised how useful Louis could be, with his money and his international influence, in local politics. He made a point of being useful in turn to the writer. For his part Stevenson was merely susceptible, though in the case of R.L.S., "merely" does not catch the full flavour of his enthusiasm when an idea infected him. In any case, the scheme had two points in its favour: Samoa's climate was better

than that of Hawaii and its communications were excellent—for a South
Sea island.

Nevertheless, it was no small thing to think of becoming a landowner.
The project might even have been accounted as foolhardy as his dream of
becoming a trader with the *Northern Light*. As ever in such circumstances,
however, Louis managed to talk himself into it. An estate would be an in-
vestment for his family and he need only use it as a base. He could return
to Britain whenever he pleased or felt able. Fanny, a keen gardener, was
eager. Moors, who seemed not to question the sense of a skinny semi-
invalid subjecting himself to the backbreaking toil involved in clearing a
plantation, was asked for advice. R.L.S. wondered to himself if the American was not a swindler but quelled his doubts. He had discovered with
the copra trade that businessmen in the islands were obliged to tread a
thin line between legal and illegal. "You may wonder," he told Baxter, "I
should become at all intimate with a man of a past so doubtful, but in the
South Seas any exclusiveness becomes impossible; they are all in the same
boat . . ."

In the meantime Joe Strong was sent to join his wife in Sydney. He was
seriously ill with a heart condition and needed medical treatment. Fanny
believed he was dying and thought it no bad thing "for himself and the
world at large . . ." A few weeks later Moors reported that he had found
a property that might be suitable.

Vailima, they called it. In one translation it means "Five Waters." For
the most part the land was a mass of forest that the natives believed to be
haunted, just under three miles from Apia town but eight hundred feet
above muggy sea level. The four hundred acres cost R.L.S. ten Chile dollars (roughly one pound) an acre. He told Baxter in a letter that he had
bought 314½ acres, but it seemed to survey as more. It was not a major
outlay then, nothing to what he had spent chartering the *Casco* and the
Equator, but by the time he died, Louis had probably spent four thousand
pounds on building work and other improvements. Fifty cattle were supposed to be included in the deal but these proved truant. Charles Baxter,
doubtless suppressing his alarm when the news arrived, was also told that

> . . . when we get the house built, the garden laid, and cattle in the place,
> it will be something to fall back on for shelter and food; and if the island

could stumble into political quiet, it is conceivable it might even bring a little income . . . We range from 600 to 1,500 feet, have five streams, waterfalls, precipices, profound ravines, rich tablelands . . . a great view of forest, sea, mountains, the warships in the haven: really a noble haven.

Moors was instructed to have some of the land cleared and a small house erected while the Stevensons sailed for Sydney. R.L.S. still had it in mind to travel to Britain to see old friends and put his affairs in order. Belle was in Australia as he had instructed. She had not seen them for six months. They left Samoa on the S.S. *Lübeck* in February of 1890, though not before Fanny had written, somewhat hypocritically, to Mrs. Sitwell complaining about all the work that would fall on her shoulders if Louis pursued his latest scheme.

Belle and Austin were waiting for them. Fanny's daughter had endured several difficulties on her arrival in Australia, not least because the funds Louis had arranged were slower in arriving at the bank than she. Only the assistance of King Kalakaua's chargé d'affaires had saved her from penury. Joe's return, equally, had been no godsend: he had been spared death but there was no reprieve from his alcoholism. When, in February, Lloyd appeared with the news that Louis and her mother were at the Victoria Hotel, Belle rushed to meet them with a mixture of relief and elation.

She arrived to find Louis in a rage. The hotel did not know who he was and its staff were being less than helpful to the odd couple who had turned up in eccentric island garb demanding a suite. Belle suggested another establishment, and R.L.S. soon had the satisfaction of spurning the Victoria's grovelling apology after the press had reported his arrival in town.

The affair did not put him off his stride. Louis meant to enjoy his return to despised civilisation. A few comforts—wine, restaurants, company, shopping—could be tolerated. The press could not get enough of him, and he, for all his protestations, yielded to their attentions. It was here, too, that he took pleasure in skewering the Reverend Dr. Hyde for his pomposity and hypocrisy. For a while he was in fine fettle.

The fact that they were having a high time of it should have been a signal. It had happened in Paris, it had happened in London, it had happened in New York: now it happened in Sydney. Stevenson seemed intent on falling mortally ill in each of the great cities of the world. Hardly had he readjusted to the lionisers than a cold struck; fever and a haemorrhage followed. He was moved to the Union Club, a select establishment, on the recommendation of a doctor with whom Belle was friendly. Fanny was allowed only to visit Louis in this gentleman's establishment, and moved in with her daughter while he recovered. It made no difference: as the weather cooled, Stevenson's condition grew worse. Soon it became clear that his only hope was to retreat to the ocean once again.

The problem was that the Sydney seamen's unions had struck and there was not a boat to be had. Fanny hunted the waterfront, increasingly desperate, until she found Henderson & Macfarlane, a small company with a steamer, the *Janet Nicholl*, whose Kanaka (Melanesian) crew were exempt from industrial action. The vessel was due to head out to the islands, but its Scottish owners refused even to consider a dying man as a passenger, even a dying compatriot. A woman was hardly more acceptable. The more they refused, the closer Louis came to death. At last, somehow, Fanny won the argument. Even Belle, in her recollections, was not sure how her mother had managed it:

> I was present when one of the owners, Mr Henderson, called on my mother . . . She was busily packing, for she had learned the *Janet* was leaving the next day. Her caller, very serious and firm, sat in a big chair, telling her, while my mother continued packing, that he couldn't possibly take any passengers . . . I left the room on an errand for my mother . . . When I got back I was astonished to hear Mr Henderson giving my mother instructions how to reach the *Janet* . . .

Ah Fu left them at around this time, promising to return after one last trip to his homeland. Louis made a gift of fifty pounds to the devoted little cook, but they never heard from him again. Meanwhile, Stevenson himself was bundled in a blanket and carried aboard the black, grimy, unstable six-hundred-ton *Janet Nicholl*. On 11 April 1890, they set sail.

Mr. Henderson was among the passengers, and soon warmed, as so many seagoing men did, to the "dying man." Also aboard were Ben Hird, a well-known islands trader, and Jack Buckland, known as "Tin Jack." He was another trader, born in Sydney, who was returning to work after his annual drunken holiday at home. He was, said Fanny, "beautiful," with a vanity that was "charmingly innocent." Tin Jack was given to practical jokes, but his own humour exhausted itself in later years when, according to Fanny, he killed himself after being cheated out of a legacy. Stevenson transformed him into Tommy Hadden in *The Wrecker*.

They made first for Auckland, New Zealand, where Fanny went shopping for trinkets to hand out to the islanders and Louis (the spell of the sea was persistent, even if he disliked the ship) completed his recovery. She recorded some of the voyage in a diary, later published as *The Cruise of the Janet Nicol* (her spelling), but it was tepid stuff—at least when compared to the events of the night they left Auckland harbour.

Tin Jack had bought fireworks and cartridges, apparently to entertain the natives on his island. Some time after ten o'clock, with Auckland still in view and Louis resting in his berth, red, blue, and green rockets began to burst from the cabin shared by Jack and Lloyd. Flames shot up and Fanny rushed to grab a blanket. The ship drifted, the helmsman fled his post, and the captain set to work trying to douse the flames. For a moment it seemed touch and go whether the vessel would survive. In the chaos, Fanny saw crewmen trying to throw a burning trunk overboard: she stopped them just as they were about to dump Louis's manuscripts in the Pacific.

Their other belongings fared less well. Lloyd was left with only the clothes on his back, Fanny had only one pair of shoes, and many of the photographs they had taken during their voyages around the islands were lost. It was a relief when the *Janet*'s hitherto sealed orders revealed that they would be stopping at Samoa.

Moors had been busy in their absence. The bridle path to Vailima was now a decent width, and workmen—many of them deserters from the brutal German plantations—were slashing and burning the undergrowth. A small house had been erected. Roots were going down in that foreign soil.

It was odd, then, that they decided to persist with their voyage. Louis was bored with life on the stuffy tramp steamer and compared its travels around the atolls of those of a hackney cab. By mid-June they were back at Apemama, to be greeted by a tearful Tembinoka; in July Louis fell ill again. He put it down to overwork and the conditions in which he had struggled to write. He would have enjoyed the voyage to the end, he told Colvin, if his health had held out:

> That it did not, I attribute to savage hard work in a wild cabin heated like a Babylonian furnace, four piles of blotting paper under my wet hand and the drops trailing from my brow. For God's sake don't start in to blame Fanny; often enough she besought me not to go on; but I did my work while I was a bedridden worm in England, and please God I shall do my work until I burst . . .

Fanny, obviously still smarting from the arguments over the South Seas book, showed remarkable deviousness by writing to Colvin and *inviting* him to blame her when Louis's work was going wrong. "He will stubbornly hold his own position, but is apt to give way if he thinks I am getting the blame," she said.

On 26 July they reached New Caledonia. Noumea was to be the *Janet's* last port of call before the return run to Australia, and Louis, though still unwell, decided to leave the ship for a while. He asked Fanny and Lloyd to go on without him—an odd, inexplicable decision given that he had been ill so recently. Fanny did not unwillingly leave him in such circumstances, and the usual explanation—that he wished to avoid the Australian winter—does not explain why they parted. Perhaps he was merely collecting material. Perhaps they had spent too long cooped up on the ship together. Years later Fanny claimed to Will Low's wife that she had fallen pregnant at one point during her wanderings in the islands. It seems unlikely—she was close to fifty—but enough is known of the Stevenson marriage to assert that it was not invariably blissful. There may have been some difficulty, sexual or otherwise. Speculation alone cannot explain why she left a husband who, not many months before, she had almost given up for dead.

At Noumea, having improvised something approaching evening dress, Stevenson dined with the governor and studied the penal colony, watching the convict band play in the square for the French officials. It was good to speak their language again, and to drink their wine, but he hated the place. Indeed, some of the horrors of Noumea were to reappear in *The Ebb Tide*, and the revulsion Stevenson felt makes it stranger still that he had separated from his wife. She, meanwhile, was having a miserable time of it on the voyage to Sydney, drifting in a storm with the coal "given out" and the captain ill, fearing for her life.

The couple were reunited in Sydney in August and Louis fell ill again: it was as though civilisation had become a virulent disease against which he had no resistance. It was clear that his exile was permanent. He wrote to Henry James to tell him so ("I cannot tell Colvin"): "I do not think I shall come to England more than once, and then it'll be to die." Typically, there was more than one explanation for his declaration. The English weather and his health were prime factors, of course. Equally, however, he admitted that there were only a handful of people in Britain or America to whom he felt a tie: "I simply prefer Samoa . . ." This exile was chosen, self-imposed in mind if not in body. It was the epitaph: *Here he lies where he longed to be* . . .

Colvin heard soon enough, of course, and seems to be have written a letter in which he at last plucked up the courage to blame Fanny for his deprivation. Louis was hurt, and said so. Had it not been S.C. who had made Fanny promise to keep Louis in any place that suited his health? Colvin had been the only obstacle to Stevenson's decision when it became clear to him that he should remain in the tropics. It was none of Fanny's doing.

Stevenson had other worries. Supporting Fanny, Lloyd, Belle, Joe, and Austin while spending so much on voyages, estates, and doctors had left him short of cash. He was exasperated to discover that Strong, the drunken painter, had managed to sell some pictures but kept the news, and the proceeds, to himself.

It was the second such episode in a matter of months. Louis had already arranged for money to be sent to Joe so that Belle could have a holiday only to find that Strong had spent it on himself. Just as Belle was beginning to behave, R.L.S. told Baxter, her husband was "the place where an innocent child has made a mess on the hearth-rug, and I wish somebody would mop it up . . ."

It ain't charity; I never was guilty of that. Only a person hates to see a pensioner cocking snooks at him, and putting himself up on top of a monument of mean, greedy-child selfishness.

Being bled dry made the business of housing themselves at Vailima more complicated than it should have been. Again, Fanny showed her better nature and suggested that they sell Skerryvore, the beloved "little nest" that Thomas Stevenson had left to her. Louis protested but she convinced him it was the only way. Lloyd was sent to Britain to supervise the sale and bring the furniture and Maggie Stevenson back with him. As his contribution to the economies, he gave up the idea of going to Cambridge. In September, Fanny and R.L.S. were aboard the *Lübeck* and on their way to Samoa.

A dozen or so acres of Vailima had been cleared, and Fanny set to work trying to make the place habitable with what little means she had. They were back to their Silverado ways, roughing it in the wilds, though this time the adventure would have no early end. Louis was swept away by it all. In November of 1890 he informed Colvin that he had gone "crazy over outdoor work, and had at last to confine myself to the house, or literature must have gone by the board."

Nothing is so interesting as weeding, clearing and path-making; the oversight of labourers becomes a disease; it is quite an effort not to drop in to the farmer; and it does make you feel so well. To come down covered with mud and drenched with sweat and rain after some hours in the bush, change, rub down, and take a chair in the verandah, is to taste a quiet conscience. And the strange thing that I mark is this: If I go out and make sixpence, bossing my labourers and plying the cutlass or the spade, idiot conscience applauds me; if I sit in the house and make twenty pounds, idiot conscience wails over my neglect and the day wasted.

As they worked, they discovered that parts of the estate had once been cultivated. The overgrown remains of a banana plantation and a taro patch were found, later a grove of frangipani. Elsewhere orchids grew wild and flying foxes roosted in the banyan trees. Far below them was the surf; behind the unspoiled jungle. In between his field labours R.L.S. continued to work on *The Wrecker* and on his poetry. He was still worrying over his South Seas book, still determined to make something of it:

> Those [chapters] that I did in the *Janet Nicoll*, under the most ungodly cir- cumstances, I fear will want a lot of supplying and lightening . . . 'tis really immense what I have done; in the South Seas book I have fifty pages cop- ied fair, some of which has been four times, and all twice written; certainly fifty pages of solid scriving inside a fortnight . . .

Stevenson was digging in, literally and metaphorically. Life at the tem- porary house was primitive, and the absurd, snobbish, and anti-Semitic Henry Adams, paying a visit to R.L.S. (who had not heard of him) cour- tesy of the American consul, thought Fanny and Louis like grubby peas- ants in an "Irish shanty." He later described Stevenson as resembling "an insane stork"; Fanny an "Apache squaw." It was all due, said the pompous ass, to the fact that the "early associates" of the Scotsman "were all second-rate." Instead of buying so much land, the couple should perhaps have invested in some soap. Louis, writing with heavy irony to Henry James of "enlightened society," demonstrated his own unique status by supplying Adams with a letter of introduction to the Tahitian royal family. "Stevenson gloats over discomforts," Adams wrote

> and thinks that every traveller should sail for months in small cutters rancid with cocoa-nut oil and mouldy with constant rain, and should live on coral atolls with nothing but cocoa-nuts and poisonous fish to eat.

Plainly, Louis had been telling of his adventures, sublimely oblivious to the impression he was making, or too polite to react to the self-satisfied grandee whose supposed achievements meant nothing to him. Adams thought their entire existence despicable. They had one servant, a Ger- man from the *Lübeck* named Paul who had begged for a job. He was barely competent as a cook and a martyr to alcohol, but the patriarch of Vailima allowed him into the clan. Fanny, always barefoot, was doing a good deal of planting (astonished at how quickly things grew) while su- pervising the pigs and chickens they had brought up from Apia. Their meals were simple in the extreme: avocado, sardines, breadfruit. Before their almost unfurnished shack the putative lawn was littered with stumps of great trees; the insects were fierce and unrelenting. Was this a writer's life?

It was for Louis. The exhilarator was exhilarated, riding up and down the steep path to Apia, watching over the workmen, sweating, slashing, weeding, digging, planning and dreaming. He was making his own place in the world, with his own hands. The sheer joy he took just in being able to ride Jack, his "island horse," meant more than he could easily convey:

> . . . at a fast steady walk, with his head down, and sometime his nose to the ground—when he wants to do that, he asks for his head with a little eloquent polite movement indescribable—he climbs the long ascent and threads the darkest of the wood. The first night I came it was starry; and it was singular to see the starlight drip down into the crypt of the wood, and shine in the open end of the road . . .

This life gave him a satisfaction that perhaps only he could really understand. All he asked was one quiet room in which to work. They hired Henry Simile, who had interpreted for Louis during a previous visit, as their overseer. "Life goes in enchantment," R.L.S. wrote to Burlinghame:

> I come home to find I am late for dinner; and when I go to bed at night, I could cry for the weariness of my loins and thighs. Do not speak to me of vexation, the life brims with it, but with living interest fairly.

In January of 1891 he went to Sydney to meet his mother and again fell sick. His relationship with the Australian city was never a happy one. Maggie Stevenson, though pleased to see her son, soon decided she could not live at the temporary house and went off to stay with relatives in New Zealand until appropriate accommodation could be constructed. That project, Louis's own design, was to become a consuming passion. They fiddled over plans, extending and reducing the scope of the dream.

For the time being, they worked on with what they had. The Skerryvore furniture and some pieces from Heriot Row which had followed Maggie Stevenson to the South Seas made the little house more comfortable. The food improved. In May, Joe and Belle joined them. Soon the clan were making friends in Apia: Moors; Clarke; Henry Ide, the American consul; Bazett Haggard, brother to Rider, the British Land Commissioner. The only cloud on the Pacific horizon was financial: expenses were high and would remain so. Louis began to think of Walter Scott, writing himself into the grave to keep Abbotsford going. If anything, he placed an even larger burden on himself. Vailima was a full-time job yet R.L.S. intended to continue as a full-time writer. Often, however, he was obliged to borrow from the erstwhile "blackbirder" Moors, but then so did everyone else: it was the source of the trader's power. Nevertheless, only Louis could have run up a debt of twelve thousand dollars, as he did when the new house was being built. The American, in turn, was overcharging Louis for almost everything he bought.

Talk of the Stevenson "clan" was not a joke; by the end Louis was head of a fair-sized community and took his duties as arbiter, provider, magistrate, and spiritual leader seriously. Often it all felt too much. Fanny was often ill, mentally and physically. (Bright's disease was eventually diagnosed); Joe was as much of a drunken disgrace as ever; Lloyd became involved with a native girl; Belle established a closeness to Louis at last but this did not always please her mother. Add to all that a staff of mixed races with their own problems.

Louis did not have the temperament always to cope with the volatile mix. Fanny and her brood were of a pattern, and sometimes they exasperated R.L.S. beyond measure. Husband and wife now had separate bedrooms, a fact which lends weight to the suspicion that his departure from the *Janet Nicholl* had had some personal motivation. Certainly her children saw fit to obliterate passages from her diary after her death. The passages were only deciphered, with difficulty, years later. They reveal a resentment of Louis that perhaps explains her objections to the South Seas books. He had said she had a "peasant soul," and in several entries Fanny returned to this slight; it gnawed at her, trivial though it was. The effect of the remark can be judged by her children's eagerness to expunge it.

By the middle of 1891 the first phase of the new house was complete, with ceilings and walls of California redwood, the floors stained and waxed, the furniture old mahogany, the carpets Turkish, the window and door frames dark green. Proceeds from *The Wrecker* added a second wing to the two-storey building; Maggie Stevenson paid for a bathhouse; the original shack became guest quarters. The roof was of red corrugated iron

and the sides blue. For Louis there was a workroom on the upper verandah where he kept a cot. It seemed like a palace to the natives but left
many white visitors, who had heard the tales of profligacy, unimpressed
with its barnlike capaciousness. Yet for the money Stevenson spent importing materials it might as well have been a royal house: the chimney
he demanded, a novelty on Samoa, cost a thousand dollars. Certainly they
entertained like minor royalty, a vice Moors attributed chiefly to Fanny
and Belle. The upkeep of Vailima was soon to run to $6,500 a year; its
income came nowhere near that figure.

Louis was often in Apia gathering material on the political situation.
He had sent his first letter to *The Times* from the *Casco* in 1889, in the
aftermath of the island war that had begun, for the most part, because of
rivalries between the Powers and their readiness to arm the factions. Louis
dived headlong into the crisis. Another war threatened, or so he heard.
Tusitala, the name his servants had first given him, stood ready. "We sit
and pipe upon a volcano which is being stoked by bland, incompetent
amateurs," he told Baxter.

Fanny was sometimes *Tamaitai* ("Madam"), sometimes *Aolele* ("Flying
Cloud"): the former was more commonly used. Occasionally they called
her the Witch Woman of the Mountain, testimony, perhaps, to the discipline she imposed on the staff; a hint, doubtless, of her odd behaviour.
In the summer of 1892 Joe Strong at last went too far and was caught
robbing the cellar and storeroom with false keys. Fanny told her diary all
about it:

> In revenge, when he found that he was discovered, he went round to all
> our friends in Apia and spread slanders about Belle. We turned him away
> and applied for a divorce for Belle, which was got with no difficulty, as he
> had been living with a native woman of Apia as his wife ever since he
> came here—an old affair begun when he was here before . . . He came up
> here late one night to beg forgiveness and asked to be taken back. I was
> so shocked at seeing him that I had an attack of angina, which seems to
> remain with me. Louis was made sole guardian of the child . . .

Belle now became close to Louis, siding with him in domestic difficulties and helping him with his work. Fanny felt the strain of it all and, feel-

ing her age, did not take kindly to the relationship between her husband and her daughter, the former only eight years older than the latter. It does not seem to have been a sexual thing, for all that sex had all but gone out of her own marriage, but Fanny—who also quarrelled from time to time with Maggie Stevenson—was not inclined to be understanding. The proof that her jealousy was needless came in August of 1892, when Graham Balfour, grandchild of John Balfour, brother to the Reverend Lewis Balfour, arrived at Vailima and Belle fell in love with him.

Still, the balance of Fanny's mind had shifted in the past. The strain of the divorce—so reminiscent of her own marriage to Sam Osbourne—had worn her out. When the Countess of Jersey, wife to the governor of New South Wales, paid a visit to Louis, Fanny's jealousy turned to venom. She carped, criticised, and nagged until the marriage seemed in real danger. It was, Louis admitted, a "wretched period." All of the envy and resentment came out, all of the insecurity and arrogance. The difference in age between them was now obvious to all. Louis was no longer her pupil; she no longer attractive. It was a bout from which she never truly recovered.

She continued to squabble with Belle, reducing her daughter to tears and rendering herself piteous in her remorse. She later wrote that *Catriona* was composed in some of the most difficult circumstances imaginable, given the threat of war. Her own behaviour must have made politics seem like blessed relief.

Margaret Mackay's biography of Fanny, *The Violent Friend*, gives the most complete account—based on previously censored letters—of the state to which Louis's wife was reduced in his last years. Late in 1892 and early in 1893 there occurred what Mackay calls "a relapse of her psychosis—much the worst." It culminated one long night when Fanny, her mind wandering, became physically violent and had to be restrained. For two hours she tried to run away while Louis and Belle held her. Stevenson decided, as usual, that a voyage would help and took his wife to Sydney, where she recovered somewhat before. "old fixations and hallucinations" claimed her again. Dr. Fairfax, the old friend of Belle's who had treated Louis previously, told Colvin during a visit to London that R.L.S. could regain his health under "good conditions." "Of *her* condition," S.C. reported to Baxter, "he thinks ill—both as to body and mind."

Dr. Funk, one of the medical men of Apia, dosed her with a variety of medicines, but, though not violent, Fanny remained in severe distress, refusing to eat, not speaking, not *smoking*, and hallucinating. She was almost out of her mind.

Louis was kind and hoped for the best, seeing signs of improvement when others saw none. But even he had to admit that, after becoming "quite sensible" again, she retained "old illusions." They were to remain, like the scars of her breakdown, for the rest of her life.

Mackay suggests that the onset of menopause, allied with guilt over her "failure" to provide Louis with children, was at the root of Fanny's illness. Certainly it could well have been the trigger. Equally, however, she might just as easily have cracked after years of strain, the continuous pressure traceable to her disastrous marriage to Sam, to the death of little Hervey, to Louis's repeated flirtations with death, to money worries, to endless upheavals, to the enmity of the London set, to the backbreaking toil of the early days on Samoa, to the ebbing away of eroticism from her marriage. Fanny Stevenson brought much on herself with her vanity and her selfishness, but much came unsought. At Vailima the past claimed her much as it claimed her husband, and just as she thought she had reached paradise.

17 *1893–1894*

There are two duties incumbent upon any man who enters on the business of writing: truth to the fact and a good spirit in the treatment.

"THE MORALITY OF THE PROFESSION OF LETTERS"

*L*ouis loved the heat. He crossed Europe, America, and the Pacific to find it. Sunlight healed him and assuaged a hunger in him. Even Hawaii was too chilly. From Apia he wrote to Baxter that "the ink is dreadful, the heat delicious." With the sound of the ocean breeze and the ocean breakers in his ears, he had found something that had eluded him all his life. Samoa, he said, was not as beautiful as Tahiti or the Marquesas. Nevertheless, it touched something deep within him, magnifying the sense of being at home he had once felt in the South of France. He was a world-famous author and already, so he had been told, a legend in Britain because of his reclusiveness—or was it elusiveness? The myth was taking shape.

He had no time for that: writing was his trade, his craft. Having lived so long with death, he had no intention of making a mystery out of art. Again he spurned the expectations of others. He really had no choice: the pressure to provide was unrelenting. In Apia the ink was dreadful; in Saranac it had frozen; Louis had written regardless, his career a paper chase that spanned the globe, illness dogging every page. Now he drove himself, working harder than he ever had, while still embroiled in domestic affairs, in business, and in politics. He hurried towards his end.

Fanny said that Louis became involved in political affairs because the profession of letters had been his second choice in life, forced on him by ill health. But then, by the time Fanny was making such remarks, R.L.S. was dead, and there was no one to prevent her shaping her saint out of plaster or rewriting the past. It is odd, if her remark had any truth in it, that in the space of a year he had completed *The Wrecker*, written *The Beach of Falesá*, all but completed *A Footnote to History*, worked on *A Family of Engineers*, and written *Catriona* while a war raged. He had also roughed out the opening of a book he called "The Justice-Clerk," later to become (though never finished) *Weir of Hermiston*. His "second choice" career held his attention well enough. "I have a novel on the stocks," he told Charles Baxter in December of 1892, "to be called *The Justice-Clerk*."

> It is pretty Scotch, the Grand premier is taken from Braxfield—(Oh, by the by, send me Cockburn's *Memorials*)—and some of the story is—well— queer. The heroine is seduced by one man, and finally disappears with the other man who shot him ... Mind you, I expect *The Justice-Clerk* to be my masterpiece. My Braxfield is already a thing of beauty and a joy for ever, and so far as he has gone *far* my best character.

He had a clarity of mind about his work now. There was less hesitation, fewer second thoughts. If he stalled, there was always another project to pick up. In May of 1893 he could boast with justification of his output to S. R. Crockett, a novelist who did so much to degrade Scottish fiction after Stevenson's death:

> Be it known to this fluent generation that I, R.L.S., in the forty-third of my age and the twentieth of my professional life, wrote twenty-four pages in twenty-one days, working from six to eleven, and again in the afternoon from two to four or so, without fail or interruption. Such are the gifts the gods have endowed us withal: such was the facility of this prolific writer.

Equally, he did not lose sight of his own place in the world of letters, as he might have called it. He corresponded with James, Barrie, Twain, and others. In December of 1892 he wrote to James:

> Hurry up with another book of stories. I am now reduced to two of my contemporaries, you and Barrie—O, and Kipling—you and Barrie and Kipling are now my Muses Three ... And you and Barrie don't write enough.

If Samoan politics were an early interest, they soon became an abiding concern. The Powers were making mischief in the Pacific—the wrecked warships in Apia harbour were proof enough—each competing for advantage. Louis, being Louis, learned Samoan and took the side of the natives.

In Honolulu he had begun a book about Samoa which Joe Strong was to illustrate. On reaching Samoa itself, however, he realised that this work would not do and started afresh, gathering evidence from witnesses to the war of 1888. By November of 1891, *A Footnote to History* was well under way. It was published in 1892 and remains an honest examination of the plight of the islands.

The tribal structure there was complicated—with kings selected from among competing high-chiefs—but essentially communal. By Stevenson's day, however, the islands were recognised as occupying a strategic position and, no less important, to be rich in copra. The United States had first shown an interest in the group in 1839, but by the 1870s Britain and Germany were also casting covetous eyes over them, with the Germans taking the lead. A conference in 1878 on the islands' future had proved inconclusive. By the 1890s Germans, notably cruel in the running of their plantations, were entrenched in one part, the British in another, and the Americans a third. Rivalry among three competing chiefs, encouraged by the westerners, had led to the war in 1888. The conference was reconvened and tripartite rule established. A German was made "President of the Council"; a "chief justice" was installed; and a land commission established, ostensibly to protect the natives from fraud.

The first actions of the German president were to build a jail and take control of the local newspaper. The Germans had also restored a chief named Malietoa, whom they themselves had deposed not so long before, and installed him as a puppet "king." Two other chiefs—the largely irrelevant Tamasese, and Mataafa, a chief who had been involved in the 1888 war—opposed the puppet. Stevenson, unsurprisingly, took the side of Mataafa, the anti-German candidate as it were, and gave him advice, visiting the chief at his armed camp despite official displeasure. The British government was less helpful, influenced as it was by the Protestant missionaries who distrusted the Catholic Mataafa. Soon the Powers had arrested several of his supporters and exiled them.

Louis reported all of this to the London *Times* and again in *A Footnote to History*. It earned him the enmity of many whites, and a threat of deportation forestalled only by the intervention of Lord Rosebery, the British Foreign Secretary, who wrote to Sir John Thurston, High Commissioner for the Western Pacific. This gentleman had threatened to imprison any British subject trying to bring about any protest against the government, whether that be "discontent" or civil war. Rosebery, who admired Stevenson, made sure that Thurston was put firmly in his place where R.L.S. was concerned. The bureaucrat was told not to bother the writer, but for a while Louis really thought the Vailima dream might be ended.

In fact, he was trying to effect a reconciliation among the rival chiefs. In August 1892 he arranged for Lady Jersey to visit Mataafa's camp, causing great consternation in government circles. There was, however, a mini-war, after which the leading rebels were banished to the Marshall Islands. Louis wrote to Mark Twain:

> . . . I wish you could see my 'simple and sunny heaven' now; war has broken out, 'they' have been long in making it, 'they' have worked hard, and here it is—with its concomitants of blackened faces, severed heads and men dying in hospital . . . the government troops have started a horrid novelty: taking women's heads. If this leads to reprisals, we shall be a fine part of the world. Perhaps the best that could happen would be a complete and immediate suppression of the rebels; but alas! all my friends (bar but a few) are in the rebellion.

Defiantly, R.L.S. sent gifts to Mataafa and the exiles. At Apia, he visited the less-important prisoners in jail, and they reciprocated with a feast held inside their compound. Stevenson was one of the few who had made such an effort to live among them and to take their part. No such present was "ever given to a single white man," he said afterwards. He believed simply that Samoa belonged to the Samoans and that the Powers should stay out of it. When, in 1894, the last of them was free, they sought a way to repay *Tusitala* for his loyalty. They decided to build him a road. Chiefs did not do such work, save for a friend like Louis. They finished the Road of the Loving Heart just before he died. Soon the same men were to carry him to his grave.

~

Amidst all this, he was working on the book that was to become *St. Ives*.
War drums were beating, wrote Belle, "but nothing stops the cheerful
flow of *Anne*" (as the novel was then known). It was to be another unfinished work. Stevenson's habit of picking up and putting down numerous projects produced this state of affairs. He was, for one thing, at all
times easily bored. But Colvin thought that fatigue after years of writing
was beginning to oppress his friend. According to Graham Balfour, it
amounted to four hundred pages a year for twenty years. In the "epilogue" to *Vailima Letters*, Colvin wrote of the arrangements for the Edinburgh Edition, intended by himself and Baxter to lift the physical and
financial burden from R.L.S.:

> To judge by these letters, [in the winter of 1894] his old invincible spirit
> of inward cheerfulness was beginning to give way to moods of depression
> and overstrained feeling . . . it was a new thing in his life that he should
> thus painfully feel the strain of literary work, at almost all other times his
> chief delight and pastime, and should express the longing to lay it down
> . . . it is . . . doubtful . . . if that ever-shaping mind had retained any capac-
> ity for rest, except, as he had himself foretold, the rest of the grave. At any
> rate he took none . . .

Colvin probably knew, of course, that the onslaught of pain and emotion from Fanny and her family had taken their toll. Moors, rarely reliable, was probably right when he said that in some ways Louis would have
been better off if he had not married. Fanny, too, entertained doubts over
the partnership, or at least over her place in it. In one diary entry, later
suppressed by her heirs, she had spoken of a desire to earn money of her
own, a natural enough feeling. The resentment at being dependent on
R.L.S. was less so:

> I wonder what would become of a man, and to what would he degenerate,
> if his life was that of a woman's: to get the run of her 'teeth' and presents
> of her clothes, and supposed to be always under bonds of the deepest grat-
> itude for any further sums.

Even such resentment approaching jealousy would have made sense if Louis had not been working as hard as he was. In September of 1894 he dropped *St. Ives*—in which, as with *Catriona*, he was mastering the art of depicting women—and turned to "The Justice-Clerk." The project excited him, as he told Belle:

> The story unfolds itself before me to the last detail—there is nothing left in doubt. I never felt so sure before in anything I ever wrote. It will be my best work; I feel myself so sure of every word!

He was writing with a rare intensity, announcing to his wife, amid these multifarious projects full of promise, that he proposed to begin yet another novel, set on Tahiti, to be called *Sophia Scarlet*. It would have a mainly female cast, as though as a riposte to those who said he could not write women (though *Weir* was proving otherwise). He also drafted *Heathercat*, a work of the Killing Time and the Covenanters. He was digging deep into himself, reaching into his past all the way back to Cummy and his Heriot Row childhood. It was almost a subconscious reaction to all that had happened at Vailima. Yet the Edinburgh youth could never be revived. The Louis who wrote now was a tougher character, more direct, searching for the core of human experience.

Much has been made of the differences between the "Scottish" work he did at Vailima and the "Pacific" work. Certainly most of his peers, and many in his audience, had no taste for the latter. Colvin, confronted with the setting, the "indelicacy" (suddenly Louis, who "could not write a woman," was in trouble for writing about sex out of wedlock) and the obvious anti-imperialism of *The Beach of Falesá*, hacked it to pieces in the absence of its author. The symbolism was obvious. But there is less of a gulf between Stevenson's Scotland and Stevenson's South Seas than London tried to pretend. Past and present were locked together around the same questions of moral choice, of how we arrive at the opportunity to make such choices. R.L.S. was in hot pursuit of truth. In September, Belle recorded something of the composition of *Weir of Hermiston* in her diary:

> He generally makes notes in the morning which he elaborates as he reads them aloud. In *Hermiston* he has hardly more than a line or two to keep

him on the track, but he never falters for a word, but gives me the sentences with capital letters and all the stops, as clearly and as steadily as though he were reading from an unseen book.

It must have been amusing to watch this young American trying to take down the speech of the elder of Kirstie, but Louis enjoyed having an amaneunsis. He had often suffered from writer's cramp—those thin arms—and physical liberty from his desk seemed to appeal to him. Company, even while he worked, no less so. Belle recorded one day's work late in September of 1894:

> Louis and I have been writing, working away every morning like steam-engines on *Hermiston*. Louis got a set-back with *Anne*, and he has put it aside for a while. He worried terribly over it, but could not make it run smoothly. He read it aloud one evening and Lloyd criticised the love-scene, so Louis threw the whole thing over for a time. Fortunately he picked up *Hermiston* all right, and is in better spirits at once.

His last year had begun with a third little war early in 1894. The male staff at Vailima were again conscripted. Stevenson advised on peace plans but these were botched by the bureaucrats, and once again he was dashing off letters to *The Times*. He also stocked up on ammunition.

Malietoa, one of the contending chiefs, came to make his peace with R.L.S. As custom dictated, he was offered a gift and demanded a pearl-handled revolver Sir Percy Shelley had given Louis. Stevenson thought he had emptied the gun, and Fanny, testing what she though was a defective trigger, almost blew the chieftain's head off before "intuition" told her there was still a cartridge in one chamber.

In the spring Louis heard that Henley's five-year-old daughter had died. Barrie had used her as a model for Wendy in his *Peter Pan*. Now R.L.S., remembering the friendship he had once had and touched beyond all measure, wrote a kind letter of condolence to W.E. In it he said that children were the one thing he envied Henley for. His friend and enemy wrote an equally decent reply, which Fanny interpreted as a bid for a loan. Louis wrote to Baxter sanctioning a payment—and mentioned a gig and a Pomeranian dog.

Louis was not rich himself, though he lived like a rich man. In one let-

ter home he admitted that he "lived on credit" at Vailima. Baxter and
Colvin began the arrangements for the Edinburgh Edition. Louis decided
to dedicate his life's work to the woman who had said, "Louis thinks he
forgives, but he only lays the bundle on the shelf and long after takes it
down and quarrels with it." Fanny, of course, was no amnesiac.

His birthday was celebrated, as usual, with a native feast. On 29 November, Thanksgiving Day, they held a dinner for Stevenson's American
friends in the great hall, with roast turkey, and sweet potatoes got up as
pumpkin pie. Sherry, Bordeaux red, and Madeira filled the Heriot Row
glasses. Cold champagne—the steamer had brought ice—was an unex-
pected surprise. Louis toasted his wife and mother and, looking at Austin,
told the company Vailima was blessed—"there's a child in the house."

One night Louis took Lloyd's unusual silence after a reading from *Weir*
as a sign he had disliked the work. The opposite was the case: he had
been struck dumb. Both men broke down in tears and afterwards sat talking late into the night. Lloyd would never repeat the conversation, save to
say that Louis had admitted to often longing for death. He had already
chosen his grave site on Mount Vaea.

On 3 December he seemed well. He lunched with Bazett Haggard and
returned in the darkness to see the lamps of his house shining through the
trees. Only Fanny was filled with foreboding, certain that evil was about
to befall someone near her—perhaps Graham Balfour, who was voyaging
in Micronesia. In a letter she told Mrs. Sitwell that she had known for
three days that "something terrible was going to happen in the house."
On the last day she was "almost insane with terror." Louis laughed and
teased her.

He continued to dictate *Weir* to Belle, before breaking off in mid-
sentence to chat, give Austin his French lesson, fetch his imported wine
from the cellar, struggle to lighten his wife's mood, and help prepare mayonnaise for supper. Lloyd's account, later published with the *Letters*, is still
relied upon.

At sunset he came downstairs; rallied his wife about the forebodings she
could not shake off; talked of a lecturing tour to America that he was eager
to make, 'as he was now so well,' and played a game at cards with her to
drive away her melancholy. He said he was hungry; begged her assistance

to help him make a salad for the evening meal; and to enhance the little feast, he brought up a bottle of old Burgundy from the cellar. He was helping his wife on the verandah, and gaily talking, when suddenly he put both hands to his head and cried out 'What's that?' Then he asked quickly. 'Do I look strange?' Even as he did so he fell on his knees beside her.

Fanny and Sosimo, his servant, helped him indoors, first to an easy chair that had once belonged to his grandfather. Maggie Stevenson and Belle rushed to his side while Lloyd saddled a horse and rode hell for leather to Apia to fetch Dr. Funk. Meanwhile Fanny called for brandy and shouted Louis's name, but he gave no sign of hearing.

In town, Funk took Osbourne's horse and started at once, while Lloyd stole another at the trading store and followed. The surgeon of the *Wallaroo* came. The medical men concurred in their diagnosis: an apoplectic stroke from a blood clot on the brain. Now lying on a little bed in the hall, his head supported by a rest given to him by Shelley's son, Louis began to fade, his breathing harsh, his eyes opened wide. The doctors were as helpless as the dozen or so Samoans who sat in a wide semicircle on the floor around their "chief." The Reverend Clarke had arrived and now began to pray. Fanny stood alone at the foot of the redwood staircase, immobilised with shock and grief, the colour gone from her dark face. Of all the illnesses feared and fought, this sudden blow had been unforeseen, a willful convulsion.

The great exhilarator died in silence. The Samoans passed one by one, kissing his hand. *"Tofa* [sleep] *Tusitala!"* said one of the chiefs. Another old man made a speech:

> When Metaafa was taken, who was our support but Tusitala? We were in prison, and he cared for us. We were sick, and he made us well. We were hungry, and he fed us. The day was no longer than his kindness. You are great people and full of love. Yet who among you is so great as Tusitala? What is your love to his love?

On doctor's orders they wasted no time in burying him. The chiefs had made their farewells; the prayers had been said. Tools were brought from Apia, and the men, dressed by Maggie Stevenson in the black cotton *lavalavas* of mourning, sweated to cut the path to Vaea's peak. All through the night the only sounds heard in the house were the chopping and slashing of trees on the mountain and Sosimo's Catholic prayers.

Light though the body was, it was no easy matter to carry it up the slope. The men of the household had been given the task of digging the grave 1,300 feet above sea level. The cortège set off at one P.M., the natives carrying the body in relays. Nineteen Europeans and sixty Samoans went with the coffin. Fanny, Maggie, and Belle, each clad in black, stood on the verandah of the house and watched the party disappear into the trees. He had yearned to be buried in Scotland but had known he would never lie there.

At the summit the Reverend Clarke performed Anglican rites, and Louis's own prayer, which he had read aloud to his own family only the night before, was recited. "Bless to us our extraordinary mercies," it asked in part, "if the day come when these must be taken, have us play the man under affliction. Be with our friends; be with ourselves."

"What ails you, miserable man," he had asked Colvin in a letter in 1891, "to talk of saving material? I have a whole world in my head, a whole new society to work, but I am in no hurry . . ." Of his old mentor Fleeming Jenkin he had written:

> He passed; but something in his gallant vitality had impressed itself upon his friends, and still impresses. Not from one or two only, but from many, I hear the same tale of how the imagination refuses to accept our loss and instinctively looks for his re-appearing, and how memory retains his voice and image like things of yesterday.

All of his friends were devastated by the news. Like Fanny, they had been expecting it for years, yet when death came, they could not easily believe it. Far away in Vermont, Rudyard Kipling was so devastated that for a month he could not bear to write a word. Henry James refused to believe it, and hoped for over a week that the reports were false. Charles Baxter, at Suez, en route from Britain, still mourning the death of his own wife, absorbed the blow in his own stout way and pressed on with his journey.

The Scotsman, Edinburgh's newspaper, received a Reuter's telegram from Apia dated 8 December saying Louis had died of "apoplexy." Another from Sydney made the same claim. "This sad news," said the newspaper on 18 December, "is unconfirmed by any private telegrams." The family had heard nothing. Aunt Jane had received a letter from Maggie early in December in which "cheering accounts" were given of Louis's health. Uncle George had had a letter only the week before from R.L.S. saying he was "never in better health" and discounted the telegram. Elsewhere, said *The Scotsman*, a "strong hope was expressed that the telegram might turn out a false one, and that Stevenson might yet live for many years to write more charming books."

James, the only one of Louis's friends to have tried to understand her, wrote a beautiful, delicate letter of condolence to Fanny:

To have lived in the light of that splendid life, that beautiful, bountiful being—only to see it, from one moment to the other, converted into a fable as strange and romantic as one of his own, a thing that *has* been and has ended, is an anguish into which no one can enter with you fully and of which no one can drain the cup for you. You are nearest to the pain, because you were nearest the joy and the pride.

Epilogue

There is Something that was before hunger and that remains behind after a meal.

LAY MORALS

And then? The narrative peters out. A tomb was constructed from slabs of cement and became, in its coy imitation of the Samoan style, part of the legend.

That grew, in turn. The chiefs made gunfire on the mountainside *tabu* to allow his spirit peace. In 1897 a plinth was added to the tomb, with two bronze plaques. One, in Samoan, identified the grave of *Tusitala*. It bore images of a thistle and a hibiscus and included Ruth's speech to Naomi: ". . . thy people shall be my people, and thy God my God: where thou diest, will I die . . ." The reverse, marking alpha as 1850 and omega as 1894, carried Louis's own epitaph: *Here he lies where he longed to be; / Home is the sailor, home from sea, / And the hunter home from the hill.*

A year before his death, pondering the family of engineers, Louis had written to Sidney Colvin. "I have a strange feeling of responsibility," he said, "as if I had my ancestors' *souls* in my charge, and might miscarry with them." Death broke the ancestral link, as he had long suspected it might. Samoa gave him his grave:

> . . . though it's a wrench not to be planted in Scotland—that I can never deny—if I could only be buried in the hills, under the heather and a table tombstone like the martyrs, where the whaups and plovers are crying!

~

His will was as complicated as his affections. Thus: estate in Britain to the value of £15,525. Half to be held by his mother until her passing; a third to cousins Bob, Katharine, and Dora, children of uncle Alan Stevenson; a legacy to Austin with a life interest to Belle. The rest, plus manuscripts, furniture, and other effects, to Lloyd, but with a life interest to Fanny. In the event of Lloyd's dying without heirs, Sidney Colvin and Henry James were to have his portion. To Fanny, of course, went the royalties and a pension from the Faculty of Advocates worth sixty pounds per annum.

Henry James, knowing Fanny only too well, evaded the task of becoming literary executor to R.L.S. He had shown in *The Aspern Papers* what he thought of biographers. The job, and the task of writing the biography, fell to Colvin.

Louis had perceived this monument chiefly in terms of the money it might provide for his heirs. He had instructed Charles Baxter, through a sealed letter to Lloyd, that S.C. should *edit* a modest volume but must on no account be allowed to "run away with all the profits" in a leisurely, pernickety progress through the past. Stevenson knew his old friend only too well. Nevertheless, the order to Baxter also implied an understanding of the crosscurrents running between his family and his friends. "See," he said, "that Colvin has justice." It was an attempt to avoid trouble and it failed.

A narrative without order. Fanny grew old and still more impossible, fighting her endless battles to present Louis to the world as she thought he should be presented. So many letters, prefaces, introductions, rows, and dreams. Neither his work nor his memory stood in her way. She never recovered from the shock of his death, and her belief in the afterlife strengthened with the years.

She lived for another two decades, always unpredictable. She rose above the old quarrel with Henley and offered him the Union Flag that had covered Louis's body; Henley, unable to rise, refused the gift. Yet Fanny also fell into vicious quarrels with anyone who disputed her gilded version of the past.

Unprepared for Stevenson's death, all she had was his legacy. It was, she told Colvin, "a thought hardly to be borne . . . what Louis had not yet arrived at the maturity of his powers. He was very near the true beginning of his work. Of that I must not speak—I cannot bear it."

Graham Balfour returned to Britain with a trunk of papers; Lloyd went on a sea voyage; Austin was sent to school in New Zealand. For a while, Fanny and Belle remained at Vailima alone, as though keeping watch for Louis to come riding up the mountain on Jack. The strain told on them. The mind of Frances Van de Grift Stevenson was a supple instrument, adaptable and capable of a multitude of passions. Yet often her emotions conflicted. Under pressure, her vivacity ebbed, her courage—and few women had more—faltered. As the months passed on Samoa, depression and illness besieged her again. When Lloyd returned, he too fell ill; Belle followed. In April of 1895 the survivors of the clan decided to travel to San Francisco.

Fanny was incapable of profound change. While in California she spent weeks going over Stevenson's papers in preparation for the biography, the monument whose construction she intended to supervise to the last detail. Meanwhile, she was badgering Colvin to secure a production of her inept play, *The Hanging Judge*, still demanding recognition for herself, still insisting that she needed money. She was not modest about the past if it could be made to seem golden. It did not take much to persuade her to allow Louis's intimate little testimonial to his soul mate to be included in the Edinburgh Edition.

> Trusty, dusky, vivid, true,
> With eyes of gold and bramble-dew,
>   Steel-true and blade-straight,
>   The great artificer
>   Made my mate.

> Honour, anger, valour, fire;
> A love that life could never tire,
>   Death quench or evil stir,
>   The mighty master
>   Gave to her.

It was how he had wanted to see her and how, in some ways, she had wanted to be seen, but it was not the whole truth. The passing years had opened a gulf between them. After Louis was gone, she tried to pretend the estrangement—her envy, his weariness, the absence of children, the isolation of exile—had never occurred.

Theirs had been a love born of several things: an invalid's dependence; a boy's fascination with the sexual secrets of maturity and maternity; a shared adversity; an alienation from the commonplace; her desire to partake of fame, his to enter, like children going into a darkened room, an erotic adventure. By the end they were evenly matched, she as much an invalid as he, crippled by her fears. It is not unjust to guess that Louis submitted to Fanny's whims and orders only when obedience aroused something in his stricken libido: he put himself in her hands. She, poor paranoid, was as forceful as anyone can be who really wants just to be admired and cared for.

Maggie Stevenson, that fond, foolish, redoubtable old woman, was unaware, to the very end, of how ill Louis had been, and how often. She returned to Edinburgh at last to live with her sister and record her son's death in the family Bible. To the brute facts she added: "I am left alone and desolate." In 1897, dying of pneumonia at the age of sixty-eight, her last words were of him.

In 1896 Lloyd had become engaged to Katharine Durham, an earnest mission-school teacher he had met in Honolulu. She resembled his mother in everything save stature and self-awareness. Katharine was tall and never admitted to error; Fanny short and capable of remorse; but their tempers were matched. At first Fanny spoke of her new daughter-in-law taking her place and wondered if the girl was up to the job. It became an academic question: the marriage had Osbourne luck.

Back at Vailima, Fanny and Katharine were alike in their instability— both fancied that séances put them in touch personally with Louis—and rancour grew. When the debunkers began their work, Katharine was their prime source, their first spy in the camp. *Fanny thought Stevenson would die and married him to get money*, Katharine averred, *she told me so.* Gosse, on the receiving end of some of this, turned his head away, but others were fascinated. There was a need to believe that R.L.S. had not been as he seemed, as though such an obvious truth was hard to guess at.

Lloyd, weak and vain, tied to his mother and deprived of the counsel and support of the stepfather whose boots he had tearfully unlaced while Louis lay dying, could not cope with the conflict. He had not the courage. Nevertheless, a child was born, and named Alan.

After Maggie died, Fanny was obliged to return to Britain and settle the estate of old Thomas Stevenson once and for all. The "stream of lives flowing down there far in the north" was to end with an irascible little woman from Indiana. Her health was bad, grandchildren could not be raised on Samoa, the estate was too much for her: so she rationalised her desire to be on the move again. She sold Vailima.

Stevenson had poured so much of himself into his kingdom that it is somehow shocking, almost personally insulting, to find that Fanny got only £1,750 for it. She kept the land around the grave on Vaea, but a retired German merchant moved into the home Louis had designed, worked, and sweated for. Worse, when the Powers again began to shuffle the pieces of Polynesia, and Imperial Germany annexed Samoa, Stevenson's old adversaries turned his house into their governor's residence. In the Great War it became Britain's Government House. When America exerted its mandate, the U.S. administrator installed himself. Civilisation, with it guns, slavery, and corruption, had won.

In 1961 Western Samoa became a republic and the house at Vailima its presidential mansion. Hurricanes struck the place hard in 1966, and again at the end of 1991, when the worst storm anyone could remember devastated Upolu. The house, like the island, is in a bad way.

Western Samoa is accounted one of the poorest nations on earth, though the natives do not define their self-sufficiency as poverty. Nevertheless, commercial loggers swarm through the forests like termites; without cash, the people cannot well resist and much of the natural habitat Louis knew is being destroyed. At his most prophetic he had warned the chiefs, when thanking them for the Road of the Loving Heart, that disaster awaited if they could not achieve economic independence. He compared their plight to the fate of his own country, a comparison anyone pondering the links between his Pacific works and his Scottish stories should bear in mind.

The messenger came into their villages and they did not know him; they were told, as you are told, to use and occupy their country, and they would not hear. And now you may go through great tracts of the land and scarce meet a man or a smoking house, and see nothing but sheep feeding. . .

I do not speak of this lightly, because I love Samoa and her people. I love the land, I have chosen it to be my home while I live, and my grave after I am dead; and I love the people, and have chosen them to be my people to live and die with. And I see that the day is come now of the great battle; of the great and the last opportunity by which it shall be decided, whether you are to pass away like these other races of which I have been speaking, or to stand fast and have your children living on and honouring your memory in the land you received of your fathers.

As I write, there are reports of Mormon missionaries purchasing a lease on Vailima. They have plans, it is said, for a museum and a "foundation," for a chairlift to the grave on Vaea, for tourism. The parliament of Western Samoa, desperate as any administration in the Third World for the tourist dollar, has not resisted this new imperialism. Like the old chiefs attempting to resist the European Powers, they have few choices. Civilisation does not negotiate, as Louis knew. Scotland too diminishes—and these days there is nowhere left to hide for the exile or the dreamer.

The Edinburgh Edition brought Fanny five thousand pounds. Returning to London in 1898, she was met from the train by McClure, Colvin, and Mrs. Sitwell. Henry James held baby Alan and thought the widow "like an old grizzled lioness . . ." Henley had rejoiced to have "his Lewis" back when *Hermiston* was published in 1896 with Colvin's sketch of the likely ending. Now, when Lloyd tried to make contact, W.E. rebuffed him. In Scotland, visits were made to Aunt Jane, now eighty-six, and to Cummy. In Surrey, the party rented a house.

They filled their time, but age and the absence of Louis annihilated contentment. Fanny began to fall out with Colvin over the biography. S.C. was maddeningly slow, and she, needing an operation for gallstones, began to fear that she would die before he had finished the book. Equally, she was desperate to ensure that the Louis and Fanny who emerged from it would be the couple of whom she approved. Efforts were made to prevent letters dealing with R.L.S.'s quarrel with his father over religion from appearing in *Letters from Robert Louis Stevenson to His Family and Friends*; a volume on Stevenson's Edinburgh days that dared to mention his youthful exploits around the town was condemned as "malicious"; the question of how much Colvin should say about Fanny's divorce from Sam was censored. Louis himself, writing to Henley before their quarrel, had anticipated "a masterpiece of the genteel evasion" from any of his admirers who might attempt to write about his youth in Edinburgh.

Fanny moved on. France, Spain, Portugal, and Madeira. "The years ahead," she said in a letter to Belle, "seem like large empty rooms . . ." At Lloyd's insistence Colvin withdrew, whimpering, from the biography project. S.C. and the family began to squabble over royalties from the *Letters* just as, before long, they would seem to compete in their eagerness to sell off R.L.S.'s manuscripts. Baxter tried to secure "justice" for Colvin, as Louis had instructed, but to no avail. Fanny and Lloyd were grasping and petty: years later Alan Osbourne revealed that they had never wanted Colvin to write the book, irrespective of Louis's wishes. In the meantime, mother and son tried to avoid granting S.C. a fair rate for the work he had done, believing that life insurance premiums first paid by Louis and then by themselves were sufficient compensation.

Colvin had been overwhelmed with work at the British Museum—a fact he did not reveal to Fanny and Lloyd, who had been waiting "patiently" for four years—and had managed only three chapters of the biography. Balfour was approached. When his two-volume *Life* appeared in 1901, Henry James noted that ". . . the work was, or *is*, the man and the life as well; still, the books are jealous and a certain supremacy and mystery (above all) has, as it were gone from them . . ."

Fanny moved back to California, trying to stay in sight of the Pacific. Bob Stevenson had died the year before Balfour's book appeared, and she had found the blow harder to take than most that had rained on her. She had been furious when Katharine's second son was born and her daughter-in-law had insisted on naming the boy Louis: afterwards she addressed the child by his middle name. Then came Henley's *Pall Mall* review and another old wound was reopened, but at least she lived on when, in 1903, her old enemy died.

Lloyd, at last, had made a career of his own from his books, slight and "humorous" though they were. His nephew, Joe Strong's boy, more than matched him, having given up landscape gardening for drama. In the end Austin succeeded where Louis himself had failed, with hits on Broadway and, later, in the new medium of film. He had not long shown his talent before Lloyd had roped him into a collaboration.

Unpredictable Fanny. She formed a friendship with a twenty-five-year-old Hearst journalist named Salisbury ("Ned") Field. He became her "secretary," though in her biography of her sister Nellie Sanchez described the protégé as a member of *Tamaitar's* household. There was gossip; the pair travelled everywhere together.

In 1907 another edition was prepared—the Pentland. Lloyd had developed an obsession with the motor car and, Ned in tow, he travelled through France with his mother, even attempting the Cévennes. Fanny, meanwhile, became increasingly obsessed with spiritualism and séances, hoping against hope for a soft Scottish voice to sound from the other side. In 1909, Katharine sued for divorce from the philandering Lloyd.

By the end of 1913 Fanny's health was fading. Just before she died, she finished putting her notes on the voyage of the *Janet Nicholl* into publishable form. It had all happened a long time ago; outliving her husband by so many years had come to seem like a punishment. As ever she had endured; but reluctantly, querulously.

She was in Palm Springs to take the desert air when a brain haemorrhage struck her, as though fate was having one last joke on Louis Stevenson and his wife. Her ashes were taken to Samoa; her estate (valued at a little over $120,000) was distributed amid some rancour; and Belle, a wilful Osbourne to the last, married young Ned Field. He was two decades her junior, but she outlived him by seventeen years and her brother Lloyd by six. When she passed away in 1953, the amanuensis was the last of the Vailima clan.

Had he lived, Louis would have sealed his greatness. Given his last works, the proposition seems impossible to doubt. He was barely into his maturity as an artist when he died with his energy undiminished. He had measured his own achievement with precision and was working at the last to enhance it. Writing was a puzzle, troublesome, intractable; it touched something mysterious and profound, as though to tell was to remake. But the phrase "had he lived" tolls like a cracked bell through every account of the career of R.L.S. No one knows *exactly* how the story might have been concluded; it was not that kind of tale.

The tide of literary fashion was running with him. Alive, he would overcome the debunkers. He had outstripped the romancers and, in *Hermiston, The Ebb Tide*, and *The Beach of Falesá*, was acquiring the prose voice for which he had worked so long. *Hermiston* suggests that Stevenson could have dragged Scottish fiction from beneath Walter Scott's coattails. If nothing else he had learned how to cut the Gordian knot of historical complexity. Yet in the Pacific he was also engaging with present reality: there is no escapism in *Falesá*, no romance. This, to Henry James, in December of 1892, when Stevenson had expected to be deported from Samoa:

> You don't know what news is, nor what politics, nor what the life of man, till you see it on so small a scale and with your own liberty on the board for stake. I would not have missed it for much. And anxious friends beg me to stay at home and study human nature in Brompton drawing-rooms! *Farceurs!* And anyway you know that such is not my talent. I could never be induced to take the faintest interest in Brompton *qua* Brompton or a drawing-room *qua* a drawing-room. I am an Epick Writer with a k to it, but without the necessary genius.

Stevenson had a view of late-Victorian imperialism to which careerist flag-wavers like Henley could not aspire. He had a better grasp of political complexity than Kipling ("And with Kipling, as you know, there are reservations to be made") or Hardy or Haggard. The writer who had scorned realism understood the truth of things *in* the world. He had lived with the people and been changed by them. Only Conrad set a higher standard. Past and present flowed together, lapping Apia and Earraid equally. The current did not reach the drawing-room door. Stevenson's attitude to history had much to do with Scotland; his feeling for the historical forces affecting vulnerable cultures was utterly Scottish. Small nations feel such tides most acutely. Yet a burst blood vessel in the skull eradicated all that potential. Alive, he might have tied together strands in fiction which have never properly been united. Dead, he became a synonym for chaste romance and the patron saint of boys' adventures.

"There have been—I think—for men of letters few deaths more romantically right," said Henry James in a letter to Fanny after it was over. That was true, but not the whole truth. Arthur Conan Doyle, a different sort of Scotsman, called Louis one of three great short-story writers: Hawthorne and Poe made the trio. Another truth. "I think Robert Lewis [*sic*] Stevenson shows more genius in a page than Scott in a volume," said Gerard Manley Hopkins, confusing species of genius.

G. K. Chesterton said two profound things about Stevenson in his 1927 study: one concerned the art, the other the life. They are worth repeating:

> The first fact about the imagery of Stevenson is that all his images stand out in sharp outline; and are, as it were, all edges . . . The very words carry the sound and the significance. It is as if they were cut out with cutlasses; as was that unforgettable chip or wedge that was hacked by the blade of Billy Bones out of the wooden sign of the 'Admiral Benbow.' That sharp indentation of the wooden square remains as a sort of symbolic shape expressing Stevenson's type of literary attack . . .

> I believe that the lesson of his life will only be seen after time has revealed the full meaning of all our present tendencies; I believe it will be seen from afar off like a vast plan or maze traced out on a hillside; perhaps traced by one who did not even see the plan while he was making the tracks.

There is nothing definitive to be said. The maze does not yield to a few words. The books, the charm, the spirit, the wilfulness, the endless travel, the illnesses, the love for people, places, and things: taken singly or together, none amounts to a summation of the man. Each portrait differs, taking its share of the essence, adopting its own perspective, greedy for facts but selective of truths. The reality of the man faded with him.

Just narrative, another story. One thing follows another . . .

A Scot, always, that was part of it. He never did escape. He took his identity with him and made a dream of exile. He found his stories in dreams, after all. Robert Louis Balfour Stevenson was a child of Edinburgh who went into the world, like so many before and since, and did not return. Time, memory, places, and dreams were his art.

It is clear and cool, just gone four P.M., and the shouting wind runs over the shoulders of the Pentland Hills, much as it always did. He can be imagined there if you wish, that bag of bones. He can be heard, too, in the speech of the Edinburgh streets. His footsteps can be detected in the patterns of sunlight and shadow on the plateau of the Cévennes, amid the peaks of the High Sierra, or in the creaking planks of the Samoan house. Images and noise, merely. A book is not a life, not even when it hunts a life lived for books: that is the problem of narrative. "What genius I had," he said, "was for hard work." At another time, weeks before his death, burdened with an "ungrateful canvas" and accounting himself "useless at literature," he wrote:

> It was a very little dose of inspiration, and a pretty little trick of style, long lost, improved by the most heroic industry. So far, I have managed to please the journalists. But I am a fictitious article and have long known it. I am read by journalists, by my fellow-novelists, and by boys; with these, *incipit et explicit* my vogue . . .

Take any volume from the shelf and the tutelary anthology composes itself, the Edinburgh voice, without edges or overtones, contradicts its owner. It says:

> To have played the part of man or woman with some reasonable fullness, to have often resisted the diabolic, and at the end to be still resisting it, is for the poor human soldier to have done quite well.

And echoes:

> What, then, is the object, what the method, of an art, and what the source of its power? The whole secret is that no art does 'compete with life.' Man's one method, whether he reasons or creates, is to half-shut his eyes against the dazzle and confusion of reality.

〜

We are each entitled to a choice.

One last and final, mine alone, a brief passage from a hurried letter Louis wrote one sick winter in Avignon to his unattainable madonna Frances Sitwell as he turned twenty-three. It has no great significance.

I hope you don't dislike reading bad style like this as much as I do writing it; it hurts me when neither words nor clauses fall into their places, much as it would hurt you to sing when you had a bad cold and your voice deceived you and missed every other note. I do feel so inclined to break the pen and write no more . . .

Edinburgh, 1992

Works Consulted

*I*t is impossible to acknowledge all the works on the life, times, and art of Robert Louis Stevenson to which this biography owes a debt. The influence of some is obscure to the point of irrelevancy. Without certain others the book would not exist. J. C. Furnas and David Daiches, in particular, rescued Stevenson's reputation from a beckoning pit in the years after the Second World War. The former's *Voyage to Windward*, published in 1952, is a benchmark for anyone trying to unravel the life. I have often disagreed with its interpretations and explanations but have found its guidance invaluable. Equally, anyone wishing to see the artist clearly cannot ignore Daiches.

Mention should be made of the extraordinary bibliographical efforts of Roger G. Swearingen. Much of Stevenson's literary remains were scattered after his death, sold off by friends and family; many works were wrongly dated. Swearingen cleared the ground and built on it. I owe thanks, too, to Jenni Calder, whose lucid portrait of R.L.S., published in 1980, and whose editorial work on the fruits of an Edinburgh symposium of that year (published as *Stevenson and Victorian Scotland*) put many matters into focus.

For my own part, I have approached Stevenson in the most unscholarly way. I am a journalist, and do not pretend to be anything else. The human factor mattered more than textual analysis. In any case, such academic equipment as I have often seemed inappropriate to a writer whose life and work refused to be separated. Equally, none of the collected editions are entirely adequate (a new one is required urgently) and there were times—amid one memorable, torrential thunderstorm high in the

Cévennes, for example—when a little Tusitala volume stuck in a jacket pocket was of more use than the Skerryvore I had been using in the library.

Adams, Henry. *Letters 1858–1891* (Boston, 1938).

Aldington, Richard. *Portrait of a Rebel—The Life and Work of Robert Louis Stevenson* (London, 1957).

Archer, Charles. *William Archer: Life, Work and Friendships* (London, 1931).

Ardagh, John. *Writers' France—A Regional Panorama* (London, 1989).

Baildon, H. B. *Robert Louis Stevenson—A Life Study in Criticism* (London, 1901).

Balfour, Graham. *The Life of Robert Louis Stevenson* (London, 1901).

Barrie, J. M. *An Edinburgh Eleven* (London, 1913).

Berresford, Ellis P. and Mac a'Ghobhainn, S. *The Scottish Insurrection of 1820* (London, 1970).

Boodle, A. *Robert Louis Stevenson and His Sine Qua Non* (London, 1926).

Brown, A. *Robert Louis Stevenson—A Study* (Boston, 1895).

Brown, C. *The Social History of Religion in Scotland since 1730* (London and New York, 1987).

Buckley, J. H. *William Ernest Henely—A Study in the Counter-Decadence of the Nineties* (Princeton, 1945).

Calahan, H. A. *Back to Treasure Island* (London, 1936).

Calder, Jenni. *R.L.S.—A Life Study* (London, 1980).

Calder, Jenni (ed.). *Stevenson and Victorian Scotland* (Edinburgh, 1981).

Caldwell, E. N. *Last Witness for Robert Louis Stevenson* (University of Oklahoma, 1960).

Carrington, C. *Rudyard Kipling—His Life and Work* (London, 1955).

Charteris, E. E. *The Life and Letters of Sir Edmund Gosse* (London, 1931).

Chesterton, G. K. *Robert Louis Stevenson* (London, 1927).

Colvin, S. *Memories & Notes of Persons and Places, 1852–1912* (London, 1921).

"Connell, John". *W. E. Henley* (London, n.d.).

Cooper, Lettic. *Robert Louis Stevenson* (London, 1947).

Cowell, H. J. *Robert Louis Stevenson—An Englishman's Re-study after Fifty Years, of R.L.S. the Man* (London, 1945).

Cunningham, A. *Cummy's Diary* (London, 1926).

Daiches, D. *Robert Louis Stevenson* (Glasgow, 1947).

———. *Stevenson and the Art of Fiction* (New York, 1951).

———. *Robert Louis Stevenson and His World* (London, 1973).

Dickson, T. (ed.). *Scottish Capitalism: Class, State and Nation from before the Union to the Present* (London, 1980).

Donaldson, I. M. *The Life and Work of Samuel Rutherford Crockett* (Aberdeen, 1989).

Edel, L. *Henry James—The Middle Years* (London, 1963).

Elwin, M. *The Strange Case of Robert Louis Stevenson* (London, 1950).

Field, Isobel Osbourne Strong. *Robert Louis Stevenson.* (Saranac, 1920).

———. *This Life I've Loved* (London, 1937).

———. *Memories of Vailima* (with Lloyd Osbourne) (New York, 1902).

Fiedler, L. *No! in Thunder* (London, 1963).

Fleming, J. R. *A History of the Church of Scotland, 1843–1874* (Edinburgh, 1927).

Fraser, M. *In Stevenson's Samoa* (London, 1895).

Furnas, J. C. *Voyage to Windward* (London, 1952).

Gosse, E. *Some Diversion of a Man of Letters* (London, 1919).

———. *Critical Kit-Kats* (London, 1913).

———. *Questions at Issue* (London, 1893).

Greene, Graham. *Yours etc—Letters to the Press, 1945–89* (London, 1989).

Guthrie, Charles J. *Robert Louis Stevenson—Some Personal Recollections by the late Lord Guthrie* (Edinburgh, 1920).

Hamilton, C. *On the Trail of Stevenson* (London, 1916).

Hammerton, J. A. *Stevensonia* (Edinburgh, 1910).

Hellman, G. S. *The True Stevenson* (Boston, 1925).

Henley, W. E. *Essays* (London, 1921).

Hennessey, James Pope. *Robert Louis Stevenson* (London, 1974).

Herdman, John. *The Double in Nineteenth Century Fiction* (Edinburgh and London, 1990).

Hinkley, L. L. *The Stevensons—Louis and Fanny* (New York, 1950).

Holmes, Richard. *Footsteps—Adventures of a Romantic Biographer* (London, 1985).

Hopkins, Gerard Manley. *Correspondance* (Oxford, 1935).

Japp, A. H. *Robert Louis Stevenson—A Record, an Estimate and a Memorial* (London, 1905).

Kelman, J. *The Faith of Robert Louis Stevenson* (Edinburgh and London, 1904).

Kiely, Robert. *Robert Louis Stevenson and the Fiction of Adventure* (Harvard University Press, 1964).

Low, Will. *A Chronicle of Friendships* (London, 1908).

Lucas, E. V. *The Colvins and Their Friends* (London, 1928).

Mackay, M. *The Violent Friend—The Story of Mrs Robert Louis Stevenson, 1840–1914* (London, 1968).

Mackenzie, Compton. *Robert Louis Stevenson* (London, 1968).

Mackenzie, N. and Mackenzie, J. *H. G. Wells—The Time Traveller* (London, 1987).

McLaren, Moray. *Stevenson and Edinburgh* (London, 1950).

McLure, S. *My Autobiography* (London, 1914).

Mair, Craig. *A Star for Seamen—The Stevenson Family of Engineers* (London, 1978).

———. *David Angus—The Life and Adventures of a Victorian Railway Engineer* (London, 1989).

Maixner, Paul (ed.). *Robert Louis Stevenson—The Critical Heritage* (London, 1981).

Masson, R. *The Life of Robert Louis Stevenson* (London and Edinburgh, 1923).

———. (ed.) *I Can Remember Robert Louis Stevenson* (Edinburgh, 1922).

Meredith, G. *Letters* (London, 1912).

Moors, H. J. *With Stevenson in Samoa* (London, 1910).

Naismith, Robert J. *The Story of Scotland's Towns* (Edinburgh, 1989).

Osbourne, Katharine Durham. *Robert Louis Stevenson in California* (Chicago, 1911).

Osbourne, Lloyd. *An Intimate Portrait of R.L.S.* (New York, 1924).

Pemble, John. *The Mediterranean Passion—Victorians and Edwardians in the South* (Oxford, 1987).

Rankin, N. *Dead Man's Chest—Travels After Robert Louis Stevenson* (London and Boston, 1987).

Sanchez, Nellie Van de Grift. *The Life of Mrs Robert Louis Stevenson* (London, 1920).

Schom, A. *Émila Zola* (London, 1987).

Simpson, E. B. *The Stevenson Originals* (London and Edinburgh, 1912).

———. *Robert Louis Stevenson's Edinburgh Days* (London, 1914).

Smith, J. A. (ed.). *Henry James and Robert Louis Stevenson, a Record of Friendship and Criticism* (London, 1948).

Smout, T. C. *A Century of the Scottish People, 1830–1950* (London, 1986).

———. *Scottish Voices, 1745–1960* (London, 1990).

Steiner, George. *Language and Silence* (London, 1967).

Stephen, L. *Robert Louis Stevenson* (London, 1903).

Steuart, J. A. *Robert Louis Stevenson, Man and Writer* (London, 1924).

Stevenson, Margaret Isabella. *From Saranac to the Marquesas and Beyond. Being Letters . . . Written . . . during 1887–88 to Her Sister Jane Whyte Balfour* (London, 1903).

Stevenson, Mrs. Robert Louis. *The Cruise of the 'Janet Nichol' Among the South Sea Islands* (London, 1915).

Swearingen, Roger G. *The Prose Writings of Robert Louis Stevenson—A Guide* (New York and London, 1980).

Swinnerton, F. *R. L. Stevenson—a Critical Study* (London, 1914).

Twain, Mark. *Mark Twain's Autobiography* (New York, 1924).

Index